D0173187

THE HUSBAND HUNTERS

BY ANNE DE COURCY

The English in Love
A Guide to Modern Manners
1939: The Last Season
Society's Queen
The Viceroy's Daughters
Diana Mosley
Debs at War
Snowdon: The Biography
The Fishing Fleet
Margot at War: Love and Betrayal in Downing Street

THE HUSBAND HUNTERS

SOCIAL CLIMBING IN LONDON AND NEW YORK

Anne de Courcy

First published in Great Britain in 2017
by Weidenfeld & Nicolson
an imprint of The Orion Publishing Group Ltd
Carmelite House, 50 Victoria Embankment
London EC4Y 0DZ

An Hachette UK Company

1 3 5 7 9 10 8 6 4 2

A CIP catalogue record for this book is available from the British Library.

ISBN (hardback) 978 1 4746 0143 6
ISBN (trade paperback) 978 1 4746 0144 3

Typeset by Input Data Services Ltd, Somerset

Printed and bound by CPI Group (UK) Ltd, Croydon, CR0 4YY

www.orionbooks.co.uk

CONTENTS

ILLUSTRATIONS

INTRODUCTION

For me, one of Edith Wharton's most intriguing novels is *The Buccaneers* – the story of four American girls, not in the 'right set' in New York, who come to England and marry into the peerage. 'The St George girls were beautiful, and their parents rich, yet fashionable New York had rejected them,' says Wharton in her book. 'It was bitter to be left out of all the most exclusive entertainments, to have not a single invitation to Newport, to be unbidden to the Opera on the fashionable nights,' thought the elder girl, Virginia St George; and still more did this ostracism rankle with her mother, desperate to see her daughters make good matches.

So when the suggestion was made of a London season, with the aid of one or two good contacts, it was eagerly taken up by Mrs St George. It was not long before her daughters' looks, beautiful clothes, confident American naturalness and sense of fun had landed them their titled catches.

Wharton, herself born into this 'right set', based her novels on what she saw around her, from personalities to places, from clothes to customs, so that they are virtually a biography of the times. In the period between 1870 and 1914 – Wharton was twenty in 1880 – 454 American girls married titled Europeans. One hundred were to British aristocrats – sixty to eldest sons, forty to younger sons, six to dukes, with 1895 the peak year for such marriages. By any standards, this was a staggering number.

It was a real invasion, and recognised as such. So well known was it that when Sir William Gordon-Cumming spotted Leonie Jerome, the youngest of the Jerome sisters, walking in Hyde Park on her first visit to London in 1882, he went up to her and said:

'Over here husband-hunting?' The year before, the *Punch Almanack* had featured a group of 'New York Millionairesses' about to start for Europe, shown studying 'not Murray and Baedeker – oh dear no! – but Burke and Debrett', making notes of all unmarried peers and bemoaning that photographs are not published as well as ages and titles. There was even a magazine to help them do this: *Titled Americans* was a New York quarterly, with a list of eligible single noblemen at the back.

For me, the interesting thing was not so much that they made these marriages, as why. Why should so many of these young women troop across the Atlantic when there were plenty of good-looking and much wealthier young men in America (where males still outnumbered females)? The obvious answer, that it was a case of cash for coronets, is from many points of view too simplistic. And what were the social and economic factors behind these marriages that made such a lasting impact on British society?

There was, on the face of it, no reason why American girls, spoilt and cosseted in their own country, should wish to spend the rest of their lives far from their families and the friends they had grown up with, plunging into marriages that surrounded them with strangers, reduced them immediately to the property of a man whose right to control their lives and money was unquestioned, and whose country was the embodiment of much that their background had taught them to disapprove of.

After all, it was only just over a hundred years since the fiercely fought War of Independence that had created the United States and given birth to its Constitution. America had supposedly freed itself from the idea of hereditary aristocrats; the Republican credo of its citizens' equality was trumpeted forth at every opportunity – often contrasted with the effeteness and decadence of these scions of the Old World – and yet here were its daughters turning eagerly towards them. It was the meeting of a whole set of diametrically opposed ethics.

The first surprise to me was that 'the husband-hunters', as they quickly became known, were often the mothers rather than the daughters. Some girls, it is true, had a firm idea that they wanted to marry an English aristocrat, and led the way towards their potential target, but more often than not it was the mothers who took this decision.

Some brought their daughters over to Europe in their early teens, sometimes because it was less embarrassing to say: 'I'm educating my daughter in France,' than 'Mrs Astor hasn't asked me to her ball,' sometimes to put a gloss on them so that these girls would shine more brightly in the marriage market when they returned to New York, and sometimes to establish a foothold so that if New York turned its back on their daughter when she made her début, she could be taken back to Europe and then, with the right connections and enough money, filtered into English society where, it was hoped, she would make a brilliant match.

Modern women might find it difficult to understand just how much of a role the mother of a marriageable girl played in finding her daughter a spouse. Although love was desirable, it did not play nearly such a large part in the mating game as it does today – far more important were other factors such as family background, money, probity and general 'suitability'. Thus many of these marriages were just as much a creation of the American mother as of the American daughter. For often, as I show in this book, it was the American mother who was the true husband-hunter, who took the initiative in seeking a match for her daughter in the Old World, rather than an adventurous daughter suggesting a trip to Europe – and who realised that a peeress daughter would be the key that allowed her mamma to unlock the gates of society back home. Even Mrs Astor would not refuse admittance to the mother-in-law of an earl. *Punch*, always a mirror of its times, has an 1890s cartoon of an American mother holding her daughter on a leash so that she has no option but to marry the insignificant little peer beside her as both stand in front of the altar.

Another aspect that emerged equally strongly from my research was the clash between the matriarchal society of the US and the patriarchal society of England, often resulting in a rude shock for the American bride, who had grown up seeing her mother do more or less what she wanted, paid for by an unquestioning husband, and who expected to do the same. For American upper-class society was run by women, for women; whereas in England it was fitted around the demands and expectations of male lives. Women may have fulfilled a vital role, but it was a secondary one – secondary to the demands of husband, estate, Parliament and sport.

The alien horde, as such girls were sometimes dubbed, was eagerly welcomed by some, in the main those who hoped to profit by it, while others felt that much of English life was being polluted. 'Seadown – marry Seadown?' says the baronet Sir Helmsley Thwarte in horror when his son Guy tells him that Lord Seadown is interested in the eldest St George girl. 'There won't be a family in England without that poison in their veins.'

Looking at it from the other side: why should a peer marry one of these girls who came from a culture so different from the one in which he had been brought up? Again, money was the obvious answer; again, it was not quite as simple as that. Today, no one would raise an eyebrow if a peer married an American girl. Then – for the peer – it was a completely different matter. 'Society' was a closed circle of around 1,500–2,000 families, most linked through marriage or cousinage. 'You were either in it or outside it,' said the critic and novelist George Slythe Street. And to stay in it, you married within it.

For centuries, the patriarchs of these families, almost invariably peers, owned most of Britain and, because of the system of primogeniture – their heirs were always the eldest son or the eldest son of the nearest male relative – the great estates remained largely intact. Not only that; through the rents raised from them or the produce of the farms on them, their owners were assured of an income that was sizeable to vast. All they had to do was pick a suitable bride from a similar family; although she might inherit comparatively little, she had the necessary breeding and training in the ways of a large house and the rest would be supplied by her bridegroom's large income.

Producing these incomes were the agricultural poor, who

worked the land and for whom life was constant hard labour. Even children helped, lifting potatoes, scaring crows, milking cows or leading horses. 'When I was ten I left school to work on a farm for £3 a year,' wrote Tom Mullins in 1873. 'Before bridges were built we often had difficulty getting our horses and wagons across flooded streams. Often my clothes were quite wet when I took them off at night and still wet when I put them on again next morning. On Sundays I walked ten miles to have dinner with my parents, and then walked ten miles back to start milking.'

Then, towards the end of the nineteenth century, there was an irreversible change in the settled order of things. From around 1873 England, and especially its countryside, suffered what became known as the Long Depression, accounted for by several interlocking factors. It began with a series of appalling harvests for seven or eight years from 1873 to the end of the decade, accompanied by a drift from the land to towns and cities,* partly because of increasing industrialisation, partly because of the dwindling number of agricultural jobs. Local trade, which had relied on the custom of these workers, migrated from the small market towns to the larger county towns, putting many small traders like bakers or haberdashers out of business, while those that were left, now in a more commanding position, began to bargain, so that landlords were forced to reduce the rents they charged tenant farmers.

Contemporaneous with the poor harvests and loss of labour on the land came a dramatic fall in the price of grain. Vast fields of wheat now waved on the prairies of America, with different types grown to extend harvest time. Early settlers from Minnesota, Ontario and Wisconsin brought spring wheat; in the Central Great Plains the original bread-grain crop, soft winter wheat, was grown, to be harvested in summer; with Turkey red wheat, brought to central Kansas in the early 1870s by German Mennonite immigrants from southern Russia, in the autumn. When refrigeration came (in about 1870), farmers who had relied on

* By 1871, 65 per cent of the population was urban.

livestock were also hit, as this meant that meat could be shipped from the great meat-producing countries like North and South America, and Australia. During those twenty years of change, the price of English wheat and barley fell by half – and landowners' incomes dropped like stones.

'That summer [1879] was followed by a severe winter,' wrote Mary Elizabeth Lucy, châtelaine of Charlecote in Warwickshire, of one of the decade's dreadful harvests. 'The Avon rose to such a height covering the marble vases on the lower steps of the terrace that Spencer lost all his meadow hay to the value of £700. The previous year too all the hay in the Place Meadow was carried away by a flood and for the last three years the harvest had been so bad that farmers were unable to pay their rent and many had thrown up their farms: Spencer had five in Hampton Lucy parish on his hands. Many of his tenants were asking for a reduction of rent, which he was obliged to grant for fear of having more farms on his hands.

'The times for agriculture are too sad! Spencer's income was reduced by more than half.'

So parlous had the state of agriculture become that in 1885 Joseph Chamberlain, then President of the Board of Trade, said that 'almost universally throughout England and Scotland agriculture has become a ruinous occupation'.

As for the aristocrats to whom this land belonged, many simply watched helplessly as their estates became burdened with debt and their houses began to crumble around them: the idea of earning a living was not something they could comprehend. They were not educated to work, they had no family business to go into (to be 'in trade' was to be outside society) – in short, they could not change their ways.

'Behind him was the English squirearchy, generations of it stretching back, his justification for the only sort of life he knew how to live,' wrote Mary Elizabeth Lucy of her son. 'When unpaid bills mounted he sold [his father's] collection of paintings piecemeal. The houses in London, taken in order to give the girls a chance to find husbands, the hunters, the shooting parties, the grouse moors in Scotland – all these were looked on as necessities; old masters were expendable.' For some of these men, an American wife, with her dowry of dollars, was a lifeline.

On the other side of the Atlantic strikingly different factors were at work, hinging largely on the idea of élitism. Where British society had its natural pecking order, its pinnacle being the Prince of Wales (later Edward VII), no such system operated in the US; there was therefore a constant struggle not only over acceptance but also pre-eminence. It was a class system based on exclusion, but none the less rigorous for that.

For generations New York society had been run by the 'Knickerbockers' – descendants of the original Dutch and English founders. Although rich, they lived quietly, managing their affairs and largely seeing only each other. No outsider was let in. Then came the great fortunes, made through speculation, mining, railways, shipping and banking, and, with them, the spending of this wealth to such an extent that it almost became a métier (something that in many ways resonates today). The Gilded Age was born.

The wives of these men, who had the same enterprising, energetic, winner-takes-all spirit as their husbands, battled for supremacy in salon and ballroom, their ambition not simply to outdo each other but to climb over the stockade into that inner circle where the absolute élite had their being. Wharton's Mrs St George was possessed by an 'almost religious zeal . . . to fight for entry into the circle of Knickerbocker families whom she revered as "aristocracy" superior to any in the Old World'. For such women, money was of no avail: they had to find another way in.

Often, their daughters – married to a peer willingly, cajoled or forced to do so – were their ultimate weapon. For once a daughter had become Lady XX, the respect for a title among New York's inner circle ensured that she would now be welcomed by them . . . and with her came her mother, who had now achieved her objective: she was 'in society'.

As Edith Wharton put it near the end of *The Buccaneers*, 'Mrs Elmsworth, Mrs St George and Mrs Closson had long since taken for granted their acceptance . . . by the best New York society as mothers of daughters who had married severally, a duke, an earl who would become a marquis, a courtesy lord who was the earl's brother, a prominent young British statesman widely regarded as a future Prime Minister . . .'

What I aim to do here is to examine the reasons behind this social phenomenon; and its lasting impact on British life.

Of the 'real' 'buccaneers', several rose to the topmost peaks of British society while others, through their marriages, enabled their families to enter the much more exclusive circle of American society – then almost impenetrable to those whom its leader, Mrs Astor, chose not to know. Much has been written about a few of them, such as Consuelo Vanderbilt, who became the unhappy Duchess of Marlborough, bringing with her an enormous dowry that would today be worth around $100 million. But there were many others who, though lesser known, achieved their titled goal – and, sometimes, even love.

So let me introduce the girls whose stories I shall be tracing here, their mothers and the major figures in their backgrounds. The one who could be called the pioneer of these Gilded Age brides was the stunningly gorgeous Jennie Jerome, daughter of 'the King of Wall Street', financier Leonard Jerome. She married Lord Randolph Churchill and became the mother of Winston Churchill.

She came from a New York where the pre-eminent family was the Astors, whose fortunes had been founded three generations earlier by John Jacob Astor, who began by trading in furs. By the time Caroline Schermerhorn Astor ('*the* Mrs Astor', as she was always known), from an 'old New York' family, had married John Jacob's grandson William Backhouse Astor Jnr, and begun to reign over New York society, the Astors were primarily property-owners and landlords, their immense wealth transmuted into 'old money' by the passage of time. Carrie, Caroline's youngest daughter, later married Orme Wilson, thus raising him to Astor heights.

Helping to keep Caroline on her throne, and laying down

the rules that governed her kingdom, was Ward McAllister, self-created social arbiter.

Caroline Astor's brother-in-law, her husband's older brother John Jacob Astor III, had one son, William Waldorf Astor who, because he was descended from the senior branch of the family, believed that his wife Mamie should be the reigning queen. Finally, after years of unsuccessful and increasingly bitter struggle with his aunt Caroline to achieve this, he gave up and left for England, where he became a British citizen and was later raised to the peerage.

On the other side of the fence surrounding the élite was an equally famous and almost as rich family, the Vanderbilts. The man who had made them wealthy was still very much alive, the tough, combative, coarse-tongued Cornelius ('Commodore') Vanderbilt, a man who would never have been welcomed in the polite society that he himself scorned. The Commodore's eldest son, Cornelius Vanderbilt II and his wife, the icy Alice, had never managed to crash the barricades. It took another daughter-in-law, Alva, married to a younger son, William Kissam ('Willie K') Vanderbilt, to do so.

She did this with a ground-breaking ball, talked of for years afterwards, ostensibly given in honour of her best friend Consuelo (née Yznaga), a 'buccaneer' who had married the Duke of Manchester's heir, Viscount Mandeville. In England Consuelo Mandeville became a close friend of the Prince of Wales.

By the time the next generation of Vanderbilts came along things were a little – but not much – easier. Alva had destined her daughter Consuelo from birth to an upward marriage and when Consuelo was seventeen Alva settled (successfully) on the Duke of Marlborough. When Alva herself had been ostracised by New York society after divorcing Willie K, Consuelo's marriage secured Alva's re-entry: as the mother-in-law of a duke she was persona grata once more.

Consuelo's first cousin Cornelius ('Neily') Vanderbilt III, son of Alice and Cornelius Vanderbilt II, did not have the same success when he made a marriage of which his parents disapproved. He was cut off from the Vanderbilt clan when he married Grace

Wilson, whom they thought an adventuress. Nevertheless, the cool and clever Grace managed to succeed Mrs Astor as the ruler of society.

Grace herself was the youngest of the 'marrying Wilsons', so known because all five of the siblings made matches that lifted them effortlessly upwards. They were the children of the handsome, dashing Richard Thornton Wilson, entrepreneur and Civil War profiteer and his wife Melissa. The eldest, May, married Ogden Goelet,* scion of a rich 'old New York' family; their daughter, also known as May, carried on the family tradition by marrying the Duke of Roxburghe. Orme Wilson, eldest of the two sons, achieved a major coup not only by marrying Carrie Astor, daughter of *the* Mrs Astor, in the teeth of her disapproval, but by winning her and the rest of the Astor family round. The next daughter, Belle, married Michael Herbert, the fourth son of Lord Herbert, and settled happily into English aristocratic society, while the younger boy, Richard, married into a rich Boston family.

Perhaps the 'best' marriage of all was made by Mary Leiter, daughter of Mary Theresa and Joseph Levi Leiter, of Marshall Field fame, who married George Curzon, to become a marchioness and Vicereine of India, where her sister Marguerite ('Daisy') met her own future husband, the Earl of Suffolk.

Others who figure in my account of those Gilded Age days are Mrs Paran Stevens, the pushy wife of hotelier Paran Stevens, and their daughter Minnie, taken round Europe to find a titled husband before marrying Arthur Paget, a close friend of the Prince of Wales. Mrs Stevens's son Harry was engaged to Edith Wharton, then Edith Jones, before Mrs Paran Stevens succeeded in bringing the romance to a halt so that she could continue to benefit from her son's trust.

Adèle Beach Grant was an American heiress who became Countess of Essex after a broken engagement to another peer, while Maud Burke, from San Francisco, married Sir Bache Cunard – later calling herself Emerald Cunard – and revolutionised the

* Pronounced Goo-lett, with the accent on the second syllable.

face of British opera. Mr and Mrs Bradley Martin migrated to Britain, marrying off their daughter Cornelia at only sixteen to the Earl of Craven, while Tennessee Claflin's shady antecedents did not prevent her from becoming the wife of baronet Sir Francis Cook. Fanny Work, Alice Thaw and Anna Murphy, who married respectively the Hon. James Burke Roche, the Earl of Yarmouth and Sir Charles Wolseley, were examples of marriages where the exchange of title for fortune brought neither partner happiness.

Other American notables were the social leader Mamie Stuyvesant Fish, a plain woman, almost illiterate, with a raucous laugh but witty, lively, irreverent and gay, the heiress Elizabeth Drexel, from an 'old New York' family and her husband Harry Lehr, social pet and jester, notably to Mamie Stuyvesant Fish.

The story of the beautiful Virginia Bonynge, later Lady Deerhurst and stepdaughter of Charles Bonynge and his wife Rodie Daniel, and the battles between Charles Bonynge and the 'Bonanza King', John Mackay and his wife, were avidly discussed in drawing rooms on both sides of the Atlantic.

Finally, commenting on all that was going on, and, thanks to its immense network of informers, an unrivalled source of information to the members of that society (and to me as well), was the witty, scurrilous and uninhibited magazine *Town Topics*.

CHAPTER I

Where They Came From

The year was 1873 and the Gilded Age was roaring into life. New York seemed to be growing by the minute, new and ever more splendid buildings rising in the centre with ramshackle housing filled by the tide of immigrants spreading outwards. (One tenement in Mulberry Street, home to eighty people, half of whom were children, saturated with filth and vermin, strewn with garbage, was typical. Here raged typhus, diphtheria and smallpox – only nine years earlier, smallpox alone had killed more than 800 New Yorkers.)

In a display of the untrammelled wealth* now pouring into the city, gorgeously dressed women, their huge hats wreathed with flowers and feathers kept in place by jewelled hatpins, strolled down Fifth Avenue in the first of the Easter Parades after attending a service in one of the city's fashionable churches, before returning to the houses past which they sauntered. Great palaces of marble, stone and brick, domed, crenellated, with balconies, spires, canopies, were springing up all around, some so huge that they took up a whole block, as did the largest New York town house ever built, that of Cornelius Vanderbilt II on the corner of Fifth Avenue and 57th Street.

As the green shoots of spring appeared, so did the inhabitants of these Fifth Avenue palaces. Between four and five in the afternoon, women put on their smartest dresses and drove in

* Income tax did not start edging its way in until 1894.

carriages along Fifth Avenue, sometimes stopping for a walk in Central Park. On the first Saturday in May the Coaching Club held its annual parade. Coaches lined up at the meeting place, the Brunswick Hotel (diagonally opposite Delmonico's) until given the starting signal by the president of the Club, women in their best dresses and most beautiful hats, men in their Coaching Club livery of check suits with black coats, tan aprons and red and white buttonholes. Even the horses wore bouquets, attached to their throat-straps.

In the winter there was sleighing and 'everyone' would drive in horse-drawn sleighs in Central Park, Mrs Cornelius Vanderbilt's sleigh a dark red, with dark red liveries for coachman and footman, dark red plumes and red and gilt tassels.

The air was full of noise, from the clashing of horses' shoes on the cobbles to ships' sirens, the postman's whistle and the explosive noise of one of the countless loose-fitting iron manhole covers as a carriage wheel passed over it. Although rubbish disposal had become a problem and manure, dried to a powder, blew into open windows and the faces of passers-by (the rich, who could afford to transport it, got rid of the manure in their stables by donating it to the city's parks and gardens), there was nothing like the sooty pollution of London.

Gone were the days just over a decade earlier when Central Park was full of Irish squatters, goats, pigs and dogs with them, and piles of rubbish – everything from tin cans to old hoop skirts – who had come to America after the potato famine had struck Ireland. With no hope at home, dying in the fields, the villages and the mountains, millions of Irish* had emigrated to America – with a good few speaking only Irish. Many of them were women, young and unmarried, for whom domestic labour was a way out of penury, as well as providing room and board. They were a prime source of servants for the rich of America, whose countrymen and women in general scorned the idea of working as a servant to someone to whom their Constitution declared them equal.

---

* Between 1846 and 1851 Ireland lost about a quarter of her population through death and emigration.

Now the poor had been pushed out of sight and the rich were busy spending their new wealth. That year saw a banquet so extravagant that it made even New Yorkers gasp: its cost was estimated at $3,000* a guest. The host, Edward Luckmeyer, was a rich importer/exporter who had decided to blow a rebate he had received from the government on a single evening.

Down the centre of the table, in a thirty-foot lake surrounded by violet-bordered brooks, grassy glades and lush plants, glided four swans. Around it, a mesh of gold wire from the city's most illustrious jeweller, Tiffany, stretched to the ceiling to prevent their escape. Inside, over the lake, hung golden cages holding songbirds. The only sour note was caused by the swans (borrowed from Prospect Park), which spent most of the evening either fighting or mating.

It was held at Delmonico's,† the most famous of New York's temples to extravagance. 'Everyone' went to Delmonico's. Lunching there daily was Mayor Oakey Hall, who might appear in an embroidered waistcoat under a green frock coat with pure gold coins for buttons; Colonel William Mann, proprietor of the society magazine *Town Topics* and anonymous author of 'The Saunterer', the magazine's dreaded, witty, malicious gossip column; and the glamorous actress Lillian Russell and her paramour 'Diamond Jim' Brady, while the most respectable and exclusive of New York's Gilded Age balls took place regularly in its red and gold ballroom.

Not all New York approved of the rash of new palaces – or new people. 'I wish the Vanderbilts didn't retard culture so thoroughly,' sighed Edith Newbold Jones (later the novelist Edith Wharton), from an 'old New York' family. 'They are entrenched in a sort of *thermopylae* of bad taste from which apparently no forces on earth can dislodge them.' (She was not much kinder about the brownstone houses in which most of the families like

* An 1873 dollar was worth about $20 in 2016. In later years this figure rose, so a rough-and-ready way of calculating the vast sums spent in the Gilded Age in today's money is to multiply by twenty-five.

† This great restaurant finally closed in 1923 as a result of Prohibition.

hers lived, saying they made the city look as if it had been coated in cold chocolate sauce.)

The words 'nouveau riche' began to be flung about and as Blanche Oelrichs, another 'old' New Yorker, noticed, her parents and their friends were constantly asking, in plaintive bewilderment, 'Who *is* he?' or 'Who *is* she?' of these wealthy incomers from unknown backgrounds. For in the grandest houses lived the ever-growing band of the city's millionaires and their wives – the would-be upper echelon of the greatest city in America. 'Would-be' is the right adjective: their struggle to achieve social success was long, hard, bitterly fought and often unsuccessful. Money, it seemed, did not always talk.

The then upper echelon of New York society consisted of the families who had lived there for generations. They were mainly of Dutch descent – the name Knickerbockers came from the knee-length trousers worn by these early settlers. They had the Dutch virtue of thrift: their solidly based fortunes were mainly in banking and large trading firms or amassed as lawyers, though increasingly real estate played a part.

The leader of this élite group was Mrs William Backhouse Astor, whose husband's great fortune had been founded a good fifty years earlier, thus classifying the Astors as 'old money'. William was a man dedicated to pleasure – horses, drink, yachting and womanising (the last two often together). His wife Caroline ('Lina') Astor was a descendant of one of the original Dutch settlers; née Schermerhorn, she came from an old-established shipping family and she was so determined that she and her husband remained socially impeccable that she tried hard to ensure that his middle name disappeared into oblivion ('backhouse' was one term for a privy).

She was tallish, dark-haired and olive-skinned, plump and imposing, and had those essentials for leadership, a commanding personality coupled with an ability to keep her thoughts and feelings hidden. Her single-minded determination to remain at the pinnacle of society was helped by the fact that her husband was seldom around.

Her 'subjects' lived in solid, unpretentious and heavily curtained brownstone houses between Washington Square and Gramercy Park, with plumply upholstered rosewood furniture and thickly patterned wallpaper; they guarded their privacy and had set ideas about what was 'done' and what was 'not done', such as appearing in public when visibly pregnant. 'We dined at Bessie Sands the night before New Years with Gen'l & Mrs Barton & with Mrs Pellow – but it is my last appearance in public,' wrote one of this caste, the pregnant Anna Robinson, to her sister Pauline du Pont in January 1880. 'I enjoyed it very much, but I think it must be so disagreeable to other people. Minnie Jones* wanted us to dine there next, but I told her to ask Beverly without me & then he would come.'

The people they entertained to their plain dinners, eaten at around 7.00 p.m., were each other; after dinner, there were often evening calls, perhaps by some suitable young man interested in the daughter of the house. The idea of a social season, of grand balls in the ballrooms of private houses, of showy, ornate carriages, of driving out to see and be seen, would have produced baffled stares.

Once married, they dressed in dark colours. 'I send you a sample of my dinner dress – it is made of gray silk,' wrote Anna Robinson to her sister, adding, 'did I tell you of my new bonnet? It is jet with two black ostrich tips and a bunch of pink roses on the side & black velvet strings.' Even if the richer among them ordered Paris dresses, these lay unworn in the trunks in which they had been sent over for a year or so – it would not do for a Knickerbocker lady to be up-to-the-minute fashionable – and were usually of sober colours. 'I took my velvet jacket from its repose & my black silk dress & appeared in them,' wrote Anna Robinson. 'I don't think they are more old-fashioned than two years ago.'

After the American Civil War ended in 1865, huge fortunes began to be made, in steel mills, steam engines, oil, mines, railroads, the

* Edith Wharton's aunt.

grain from the prairies and cattle from the west, preserved meats to feed soldiers, the installation of the telegraph, armaments and real estate. And for those with social aspirations – which meant most of the wives of these men – there was only one place to be: New York. It was quite true that the seat of government was Washington, from which emanated federal laws, but few of the newly rich were interested in politics – in any case, they were too busy making money – and their wives certainly were not. For them, New York was the most exciting and cosmopolitan city in America; and with their millionaire husbands, whose fortunes were growing daily, allowing them free spending on whatever they liked, surely all doors would be open to them?

They soon found that this was not so. If Mrs Astor did not know you, no invitation would ever come your way. Sometimes a son would slip in: an enormously rich young man could perhaps be a husband for one of the plainer or less choosy among the Knickerbocker girls, helped by the fact that there was a perennial shortage of men in New York. 'Poor Victorine has had a dreadful time about the ball tomorrow night,' wrote Anna Robinson. 'It appears it was arranged (without contacting her) that she should take Emily Lesser, Minnie Dale, Clara Elliot & Marie Gothout . . . Mr Mane, who is head & front of it, flattered himself that all the ladies are buying new dresses for it . . . Of course it will be a great sight but I am afraid apart from that it will be pretty sad not to know a man.'

Huge fortunes did not always help towards social inclusion. Many of the wealthiest families, such as the Rockefellers, Carnegies and Goulds, had to remain outside the palisades. If Mrs Astor did not want to know you, she did not know you.

One such family, the Stewarts, went as far as building a mansion opposite that of Mrs Astor so that she could not avoid seeing them. What perhaps they did not realise was that she so guarded the exclusiveness on which her myth was founded that she would not even go near her own windows lest the crowds that thronged Fifth Avenue hoping to catch a glimpse of the rich and famous should see her.

*

Yet at that very moment, as the Gilded Age began, a new social format was being created that would give shape and structure to the fashionable world for the next few decades – and launch those daughters of the newly rich, the real-life 'buccaneers', across the Atlantic. At the heart of the stratagem designed to create what would become known variously as 'Society' and the 'Four Hundred' was one man, a Southerner named Ward McAllister.

As a young man McAllister had been remarkably handsome. At the time he began his remodelling of New York social life, his brown hair was receding and beginning to go grey. His eyes were blue and kindly, his forehead high, his nose aquiline, his chin firm. He was not tall – he was about 5ft 9ins – but he was square-shouldered and stood straight, so that his clothes hung well. He dressed conservatively, with a tall hat and cutaway coat of dark material. Even in an age of social striving, he was known as a snob.

Connected by birth to some of the old New York families, in 1852 he had married an heiress and a few years later had settled in Newport, where his style of entertaining soon began to be copied. He had had a good deal of relevant experience, gained from looking after his family, even down to going to the market – followed by a couple of boys each carrying a huge basket – and thus acquiring a thorough knowledge of game, fish and vegetables, the best time to eat them, and the best way of cooking them. He had also travelled extensively in Europe, where he soaked up everything he could about court and aristocratic customs. On his return to America he determined to become the self-appointed arbiter of its society and the customs it should follow.

He had already been successful in shaping the society of Newport.* Now, he decided, it was time to tackle the one city in America pre-eminent in wealth, drawing power, sophistication and general glitter: New York. A man might have made a fortune by planting a Midwest prairie with wheat – but it was to New York that his wife, avid to spend this new wealth, now insisted they move.

---

* See Chapter 8.

McAllister's cleverness lay in realising that the newly rich were there to stay; more and more millionaires appeared each year and the relentless tide of wealth would soon flood the passive Knickerbockers completely – unless something were done about it (not for nothing were these newcomers known as 'the Bouncers'). He also recognised that any society had to have a leader, whom everyone would accept without question – if not, it would degenerate into a formless mass riven by bitter internal struggles.

There was only one person fit for this position and she, although beleaguered by the strivings of 'Bouncer money', as parvenu wealth was called, already occupied it. Caroline Astor would continue to be the queen.

He decided to use the most desirable members of both old and new as the foundation stones of the new order. To select these, he formed a small committee ('there is one rule in life I invariably carry out – never to rely wholly on my own judgment'); a little band that met every day for a month or two at McAllister's house, making lists, adding, whittling down, forming judgements.

Eventually, twenty-five men, all wealthy, some from old families, some from the new rich but all considered to be men of integrity, were chosen and invited to become 'Patriarchs', as they would in future be known. They would give two and sometimes three balls a season, as exquisite as possible, with each Patriarch in return for his subscription of $125 having the right to invite to each ball four ladies and five gentlemen, this number to include himself and his family; all distinguished strangers (up to the number of fifty) would also be asked, their names to be run past McAllister. Everyone asked to be a Patriarch accepted immediately.

As McAllister had rightly foreseen, the exclusiveness of these balls was what gave them their magnetic power. 'We knew . . . that the whole secret of the success of these Patriarch Balls lay in making them select . . . in making it extremely difficult to obtain an invitation to them, and to make such invitations of great value [so that] one might be sure that anyone repeatedly invited to them had a secure social position.'

The first of the balls was given in the winter of 1872. With them, McAllister achieved absolute social power.

Applications to be made a Patriarch poured in, the great majority turned down but often with the door left tantalisingly ajar. Soon McAllister realised that there was one significant omission from his otherwise highly successful plan. With places at the balls at such a premium, most of the women who came were married – you could not ask an invited husband to leave his wife behind – so that the daughters of even the top families were squeezed out. Such was the press of those anxious to be part of this inner circle that it was clear something would have to be done if rival upstarts were not to launch competition.

Accordingly, McAllister introduced the Junior Patriarchs – known as the Family Circle Dancing Classes – in which all the debutantes were to dance in identical white tulle or, sometimes, in fancy dress. One result was that every morning he was besieged by a stream of mothers desperate to get their daughters in. Well aware that, as for the senior Patriarchs, exclusiveness was vital if the balls were to maintain their prestige and the cohesive social nucleus were not to splinter, he used all his charm and diplomacy to keep mothers at bay.

'My dear Madam,' he would say as he sprang up from his chair and bowed low. 'Say no more . . . you have a daughter and want her to go to the Family Circle Dancing Classes. I will do all in my power to accomplish this for you but please understand that in all matters concerning these little dances I must consult the powers that be. I am their humble servant, I must take orders from them.' Upon which he would delicately try to find out more of the family's background – a grandmother from one of the great families, say, might mean the door should be left open a chink. Jewish blood, divorce or an appearance on the stage meant instant exclusion; when the internationally acclaimed actress Sarah Bernhardt came to America in the 1880s the hostesses who gave receptions for her would not allow any unmarried girls to be invited to meet her.

McAllister's remoulding of society occupied his whole life. He had studied the customs of every court in Europe, he had read books on heraldry and precedence, he was aware of many of the nuances of English society. As a social arbiter he watched carefully to see who was being received by whom, he made the rounds of all the boxes at the opera on Monday nights, he gave advice on everything from the flowers to choose for a ball to the colour of writing paper.

Every afternoon at the same hour he would walk up Fifth Avenue with a fresh flower in his buttonhole, his moustache and imperial brushed to the correct courtly point, greeting those he was prepared to recognise and cutting dead those outside the Astor perimeter. An ordinary business acquaintance, whom he would greet affably in his downtown office, he would pass with a cold stare on his walk to the Union Club. He declared that he would not recognise plebeian people on Fifth Avenue.

He sent the fashionable to the opera on Monday and Friday nights, always to arrive at the end of the first act. During the second interval they would visit the boxes of friends and converse – 'chat' is too flimsy a word for this ritual social intercourse – with their friends. On some Mondays 'everyone' went on to one of the Patriarchs' Balls, an Assembly Ball – chic subscription balls that gradually superseded the original Patriarchs' Balls – or a Family Circle Dancing Class, all held at Delmonico's. If a dance floor of wood was too slippery to dance on, McAllister would order it to be sprinkled with powdered pumice stone ('nothing else to be done'), if covered with a heavy coat of varnish, corn meal put down then swept away.

The third Monday in January was devoted to the most sacred and exclusive social event of all: Mrs Astor's annual ball. The initial list of names was pruned and pruned again by Caroline Astor and her faithful acolyte Ward McAllister until those left were the crème de la crème. Then the invitations, written in Gothic script, were sent out.

Even receiving an invitation written so elegantly was an upward move in the status game. The only woman capable of these stylish superscriptions was Maria de Baril, the scion of an old but impoverished Peruvian family, who was herself extremely conscious of social gradations. Only if she decided that those to whom she was addressing invitations were sufficiently 'bien' did she consent to write and address such cards, so that receiving an envelope embellished with her decorative calligraphy was in itself a sign that you were one of the elect.

Those who did not receive this coveted bit of pasteboard resorted to various stratagems to prevent their friends from finding out. Some would persuade their doctors to recommend trips to the Adirondacks for health reasons, others invented funerals of distant relatives or took to their sickbeds; still others left for Europe.

For the ball itself the keynote was lavishness and ceremony. The huge and magnificent Astor mansion blazed with lights and was filled with flowers, the servants were in their full livery of green plush coats, white knee breeches and red whipcord waistcoats with brass buttons stamped with the coat of arms and motto (*Semper fidelis*) that the Astors had bestowed upon themselves, and Caroline received like a presiding goddess.

By now her rule was supreme and unquestioned. Even the man – or more likely, the woman – in the street knew this. 'She ruled with a strong hand,' said the *New York Times*. 'Her visiting list was the index of the socially elect.'*

Caroline Astor filled her role admirably. A woman of commanding presence and deportment, she was made more impressive by whatever magnificent Worth gown she wore – education in a French-run school and visits to France had given her a love of French clothes, cooking, furniture, paintings and architecture. Her hair was always done high on her head – in later years, this effect was achieved with a black wig – emphasising the appearance of majesty, as, even more, did her jewellery, worn in intimidating abundance. She was hung about with diamonds – a diamond tiara finished with diamond stars, a triple necklace of diamonds, a stomacher of diamonds originally worn by Marie Antoinette and so large that it was almost a breastplate flashed

* The phrase 'the Four Hundred' did not become shorthand for 'society' until 1892, when McAllister provided the press with the names of 400 of society's most distinguished members.

rays of light through the chains of diamonds embellishing her corsage.

She wore this great fortune in gems with the air of an idol bedecked for a ceremonial, carefully cultivating the mystique that had served her so well by refusing interviews, never allowing photographers into her home, keeping her opinions to herself and almost never dining out; if she did, she insisted on having the seat of honour at the host's right hand. Her splendid entertainments had the air of regal receptions: you did not go there for the conversation – it was enough just to be there.

Night after night there were parties – balls, dinners, musicales, the opera, in houses filled with the spoils of treasure-hunting in Europe and smothered in flowers. At the first Patriarchs' Ball in 1872 flowers were hardly thought of, but within thirty years massive displays of blooms, shrubs and tropical palms were mandatory in the houses of the rich. Caroline Astor draped chandeliers and filled window seats with roses as well as splashing them over tables and mantelpieces.

Everyday life for the smart set was hedged about with ritual. Dinner invitations were always sent by hand, although invitations to a ball or reception could go by mail. Calling had an etiquette all its own. Posture was all-important: backs had to be straight, heads upright; if invited into a house the visitor only stayed a set number of minutes. 'Children, remember that no lady crosses her knees,' said one teacher. 'She may cross her ankles, but never her limbs.'

While men could go anywhere, certain areas were forbidden to respectable women. One favourite place for them was the 'Ladies' Mile', which intersected Broadway, Fifth Avenue and 23rd Street, and had fashionable shops, hotels, the jewellers Tiffany and restaurants where smart women would meet each other. Even this had its dangers in those days when reputations had to be hyper-clean: it was also the haunt of demi-mondaines, usually as elegantly dressed as society women and frequently the mistresses of their husbands.

So well known had McAllister become that his comments on

matters social had the force of canon law.

'A gentleman can afford to walk; he cannot afford to have a shabby equipage.'

'If you want to be fashionable, be always in the company of fashionable people.'

'If you see a fossil of a man, shabbily dressed, relying solely on his pedigree, dating back to time immemorial, who has the aspirations of a duke and the fortune of a footman, do not cut him; it is better to cross the street and avoid meeting him.'

'The value of a pleasant manner is impossible to estimate.'

'When you entertain, do it in an easy natural way as if it was an everyday occurrence, not the event of your life.'

'A dinner made up wholly of young people is generally stupid.'

'If you are going to refuse, do so at once, but remember that a dinner once accepted is a sacred obligation. If you die before the dinner takes place, your executor must attend the dinner.' After every lunch, dinner or ball, calls had to be made.

'If you are stout,' he told his male audience, 'never wear a white waistcoat or conspicuous watch chain.' 'If you go to an opera box with ladies, wear white or light French grey gloves, otherwise gloves are not worn.' 'A boutonnière of white hyacinths or white pinks is much worn, both to balls and the opera.'

And the clincher: 'My dear sir, I do not argue, I inform.'

What was to be eaten – or not eaten – at a dinner was equally important: never two white or two brown sauces in succession, one soup rather than (the more usual) two, hot salmon only in spring and early summer. For a dinner of only twelve or fourteen, 'one or two hot entrées and one cold is sufficient', sorbets should never be flavoured with rum but always with maraschino or bitter almonds, omit a pudding but serve an ice, 'preferably Nesselrode, if good cream is used'.

There were even instructions for icing champagne, beginning to be the favoured drink for all lavish or ceremonial occasions on both sides of the Atlantic, thanks to an unremitting sales and publicity campaign by the French. 'Put in the pail small pieces of ice, then a layer of rock salt, alternating these layers until the pail is full . . . keep the neck of the bottle free from the ice . . .

if possible turn it every five minutes. In twenty-five minutes from the time it is put in the tub it should be in perfect condition and served immediately.'

The society over which Caroline Astor reigned was one built on exclusion.* As McAllister had foreseen, to be a success in New York or Newport society meant constant social striving and a rigorous adherence to the forms and customs deemed correct. Where an English grandee, his wife and their children could retire to his estate for several months, confident that their place in society would be unaltered when they returned, the American social leader could not afford to be absent: the ferocious competitiveness of American society ensured that in her place, others would instantly rise up – and how to struggle back?

The result was that 'everyone' did the same thing at roughly the same time in a routine of what – seen from the perspective of today – seems not simply pointless but, without any other distractions, ineffably dull. The sole sport – if sport it could be called – lay in watching the struggles to be accepted by those on the outside.

Already the daughter as social weapon was coming into her own. Great beauty accompanied by faultless style (and, of course, great wealth) was a powerful lever into the top social circles. Each season usually brought forth one or two such girls, known as 'belles'.

To be a belle was the equivalent of having the necessary patrician background. As belles were a recognised feature of American society a girl tabbed as one could gain entry to it by dint of her looks and general air of distinction, even if not from a society family. The belle had to be seen everywhere, her presence was required at all important dinner and dances. No ball was complete without her; it was considered her duty to be present at all public or semi-public events – and where she went, of course her parents had to come too, for whereas in England a daughter's place in society was dependent on her parents, in America a

* The census of 1900 showed that there were more than three million inhabitants of New York but no more than .001 per cent were 'in society'.

daughter could often elevate the status of her mother.

Mary Leiter, the daughter of Joseph Levi Leiter, was the supreme example of the belle who swept all before her. She was a tall girl with a curvy figure, large grey eyes, glossy chestnut-brown hair and small, elegant hands and feet; almost as important was her poise, charming manner and air of distinction. Her family was neither old-established nor, originally, particularly wealthy. Her father had begun life as a clerk in a dry-goods company and then made most of his fortune in real estate; as a self-made man with wealth of such recent origin, and without benefit of any connection to the New York élite, neither Leiter nor his wife would have had any hope of a welcome from them. But Mary's beauty, presence and accomplishments – she had learnt dancing, singing, music, French and art at home from tutors and a French governess, history, arithmetic and chemistry from a Columbia professor – took her effortlessly over these hurdles. Her grace and polish charmed everyone including, later, her future husband George Curzon. She finished up a marchioness and Vicereine of India.

But for those outside the charmed circle of society, what then? For the more enterprising and determined, it was a case of an assault on another front. A visit to Europe was an excellent excuse for not being seen at, say, an Assembly Ball or a Newport picnic – especially as rich, good-looking American women were warmly welcomed on the Continent. The 'buccaneers' were on their way.

CHAPTER 2

The 'Buccaneers'

From the first tide of invaders, as the Gilded Age began, Englishmen from the Prince of Wales downwards tended to find American girls irresistible.

The American girl was completely different from her opposite number, the girl that one of these peers would otherwise have married – perhaps the sister of one of his friends, perhaps a distant cousin, but certainly drawn from within the tight little circle that the English aristocracy then was. The transatlantic visitor's looks were polished, her clothes impeccable and – within the bounds of complete propriety – her manner was inviting and lightly flirtatious. She also exuded that compelling quality, complete self-confidence.

For she did not, like an English girl, regard herself as a second-class citizen, nor had she been treated, as English girls were from birth onwards, as much the least important member of the family. All her circumstances conspired to make her feel that she was mistress of her fate – or to believe that she was. 'She expects to be worked for, worshipped and generally attended to – and she gets her way,'* said the best-selling novelist Marie Corelli.

In England, primogeniture meant most of the focus was on the eldest son, with a certain amount on any brothers he might have – after all, in case of accident, one of them might inherit – while

* In *Free Opinions, Freely Expressed*, Archibald Constable, 1905.

his sisters were treated very much as subsidiaries, remaining so when they married, for as far as the law was concerned, husband and wife were one person, and that person was the husband. A married woman could not own property, sign legal documents or enter into a contract, obtain an education against her husband's wishes, vote or keep a salary for herself.

American girls, by contrast, were brought up to believe in themselves, to demand respect, even veneration, from their men, whom they treated as equals. In front of them, all the time, was the example of their formidable mothers, women who reigned over their households and their husbands alike, women who perhaps two generations earlier would have stood shoulder to shoulder with their men as they carved out the beginnings of a fortune in their brave new world. Marriage in the early republic had been thought of as a partnership, perhaps not of equals, but of two mutually supportive people, each of whom contributed complementary and equally valuable skills, and this spirit still infused the American household.

It was said that American husbands were the best in the world, and from the standpoint of American women this was true. For the early part of the century, men had greatly outnumbered women and the value attached to this scarcity still lingered. American daughters saw their mothers make decisions on everything, from the building of a house to where in Europe the family should visit that spring, with the funds to do so automatically handed over.

'American women are more indulged than English women because they eclipse English women in their ability to inspire their husbands; and they are also more extravagant in their personal expenditure, but in this particular they are encouraged by their husbands,' confirmed John Morgan Richards, an American who had come to England at eighteen and spent the next sixty years living there, interspersed with visits to the States. 'In all matters of pleasure-making, amusements and travelling the American woman sets the pace.'

Sons were of course welcomed, especially as able successors in the care and increase of family wealth, but daughters were seen as the way forward, the family member who could boost the status and fortunes of a whole generation. The girl who made a successful marriage could lift herself and her whole family upwards, so that daughters were cosseted and cared for like hothouse plants, cherished not only for themselves but for their potential. Almost from birth they were educated in everything, from riding to music, languages, painting, history and dancing, that was supposed to fit them for a position in American society – or for marriage into the English aristocracy.

To a father, accustomed to the position of power held by women both in his own home and in society, a daughter was often a little princess rather than, as in England, a somewhat disregarded junior member of the household. As Juliette Adam put it (in the *North American Review*): 'The young girl is the aristocracy, the luxury, the art, the crown of American society.' As such, American daughters were used to demanding – and having their demands met.

Thus when Grace, the daughter of Richard Wilson,* cabled her father from Paris: 'Father, what shall I do? I'm supposed to sail on the *Teutonic* and Worth doesn't have my dresses ready,' he did not hesitate but immediately sent for his brother-in-law, who worked for him, and despatched him to Paris that afternoon to pay whatever was needed to secure Grace's dresses and allow her to sail as planned. It is impossible to imagine the owner of a stately home in England doing the equivalent: sending his agent to Paris to chase up a daughter's dresses – if only for the very good reason that such a daughter would never have been lucky enough to have a Worth dress. Any spare cash would have been spent on the estate, or perhaps a couple of new hunters for his sons.

In 1890 George W. Smalley, the American correspondent to *The Times*, was writing that 'in matters of costume the Englishwoman of today is a far more admirable person than she was ten years ago,' as he marvelled at the chic of the women in the Sunday-morning promenade of the smart in Hyde Park. It was, he concluded, because 'the American has taught her English

* The father of the 'marrying Wilsons'.

cousin how to dress, and her cousin has learnt the lesson and now dresses almost as well as her teacher'.

For to young American girls wonderful clothes were not a luxury but a necessity, making them infinitely better, and more seductively, clad than their English counterparts. After a ball she went to in Cowes where she wore a beautiful grey tulle dress, Belle Wilson wrote to her sister: 'it was so lucky that I had pretty dresses as everyone talked so much about our clothes . . . I don't believe I should have found it [Cowes Week] so amusing if I had not worn my best clothes and been conscious that we were *decidedly* the best-dressed women there.' She ruined most of her dresses walking in the gardens afterwards and said Cowes was harder on clothes than Newport – but no matter, she had a devoted father to buy her more.

The equality of the American girl with her brothers was reflected in her financial status. American fathers often left sons and daughters equal portions or, if they did not, made sure the girls were handsomely provided for. By the time the Gilded Age dawned the American girl's individual rights were enshrined in law: by about 1850 most states had given married women the right to hold on to their own property (in England the Married Women's Property Act was not passed until 1870, nor, once married, did a married woman have a legal identity).

Women in America were powerful entities; in a few states they even had the vote. And as the novelist Elinor Glyn wrote: 'The traditional contempt for woman, as the weaker vessel, which the average Englishman has inherited as a second nature, was cancelled in America by genuine respect for the gallantry of the women who endured the hardships and shared the risks of pioneering days, and the chivalrous feelings natural to virile men were fostered to a wonderful degree in their sons by the influence of Victorian idealism.

'The second cause . . . of the enslavement of American men by their women is very easy to understand . . . The American woman is unquestionably the most beautiful, the best-dressed, best-turned-out and consequently the most attractive of all women. She takes infinitely more trouble about her looks . . .'

It was quite true. Preserving their complexions, all-important in those days when little or no make-up was worn, was an article of such faith among well-off Americans that often even little girls wore veils when sent out to play to avoid the damaging rays of the sun. Silk gloves protected the hands, and veils were worn by smart women during most of the summer, including for activities like tennis and swimming; porcelain skins were the result. This freshness, often with vivid colouring thanks to their more athletic lives, was one of American girls' chief beauties. It compared favourably with the 'enamelling'* used by some Edwardian beauties (including Queen Alexandra), often dusted with a light veil of pearl powder. Make-up was considered 'fast', but women often used aids like burnt matchsticks to darken eyelids or Indian ink to draw in eyebrows – a focus of beauty for Edwardian women – with belladonna to brighten eyes and enlarge pupils.† Some used geranium or poppy petals to stain their lips.

Later on in their lives, American women, always to the forefront, spent time dyeing their hair. For redheads, as red hair holds its pigment longer than any other colour, this was particularly difficult, as the process took two days: first the hair was dyed black, then green, then finally red (Alva Vanderbilt and other russets would retire from society for forty-eight hours to accomplish this, a disappearance tactfully overlooked by everyone else).

Another trait that allured Englishmen was the American girl's ability to talk to boys, a skill she had been practising all her life. While English boys went to boarding school and their sisters, taught mainly by a series of governesses, spent their days in a large house often down a long drive with no nearby playmates, and very few other children deemed 'suitable' as friends within carriage-driving distance, young Americans, especially girls, were groomed during their teenage years in preparation for the adult social life awaiting them, meeting boys on an easy basis from childhood on.

'This afternoon was dancing school and I wore my white

* Enamel was a white face paint made with white lead (now known to be toxic).

† Enlarged pupils are now considered a sign of sexual arousal.

dress and some lilies of the valley,' recorded the sixteen-year-old Gertrude Vanderbilt in her 1891 diary. 'The nice fellow who asked me last week for the german danced the lancers, the court quadrille and several round dances with me. The one who has no ear for music I danced several round dances with (he is beginning to improve) and the german. I danced with a good many other fellows that I don't often dance with.' And a week later: 'Alfred had a party of fellows and we went to the circus after lunch.'

Teenage Americans also learnt many of their social skills through a series of small parties almost like a junior 'season', such as the one noted by Gertrude Vanderbilt: 'Bill had a dinner of young girls and fellows tonight.' These gatherings, called 'Sociables', were groups of forty or fifty young people who played parlour games, sang songs and danced or in summer went driving or picnicking. There were no such excitements for their English upper-class opposite numbers.

Although they saw plenty of the opposite sex, these young American girls were always chaperoned, with mothers ever vigilant. Even at twenty, when Gertrude, clad in a black jacket and dark sable furs, wanted to go for a walk with a young man with whom she had made an afternoon date hoping her mother would be out, she had to resort to subterfuge.

'I had come in from lunch hoping to find Mama out. It was on the strength of that I made the appointment. The man at the door, in response to my question, informed me she was not out and had not ordered the carriage. I saw the only plan for me was not to go upstairs for to get to my room I would have to pass Mama's boudoir, where she would almost certainly be.' They managed to slip out and 'we no sooner got outside the door than his whole manner changed. His face lit up and he began to laugh. I did the same, out of pure happiness being out alone like this, and without Mama having discovered.'

Spending so much of their time with their contemporaries, with more freedom and far fewer restrictions than in Europe, gave these future American debutantes a social confidence and ease of manner missing in their English contemporaries – and helped them develop the quickness and repartee so fascinating to

Englishmen. In contrast, many English girls had hardly spoken to a young single man – the sort that in a year or so they would be expected to marry – before they had 'come out', so that they were shy and nervous rather than natural and friendly.

As Corelli remarked of the American girl: 'Perhaps the chief note in the ever-ascending scale of her innumerable attractions is her intense vitality . . . She is full of energy as well as charm. If she sets out to enjoy herself, she enjoys herself thoroughly. She talks and laughs freely . . .'

Their very Americanness was another point in their favour. A young English girl from a lower level of society who had been married for her money could shame the aristocrat in many ways, from insisting that her parents be produced on public occasions to speaking with the wrong accent – to sum up, by obviously coming from a different class. As for accent, the only American accent that some English recognised was a Southern one, which was regarded as gentlemanlike – many younger sons had settled in the South to try for a cotton fortune – and to the average untuned English ear it was impossible to place any other.

Few of these perceived drawbacks affected the American girl. 'We are apt to accept without further enquiry, provided they come from a sufficient distance, people who are charmingly dressed, appropriately housed, and boundlessly hospitable,' said the magazine *Vanity Fair.* 'It has happened that members of that exclusive body, the "Four Hundred", have been dreadfully shocked to find some compatriot who is taboo on the other side of the water received with open arms in Mayfair and Belgravia.'

American parents were usually too far away to embarrass. 'The American mother is a tedious person,' wrote Oscar Wilde.* He could have been speaking of Mrs Leiter, mother of the beautiful Mary, whose malapropisms were a byword. She expressed admiration for a sharp-witted person's quickness at 'repertoire'; when she received someone in her negligée she begged their pardon for appearing in her 'nom de plume'; and when told by someone at

* In 'A Dramatic Review of *Olivia*', 30 May 1885.

Newport that Mary looked too delicate to sit on the porch in the evening, replied: 'You are mistaken, my daughter is one of the most indelicate girls you ever knew.'

The American father, thought Wilde, was better, largely because he was never seen in London. 'He passes his life entirely in Wall Street and communicates with his family once a month by means of a telegram in cipher,' while Americans were so different and so far from the English system that the word 'class' was meaningless when applied to them. Their very openness and lack of shyness emphasised this. As Frederick Martin, socialite and writer, observed of his young female compatriot: '[she] starts her social progress unhampered by caste and tradition'.

This freedom, however, did not extend from the social to the moral sphere. Sons, and particularly daughters – destined to be the moral compass of the home – grew up with the ideals of purity and innocence. For girls, even their names added to this impression of flowerlike innocence – Daisy, Violet, Pansy, May, Rose, Lily; Lilian Price, aware of this, changed her name to Lilly when she came to New York and added to her aura of fragrant purity by invariably dressing in white. She would create a sensation when she arrived at the Coaching Club Parade, dressed in foaming white, from the ostrich feathers curling over her huge hat to the tips of her shoes. Once in her seat, she would open her white silk parasol, conscious of the effect she was producing.

This ideal of blameless, rigorous morality naturally carried on into marriage. With society ruled by women, for whom the retention of a rich spouse was all-important, fidelity – or rather the appearance of fidelity – was everything. Nowhere in the American ideal of marriage was there room for the discreet affairs and liaisons between members of the same social set that took place across the Atlantic in the Prince of Wales's circle or among the Souls*, with the tacit complicity of those around them.

Most young American girls were ferociously chaperoned, their

---

* A loose-knit group of friends who, though drawn mainly from the same background as the Prince's set, set store on wit, cleverness, originality and romance rather than on racing, gambling and card-playing. Their members included many of the most distinguished English politicians and intellectuals.

mothers sticking to them like burrs and any contact that could possibly sully their purity forbidden, including, of course, any mention of sex. Edith Jones, brought up in the heart of well-bred American society, was so ignorant of, and so dreading, 'the whole dark mystery' that just before getting married she summoned up the courage to question her mother, who had always refused to allow any mention of it.

'[I] begged her, with heart beating to suffocation, to tell me "what being married was like". Her handsome face at once took on the look of icy disapproval which I most dreaded. "I never heard such a ridiculous question!" she said impatiently, & I felt at once how vulgar she thought me.

'But in the extremity of my need I persisted. "I'm afraid, Mamma – I want to know what will happen to me!"

'The coldness of her expression deepened to disgust. She was silent for a dreadful moment; then she said with an effort: "You've seen enough pictures & statues in your life. Haven't you noticed that men are – made differently from women?"

'"Yes," I faltered blankly.

'"Well, then?"

'I was silent, from sheer inability to follow, & she brought out more sharply: "Then for heaven's sake don't ask me any more silly questions. You can't be as stupid as you pretend!"' And that was all.

It was not difficult to be ignorant in those days when no one, ever, talked openly about sex to the young. 'Girls know absolutely nothing until they are married,' wrote the seventeen-year-old Lady Emily Bulwer-Lytton to her confidant the Rev. Elwin Whitwell. 'They are taught that everything is wrong, and then plunged suddenly right into the middle of it.'

Even Leonie Leslie, brought up with the other Jerome sisters in the more free-and-easy atmosphere of France, shirked the issue. She had taught her four sons to walk on a drawing-room sofa above which hung a Poussin, *The Marriage of Thetis and Peleus*,* in which, as she remembered, 'debauched cherubs are

* Now in the National Gallery.

lowering a red canopy over the amorous couple while sunburned satyrs carry off white-thighed Bacchantes with obvious intent'. When the children asked 'But what are they doing?' Leonie could only reply: 'Having a lovely picnic.'

Another factor in the popularity of the American girls who came to England was that they were ready and able to talk to anyone on equal terms. 'There would be great difficulty in finding an American woman who would be prepared to take a back seat,' said John Morgan Richards, the American entrepreneur who lived in England most of his life. Such girls also had more to talk about, as most were more cosmopolitan. Some had travelled around Europe in their fathers' yachts, usually accompanied by friends of their parents, so that they had lived in a sort of floating house party, with visits to places of interest en route – all good conversational material.

Most were better educated than English girls, taken by their mothers to Europe to learn languages and study art and music. When Consuelo Vanderbilt was sent to spend time with the youngest Lansdowne daughter, while her parents were staying with the Viceroy and Vicereine of India, Lord and Lady Lansdowne, at Government House, she was surprised to find 'how scanty was her knowledge. Little time or trouble was spent on the education of English girls. It was still customary for them to have a good homespun governess. They read Miss Young's History of Greece. But Virgil, Gibbon, Hallam and Green were unknown to them. I pitied the limited outlook. Later on I was to find that English girls suffered many handicaps.'

What Consuelo did not then realise, of course, was that English education was of a different sort – though often scanty in the schoolroom, it was a good training for the kind of life they hoped and expected they would lead: marriage to a 'suitable' young man, with a future life spent largely in the country, with perhaps seasons in London. That is, very much like that of their parents.

Although confined largely to the schoolroom, the daughter of an English landowning aristocrat (and most aristocrats *were* landowning) absorbed much of the expected behaviour of the wife of such a man from her mother. With her mother she would take food to cottages, visit the sick, attend fêtes, and as she grew older gradually join gatherings of her parents' friends or meet them during some of the long country-house visits exchanged between cousins, friends and connections.

In these parties, she would hear constant political conversations – most of the landowners were in government – analysis of questions of the day, discussions about the party leaders and their MPs as well as more general chat about sport or the estate's affairs. When Jennie Jerome, newly married to Lord Randolph Churchill, arrived at Blenheim she quickly discovered that in the morning an hour or more had to be devoted to the reading of newspapers, 'a necessity if one wanted to show an intelligent interest in the questions of the day, for at dinner conversation invariably turned on politics'.

Chauncey Depew, a witty lawyer working for Cornelius Vanderbilt and later a senator, said that in American society conversation was not 'thoughtful, profound, or argumentative; it is but the contact of the moment, a dinner, a reception, or a call, and we separate'. But as the English often visited for up to four months at the same house, met the same people and lived intimately together, 'conversation becomes discussion of serious and weighty considerations'.

At a London dinner party, though – and it was usually in London or at least in an urban setting that an American girl met a future English husband – it was the American who glittered, with her looks, her polish, her sparkle, her original remarks, while her knowledge of Europe and its languages made her in demand if ambassadors were to be entertained.

There was no doubt that American girls swept all before them: between 1870 and 1914, 102 American women married into the peerage. As one verse of the day put it:

. . . For there were the strangers, delightful and wild.
With twang well developed and dollars well piled.
And the mothers of Mayfair are loud in their wail,
As their schemes matrimonial hopelessly fail,

Each match of the season, duke, marquess, or Lord,
Is caught in the coils of the alien horde.

How did they meet the men they married? Thanks to the matriarchal character of the society from which they had sprung, American women who had already made good marriages often introduced their countrywomen – provided these measured up to their exacting standards – to London life. As *Vanity Fair* pointed out (on 6 July 1905): 'The American hostesses who really play a part in London society are not very numerous . . . But they entertain with an originality, an *entrain* and above all with a splendid disregard for money, which our sadly handicapped aristocracy cannot afford to imitate.'

Lady Paget, born Minnie Stevens, daughter of Mrs Paran Stevens, for instance, was a close friend of the Prince of Wales. 'Once greetings had been exchanged I realised with a sense of acute discomfort that I was being critically appraised by a pair of hard green eyes,' wrote Consuelo Vanderbilt, whose mother Alva was a friend of Minnie's mother. 'I felt like a gawky, graceless child under her scrutiny.' At the next dinner party at her house, Consuelo was seated next to the Duke of Marlborough, 'a rather unnecessary public avowal of her intentions,' thought Consuelo.

Sometimes money changed hands. Many well-born Englishwomen were much worse off after the agricultural depression and the drop in income to the great estates. When in 1894 Elizabeth Banks, an enterprising young American journalist, pretended to be an American heiress looking for a chaperone ('A Young American Lady of means wishes to meet with a chaperon of Highest Social Position who will introduce her into the Best English Society', ran her advertisement), she received eighty-seven responses, almost all from genuinely well-connected women, some of them impoverished peeresses, all promising to launch her and some to present her at court. Their prices ranged from £500 to £10,000.

She went to call on one, 'who had intimated her willingness to chaperone me for £2,000'. Elizabeth arrived, dressed elegantly, at a smart address and found, not the cold-blooded bargainer she had expected but 'a more aristocratic, refined and interesting woman I had never met. She candidly explained that she was in great need of money, and was obliged to either increase her income or diminish her expenses.'

Elizabeth, still in her persona of wealthy heiress with no social connections, also got several proposals of marriage, some veiled, some explicit. 'You would possibly desire to marry an Englishman of high social position, who could place you in a certain circle where you would lead others,' wrote one man. 'I am a country gentleman, have a fine place, house and estate, have been an officer in a distinguished regiment, and know many people of position and rank.' He informed her that he would treat her 'with all honour and respect' – including silence on the matter – but added, 'it would be an absolute necessity that you should be a lady of considerable fortune'.

She agreed to see him and when they met thought he was 'a fine-looking aristocratic man of middle age', and 'a thorough English gentleman'. She discovered that he was a widower and, to her surprise, found when she investigated him that he was exactly what he said – from a titled family and with a large place in the country but whose fortunes were 'decaying', as so many were. Another, who thought he 'might be able to suggest a way by which she could even more than gratify her ambition for a place in English society', turned out to be a young man she had already met (who was also exactly what he claimed to be). In this case the embarrassment of meeting him in her guise as a coronet-hunter would have been too much and she simply threw his letter into the fire.

Some women advertised openly. 'A lady of title wishes to borrow £1,000 for six months. Would act as chaperon to young lady.' Everyone, found Elizabeth, was prepared to overlook her own lack of background and ancestry in return for cash. 'Had I carried my experiment further and been introduced and presented at court, I should only have been one of numerous Americans who have walked on a golden pavement to the Throne Room of Buckingham Palace.'

Elizabeth Banks also discovered a man prepared to concoct pedigrees, crests and coats of arms for affluent visiting Americans who wanted 'ancestry' to go with their new wealth. He warned them, however, only to use one of his creations in America, 'where people will not put it to a close scrutiny'.

One of those who made full use of the introductory process was Adèle Beach Grant. Her determination to marry a peer and thus enter the highest society clearly shows through the ins and outs of her romantic history; what is unusual is that once she had succeeded she refused adamantly when asked to perform a similar service, despite a huge financial inducement.

The beautiful Adèle was born in New York, the daughter of David Beach Grant of the Grant Locomotive Works and, as one society paper put it: 'she belongs to the English set in New York, rides to hounds, is a notable lawn tennis player, and a famous horse-woman in a town said to boast the most fearless and reckless of women riders in the world. The Grants have entertained a great many Englishmen of distinction, the last one being Sir Arthur Sullivan, of *Pinafore* and *Mikado* fame.'

Sir Arthur, indeed, was so assiduous in his escorting of Adèle that it was said at one time that they were engaged. Her looks were exactly those that fitted the Edwardian ideal of beauty: she had a mass of black hair, a creamy complexion, vivid colouring and lustrous eyes; so lovely was she that she was later the model for Hubert von Herkomer's portrait *Lady in White*. When she made her début in New York society during the season of 1883–4, at the first Patriarchs' Ball, held in Delmonico's, she was the acknowledged belle of that season.

What was not so generally known was that her father was a notorious drunkard. During her coming-out ball he had been returned, drunk and dishevelled, by the police, to be smuggled up the back stairs, given a sedative and locked in his bedroom. Enough, Adèle must have decided, was enough. She managed to transport her family – mother, younger sister and brother – to Paris, where she spent a year at the Sorbonne.

The next season, staying in Pau,* she met the twenty-five-year-old

* There was a large English colony in and around this town, with English sports like fox-hunting.

Lord Garmoyle, son of the 1st Earl Cairns, a former Lord Chancellor and distinguished Conservative politician, but the romance did not start until a few months later when Lord Garmoyle arrived in New York and saw her at a ball given by Mrs Bradley Martin.

Cairns was in New York to escape the furore caused by the result of a breach-of-promise action. When he was twenty-three he had met a lovely young actress who performed under the name of May Fortescue, whom he had first seen on stage in Gilbert and Sullivan's *Iolanthe*. May had joined the D'Oyly Carte Opera Company in 1881, when she was nineteen, and quickly became both admired for her beauty and a protégée of W. S. Gilbert.

Garmoyle fell in love with her, and proposed marriage (in August 1883) and she left the theatre. It was a time when marrying out of one's class was *mal vu*, and when an aura of immorality still clung about the stage; nevertheless, his family accepted her. His friends, however, were a different matter and this meant so much to him that he broke off the engagement in January 1884, and went travelling in Asia. When he returned she sued him for breach of promise – W. S. Gilbert paid for her lawyers – won the case and £10,000; and went straight back into the theatre, starting her own theatre company.

In New York, with the case behind him, and by now Earl Cairns (his father had died that April), he began to pursue Adèle, following her to Europe. 'He has no indication of the possession of any intelligence beyond that required for the customary languid intercourse of fashionable society,' wrote the *Daily Alta of California* scornfully in June 1886. 'In dress, manners and expression of feature he is nothing more than the typical English youth of fashion.' Nevertheless, the idea of being a countess clearly overwhelmed any scruples Adèle might have had, and in the summer of 1886 she accepted his proposal. Nor was he taking any chances: for the 'Battle of Flowers' at the Nice carnival, he went as far as Genoa to buy camellias, filling the carriage of his new fiancée fuller of flowers than any other in the procession.

The invitations to the wedding were sent out to all the bride and groom's friends in London and New York, a splendid trousseau was ordered in Paris, wedding presents poured in

– including expensive jewellery from Lord Cairns – and a house taken in Grosvenor Square for the wedding breakfast.

Then, suddenly, the marriage was called off. The reason, everyone agreed, was financial; some said it was because of the prospective bridegroom's extortionate demands for a settlement, others that he was so hopelessly enmeshed in such deep financial complications that Adèle's relatives did not think it worthwhile to extricate him for the sake of gaining her his coronet and title. Although she had to send back the presents and cancel the house, the trousseau, at least, was not wasted: during the following London season she appeared in the gowns ordered for it.

She was steadily moving upwards in English society, by now being helped by Consuelo Mandeville. Lady Mandeville, unhappily married to the Duke of Manchester's heir, who was flagrantly unfaithful and gambled much of her money away, had decided to make a life for herself in England. The first step was to become a close friend of the Prince of Wales, which she managed quickly and successfully. The second was to accept large fees to groom and school American girls anxious to enter English society – provided they measured up. Adèle's wealth and exceptional beauty ensured that she did.

In 1891, Consuelo Mandeville had succeeded in having Adèle and her mother, now living in Cumberland Place, presented at one of Queen Victoria's Drawing Rooms by a Mrs Lincoln, and by the following year Adèle had been introduced to the widowed Earl of Essex, then thirty-four. He was a strikingly attractive, well-dressed man, who turned up the ends of his moustache every morning with a tiny pair of curling tongs while his valet waited for him to select a buttonhole from a tray holding a rose, carnation and violets. But he was also, as his daughter Iris recalled, 'first and foremost, an angry man', often breaking anything that happened to annoy him – clouting his caddy over the head if he moved by the tee or breaking his putter over his knee if he missed a shot on the green.

His family seat, Cassiobury Park, an Elizabethan house in Watford, Hertfordshire, was one of the showplaces in eastern England, with a wonderful collection of porcelain and pictures, some by Sir Joshua Reynolds. He was not, otherwise, considered a rich man, and Adèle's fortune as the heiress of her wealthy uncle

Suydam Grant helped offset some of his financial problems.

Their wedding at St Margaret's, Westminster, in 1893 was the social sensation of the year, with Adèle's old admirer Sir Arthur Sullivan accompanying his own anthem 'Sing O Heavens' during the signing of the register. The town of Watford was illuminated and decorated with triumphal arches. An escort of the Herts Yeomanry Cavalry, of which Lord Essex was Captain, met them at the station, and after they entered their carriage the horses were unharnessed and the equipage was drawn by tenantry the two miles to the gates of Cassiobury.

As Lady Essex, Adèle quickly made her mark in society, her beauty smoothing her path and forming a pleasing contrast to the coarseness of her husband, whose ribald conversation once made Balfour leave the room – although it did not stop his visits to Cassiobury. When Edith Wharton, a great friend, went down to Cassiobury one Sunday at the end of the season she found there Balfour, Lady Anne Dickson-Poynder (later Lady Islington), John Singer Sargent, Henry James, Lady Elcho and Lady Desborough – Ettie Desborough thought Adèle 'top' for elegance of any woman she had ever known.

Along with the Duchess of Sutherland, the Countess of Westmorland, the Countess of Lytton and the Countess of Warwick, Adèle was one of the so-called 'Lovely Five', and she was a favourite of the Prince of Wales, a friendship that continued when he became king. In 1905 there she was, in a house party arranged for the King, Queen and Princess Victoria at Chatsworth, that included the King of the Belgians, Arthur Balfour, the Marquis de Soveral, the Earl and Countess of Mar and Kellie, Lord and Lady Elcho, Evan Charteris, Consuelo Duchess of Manchester, Lord Montagu, Mr R. Cavendish MP, Lady Moyra Cavendish and the Earl and Countess de Grey, who wrote of it to her brother Mungo.

'We had a very pleasant weekend at Chatsworth last week. The old King of the Belgians . . . made propositions to all the ladies, and even non-plussed Ettie who is pretty clever at warding off awkward requests! But he had no success with anyone. Hugo walked into his bedroom by mistake one evening, & said he was only made aware of what he had done by hearing a bitter groan of disappointment from the bed.'

Her own experience did not, however, encourage Adèle to help others up the social ladder. When her husband's aunt by marriage, Lady Meux, the immensely rich widow of the brewer Sir Henry Meux (Lord Essex's uncle), asked her for such help she refused to give it. As Valerie Reece, Lady Meux had been a bar girl – and possibly worse – before becoming a burlesque star. Sir Henry, heir to something like £3 million, doted on her and when he died she inherited everything he possessed, from two estates and wonderful jewellery to 15,000 acres of land.

Valerie Meux was a controversial figure, given to driving herself around London in a phaeton drawn by a pair of zebras. Never accepted by her husband's family or by the social world in which they moved, she must have felt that now, bejewelled, independent and enormously rich, was her chance; and all she needed was the entrée. She begged Adèle to introduce her to polite society, saying that she would make Lord Essex her heir if she did so. But Adèle's disapproval of the flamboyant widow was such that even this bribe failed to move her.

Chauncey Depew neatly summed up the reasons why Englishmen selected American wives: 'I should say that the American girl has the advantage of her English sister in that she possesses all that the other lacks. This is due to the different methods in which the two girls are brought up . . .

'The American girl comes along, prettier than her English sister, full of dash, snap and go, sprightly, dazzling, and audacious, and she is a revelation to the Englishman. She gives him more pleasure in one hour, at a dinner or a ball, than he thought the universe could produce in a whole lifetime. Speedily he comes to the conclusion that he must marry her or die. As a rule he belongs to an old and historic family, is well educated, travelled, and polished, but poor. He knows nothing of business, and to support his estate requires an increased income. The American girl whom he gets acquainted with has that income, so in marrying her he goes to heaven and gets – the earth.'

CHAPTER 3

Jennie

One of the women who turned towards Europe was Clara Jerome, wife of Leonard Jerome, a flamboyant, sporting financier who made and lost several fortunes. Unable to achieve the social success she longed for in New York, on the flimsy pretext of benefiting her health she took her three daughters to Paris, where entry, through them, would be much easier. It was a stratagem that worked out perfectly both for Clara and the Jerome daughters.

Once in Europe, the most popular destination for Americans was Paris – the Paris of the Second Empire, under the sway of Louis-Napoleon (Napoleon III) and his wife the Empress Eugénie – and here the four Jerome women arrived in 1867.

Louis-Napoleon was born in 1808, the son of Louis Bonaparte, King of Holland and of Hortense de Beauharnais, the Empress Josephine's daughter by her first marriage. He was physically unattractive, though with great charm and a kind nature. He had seized power in a coup d'état in December 1852, declared himself Emperor a year later and then set out to make Paris the most glorious capital in Europe. Until then it had been a medieval city, with narrow streets, winding alleys, slums and open drains in the middle of each road. Under the Emperor, by the 1860s it had been transformed into the Paris we know today, with splendid boulevards designed by George Haussmann. The same year that Louis Napoleon declared himself Emperor he took the step that made his court the most glamorous in Europe: he married the beautiful twenty-seven-year-old Spaniard, Eugénie de Montijo.

Eugénie was tall and slim, with tiny feet 'smaller than those of a twelve year old child', according to one lady-in-waiting, with a graceful walk, a perfect complexion, tawny hair and sparkling violet-blue eyes. Her love of fashion and elegance made her court the centre of all that was glamorous and exciting in Europe.

Her first-floor apartments at the Tuileries reflected this. The *salon vert* had green friezes on a green background, with green parrots and woodpeckers over the doors, and an enormous mirror reflecting the gardens. The waiting room was hung with rose silk; all the rooms were lit by wax candles in rock-crystal chandeliers and filled with clocks, bronzes and Sèvres porcelain. The four outfits she would wear that day descended on a lift through a trapdoor in the ceiling. Winter and summer, orchids, roses, carnations, geraniums and ivy, for which she had a passion, filled the many vases.

Her favourite colour was mauve, her court was relaxed and gay, her ladies-in-waiting wore scarlet jackets and cloaks, the gentlemen of her household her uniform of pale blue coat and white silk breeches. She gave endless balls and fêtes, at which ladies wore gowns of tulle, velvet or gauze, trimmed with lace and embroidery, with trains, between three and four metres long, depending from their bare shoulders.

She insisted on glamour, ruling that no woman was to appear at court functions wearing the same dress twice. In 1869 the wife of an American banker fell foul of these demands and was 'notified by the master of ceremonies of the Empress Eugénie that the permission formerly granted [to her] to appear at the Monday evening receptions of the Empress has been withdrawn'. The cause: 'unbecoming dress at the last soirée in the Tuileries'. She also hated women to dress too young: when a countess of seventy-two appeared dressed in white tulle with red bows, and a crown of white roses in her hair, 'the Empress was greatly annoyed and avoided speaking to her the whole evening'.

Sometimes Eugénie would drive down the Champs-Elysées in an open carriage drawn by four high-stepping horses, a postilion on one of the leaders and two tall footmen standing behind her, as she leant back in her flounced dress of bronze taffeta, a tiny black lace bonnet perched on her auburn hair and a tea rose above one ear.

After marriage, it did not take long for her husband to stray, as Eugénie found sex with him 'disgusting'. It is doubtful that she allowed further approaches from him once she had given him an heir, as he subsequently resumed his *petites distractions* with other women. From then on she focused on being an Empress.

Her influence was pervasive. Everywhere there was velvet, marble and gilding, bright flowers, opulence, rooms scented with vetiver and patchouli. This limitless extravagance extended to another feature of the age, the great courtesans, some of whom even dyed their hair red (with ammonia and brick dust) in tribute to Eugénie, and almost all of them, like her, went to Worth for their clothes.

Sexual undertones were everywhere; the music heard at court was by Offenbach, whose operettas were popular, gay and often satirised goings-on at court or the regime. In *Orphée aux Enfers* the life led by the gods on Mount Olympus, with its intrigues and sexual liaisons, was clearly supposed to reflect that of the court: the lustful Jove wore a beard and waxed moustaches just like the Emperor, a notorious philanderer.

It was not surprising that American girls who came to France, like the Jerome sisters, learnt that affairs were normal, in contrast to the strict morality of their own country; and no doubt became aware of the demi-monde, since its stars, beauties like La Belle Otero and Liane de Pougy, were seen wherever fashionable people gathered – at the opera, driving in the Bois, at the races, where their wonderful toilettes and their jewels made them the cynosure of all eyes.

Naturally, there was an etiquette even in relationships with a courtesan. Passing a stylish equipage in which was seated one of these gorgeous creatures, it was not done to recognise either her or the man who was escorting her, even if he was one of your greatest friends and had dined at your house the previous night. In the early days of the century, if a man was driving with his wife, or some other lady of spotless reputation, she always sat on his right; if he was with a mistress she sat on his left so that friends and acquaintances knew when to ignore the couple. Similarly, if he was in a carriage with his courtesan-mistress, it was a social solecism for him to acknowledge any other woman; when a Danish diplomat bowed to the Empress when with his mistress, the Empress complained formally to his embassy of his behaviour and he was severely reprimanded and temporarily suspended from his duties.

In contrast to the puritan ethic of their own country, where in polite circles sexual matters were never mentioned or alluded to in front of a young girl, young American girls in France who witnessed the courtship rituals, the glittering lives of the successful demi-mondaines and the endless discreet love affairs in French court circles must have absorbed the idea that sex was something agreeable to be enjoyed by both men and women.

And for girls who moved on to England, as did the Jerome sisters, the ideal of perfect monogamy must have grown ever more shadowy and the goings-on in Edwardian high society a sport in which they, too, might one day join.

Between January and Lent the royal couple held four grand, official balls to which four or five thousand people were invited. They were gorgeous, sumptuous affairs: the Emperor's chamberlains were in scarlet swallow-tail coats with broad gold embroidery, the equerries in green and gold, the prefects of the palace in amethyst and gold and officers in white breeches danced with bejewelled women in silks and velvets.

At nine o'clock precisely, the Emperor and Empress made their entrance, slowly progressing towards their chairs, nodding and smiling. Dancing began at 10.30 but the Empress would remain standing the whole time, going from group to group to talk. She would take leave of her guests by shaking hands with those nearest to her and then, when she reached the door, turn and sweep everyone a curtsey. American women, good-looking, wealthy and always superbly dressed, were warmly welcomed. If presented at court, they could then be invited to private receptions and to the Château de Compiègne, in Picardy.

Here those who hunted in its huge forests wore the royal

colours, the men green coats and the gold hunt button, the ladies flowing green habits and tricorne hats. Every night from sixty to one hundred guests sat down to dinner, which the Emperor never permitted to last more than three-quarters of an hour. Sometimes magnificent gold plate adorned the table, sometimes precious *biscuit de Sèvres*. After dinner came dancing. At the close of the visit there was a grand lottery, in which all tickets won prizes. The Emperor stood near two great urns, from which the numbers were drawn, and as each guest received one he wished him '*Bonne chance*'. Here seventeen-year-old Clarita, the eldest of the three Jerome sisters, got an inkstand shaped like a handkerchief, filled with gold *napoléons*.

But with the defeat of France in the Franco-Prussian War of 1870 this glamorous life came to an end. Mrs Jerome, well aware that her daughters would stand better matrimonial chances in Europe than in the closed circle of American society, began to think of England, and there their father took them, renting a house at Cowes on the Isle of Wight. As the yacht-racing capital of the world, it was an excellent choice as all fashionable London flocked there for the Regatta, in the train of the Prince of Wales.*

The Jerome girls were well prepared. They were good-looking, extremely well educated, trailing the glamorous, sophisticated aura of the French court and infinitely better dressed – a point that cannot be over-stressed. For American husband-hunters, whether mother or daughter, clothes were not simply a matter of covering their bodies decently and reasonably attractively, but a lethal weapon and a walking advertisement of status and of husband or father's wealth and success.

Choosing, fitting, putting on and wearing their clothes was virtually a full-time occupation, and vital if they wished to rise to the top – or marry someone who could elevate them. Dressing badly, or worse still, shabbily, was not an option. It was not so much that wearing elegant clothes helped you rise, more that 'bad' ones (especially ones that denoted a drop in income) facilitated descent down the ladder. With enough money, if a woman

* Later to become Commodore of the Royal Yacht Squadron.

had no taste, she simply left it to her dressmaker.

No other dresses equalled those of Charles Frederick Worth, couturier supreme to the Gilded Age. His base was Paris, regarded as the centre of all things luxurious, fashionable and elegant, but his reach stretched over almost the whole of the western world. He was an unlikely person to have taken Paris, the centre of fashion, by storm. Born in 1825 to a family of Lincolnshire solicitors, he served as a shop assistant at Swan & Edgar in London from the age of twelve until he was nineteen, sleeping under the counter when he was not working (shops opened from 8.00 a.m. to 8.00 p.m., six days a week). At twenty, with £5 in his pocket to keep him while he looked for a job, he left for Paris. For two years he nearly starved; for the next eleven he sold fabrics. Gradually he rose, until at thirty-three he set up on his own.

One morning, a desperate woman, invited to a royal reception that evening and hating the dress produced by her dressmaker the evening before, arrived at the Worths' house at dawn. She was ushered in, greeted by Worth in his dressing gown and taken to discuss her problem with Worth and his wife – still in bed and enveloped in layers of lace. Worth, leaning against one of the bedposts, described the dress he would like to make for her: a gown of lilac silk covered by puffed-out lilac tulle caught by knots of lily of the valley. She was delighted; and by evening it was ready.

At the palace reception the Empress Eugénie stopped in front of her and, after complimenting her on her toilette, asked the name of her *couturière* – all dressmakers then were women. But when she heard it was a man Eugénie moved on: to have a man supervise fittings of an evening dress would have been considered highly indecent for an empress or her circle – so the Worths were still no nearer to finding the necessary glittering patroness.

One morning they took a bold step. Madame Worth nervously approached the Princess von Metternich, the daring, avant-garde wife of the Austrian Ambassador and the Empress's great friend. The Princess decided to give the new House a try and ordered two dresses. When they came she was delighted with them and wore the evening gown – white tulle spangled with silver and garnished with daisies that had pink hearts – to a State Ball. The Empress, fascinated, stifled her objections and demanded that Worth call on her the following morning. He was launched.

That a man should see women in their underwear, that he should touch their bodies in the course of fitting a dress, seemed outrageous to the more prudish, whose disapproval was profound and frequently voiced. It was an era when no lady showed an inch of flesh – except for face and hands – in the daytime, yet was happy to wear a plunging décolletage at night.

But no moral indignation could stop Worth's meteoric rise. By 1860 he was famous in all the capitals of Europe and his dresses were even being ordered from New York. The Empress Eugénie was still his best client, because she never wore a dress more than once and needed new ones for any official occasion, and soon this was also a rule for all her court (their discarded clothes were given to their servants, who sold them). No evening toilette could ever be too elaborate for Eugénie – once she had the French crown jewels worked into the border of a ballgown, so that it glittered with rubies, emeralds, sapphires, turquoises, topazes and innumerable diamonds.

Worth was a true innovator – the first to introduce the concept of shop as house and showroom. Visitors were greeted at the door by polite young men in frock coats, led up a grand, red-carpeted staircase and shown into, first, a room containing only white and black silks. In the next salon were silks of all colours, and in the third velvets, wools and plush. In a mirrored showroom were his latest creations, with house models ready to display them. The last room, the *Salon de Lumières*, was lit artificially, so that the client could see what a dress might look like at an evening party.

He also impartially dressed all the top cocottes. Well aware of the value of publicity, he allowed actresses like Sarah Bernhardt, Eleonora Duse and Nellie Melba to order his clothes at a special *prix d'artiste*.

What marked a Worth gown were the exquisite, luscious fabrics in wonderful subtle colours, and the beautiful embroidery and decoration. Everything, he believed, had to be of the best and with his background in the textile trade he was able to handpick superb fabrics for his clients.

With the number of different outfits needed every day and the requirement for these to be new and fresh, keeping up with court circles was an expensive business. Lillie Moulton, a young married American woman living in Paris, invited to the Château de Compiègne in 1866, noted in her memoirs that an invitation received twelve days earlier 'gave me plenty of time to order all my dresses, wraps and everything else I needed for this visit of a week to royalty'.

As no one was allowed to wear a dress more than once, what Lillie was 'obliged' to have were about twenty dresses, eight day costumes (1,600 francs), the green cloth hunt dress, seven ball dresses (each costing 2,500 francs) and five tea gowns. Her morning clothes were black velvet with sable hat and muff, brown cloth with sealskin, grey velvet with chinchilla hat, muff and trim, dark blue and purple. As the number of guests invited was around a hundred, fifty ladies would arrive at the imperial château with about a hundred trunks.

Because dresses were so expensive, women – or rather, their ladies' maids – did what they could to protect them. Keeping clothes clean was an endless preoccupation, although dresses themselves suffered very little from what one can politely call 'body dirt', largely because so many underclothes were worn beneath them – chemise, camisole, petticoats – and often had removable collars and cuffs that could easily be washed. In Paris scented flannel, said to keep its perfume for six months, was sold by the yard for women to lay in their underclothes drawers.

Dresses too tight for a camisole often had shields, known as dress preservers, sewn lightly into the underarms of the bodices, which could be removed later and washed; similarly, ruffles were sewn onto the hem, inside the skirt – falling a fraction below the hem, they picked up most of the mud and dirt in the street and could be unpicked and washed or replaced.

Large houses had their own laundry, but all lady's maids were supposed to know cleaning techniques. Velvet, for instance, could be cleaned with turpentine rubbed on gently with a piece of clean flannel; a silk dress might be sponged over with a strong infusion of black tea, or a mixture of gin, water, honey and soft soap or gin mixed with egg white to remove stains. Lace, meant to be creamy rather than white, was dipped in cold coffee or tea after washing. There were also recipes for fireproofing silks, satins and muslins – at balls there were both fires and candles and a too-vigorous *valse* might risk incineration.

With the Franco-Prussian War of 1870, the fall of the Second Empire and in 1871 the surrender of Paris to the Prussians, Worth was initially ruined. However, shrewdly judging that the appetite for luxury in the New World could only increase, he reopened in June 1871. With the establishing of the Third Republic, trade began to pick up. Soon he was as busy as before, but with much more foreign custom: now, in swept the wives and daughters of American millionaires, each anxious to outdo the other. As Felix Whitehurst of the *Daily Telegraph* pointed out: 'The men believe in the Bourse and the women in Worth.'

As new money poured into New York and the houses of the rich filled with everything that could be considered indicative both of wealth and of good taste so clothes, too, vastly increased in importance. As the *New York Times* noted (on 28 June 1875), 'a man is rated by his money, a woman by her dress'. (Edith Wharton realised this early on. When asked as a child by an aunt: 'What would you like to be when you grow up?' Edith replied: 'The best-dressed woman in New York.')

As no dresses were more stylish or expensive than those by Worth, possessing a Worth gown showed you were a woman of fashion, taste, discrimination and, of course, wealth. American women went in spring and autumn to choose their dresses and those of their daughters, have them fitted and enjoy Paris, paying as much as $20,000 dollars annually for a Worth wardrobe, plus another $10,000 in the regulation 50 per cent tax when the clothes arrived. Others, when their measurements were known, chose from photographs. The dresses came over in trunks swathed in tissue paper, and were held above the dress below by tapes stretched across the trunk so that creasing was minimal.

Consuelo (née Yznaga) with her husband Viscount Mandeville, the Duke of Manchester's heir, at Tandragee Castle, the Manchester estate in Ireland, in around 1875.

Consuelo Vanderbilt, before she was forcibly married to the Duke of Marlborough.

The Vanderbilt mansions dominated New York City's Fifth Avenue.

Cornelius Vanderbilt II's New York mansion

Left to right William K. Vanderbilt and Oliver Belmont, Alva's first and second husbands.

Sexy, aggressive, iron-willed: Alva Vanderbilt was the supreme embodiment of both husband-hunter and social climber.

Alva Belmont (formerly Vanderbilt) (*second from right*) in her later years, still dripping with jewels, at the 1915 Women's Voter Convention as a keen supporter of women's franchise.

The Marble House, built by Alva and William K. Vanderbilt, where their daughter Consuelo was kept a prisoner until she agreed to marry the man her mother had chosen for her.

Newport's most famous 'cottage', The Breakers, built by Cornelius Vanderbilt II and his wife Alice. It had seventy rooms, thirty-three of them for the necessary servants.

A game of mixed doubles at the Casino, Newport, Rhode Island. The Casino was built in 1880 and its first tennis championship held in 1881.

Swimming in the sea for ladies who wanted to cover themselves and preserve their pale complexions was a difficult affair.

Consuelo Vanderbilt's brothers Willie K. Vanderbilt II (*left*) and young Harold Vanderbilt (*middle*) bathing at Newport's Bailey's Beach with Harry Lehr, the smart set's joker.

Above left Newport harbour, with the yachts of the New York Yacht Club at anchor, and *above right* spectators watching a yacht race.

Mrs Jerome and her three daughters before their marriages, at the house they rented in Cowes. Eighteen-year-old Jennie stands on the right, the eldest daughter, Clarita, holds her mother Clara's hand and Leonie stands behind.

'More panther than woman': Jennie Jerome and her first husband, Lord Randolph Churchill.

Jennie Churchill with her two sons, John (*left*) and Winston.

Left May Goelet at the time of her marriage to the Duke of Roxburghe, shown here in his uniform of the Royal Horse Guards, and *below* the huge stack of trunks and dress baskets containing May's trousseau.

It was all a great contrast to the English attitude, particularly to the clothes of a *jeune fille*. 'They still seem to be struggling with Barbara's clothes; she has as yet not one cotton frock against the hot weather,' wrote Lucy Graham Smith the day after her niece Barbara Lister (the eldest daughter of Lord and Lady Ribblesdale) was presented at court.

The importance of dressing well was a lesson the Jerome women learnt early; and whatever her financial circumstances later, never did Jennie compromise on her clothes. To her sister Clara they were so important that she would write long descriptions home of the outfits she had seen at parties and of her own ('I wore the blue chosen by Leonie and Jennie her black gauze').

Their beautiful clothes, often contrasting unhappily with those worn by English girls, made these young Americans stand out. It was while she was dancing at a ball at Cowes that Jennie, by now a stunning beauty with the dark hair, lustrous eyes and strong colouring so admired then, was noticed by Lord Randolph Churchill, the third son of the 7th Duke of Marlborough, who asked to be introduced to her. The spark between them was instant: the two fell in love so quickly that a mere three days after their first meeting Lord Randolph proposed to Jennie and was accepted.

After a battle with both their families, Lord Randolph's charm offensive won Mrs Jerome over, while the promise of a substantial dowry mollified the Duke of Marlborough and, with the proviso that Randolph enter Parliament, the two were allowed to marry in April 1874.

When Jennie, aged twenty, first arrived at her new husband's ducal home, Blenheim, far from being overawed by its hugeness and splendour and the grand title of its owner, her near-patronising attitude quickly made her unpopular with her sisters-in-law. She had been her father's favourite, her sense of entitlement was at least the equal of theirs and, thanks to her astonishing beauty which brought with it the confidence of sexual desirability, she had a natural arrogance. Nor did she hesitate, in her letters home, to point out the deficiencies of taste in both the house and her in-laws' clothes: the thick tumblers on the dining tables were 'the kind we use in bedrooms', the table mats were the wrong shape and so were the shoes the females of the family wore. She mocked the frumpy clothes of her English sisters-in law – she herself had twenty-three Paris dresses, eighteen of them from Worth. When Lady Wilton appeared one morning in a dress of electric-blue velvet and, on being asked who made it, answered with an air of pride: 'It's a Stratton' as one would say 'It's a Vandyke', Jennie admitted to 'laughing immoderately'.

She was also far better educated. Used to practising four or five hours a day, she played the piano better than anyone at Blenheim; thanks to the exhausting hours spent with French and German governesses she was fluent in both languages and she was very well read. No wonder they resented her. 'It is no use disguising it,' she wrote to her mother, 'the Duchess hates me simply for what I am – perhaps a little prettier and more attractive than her daughters. Everything I do or say or wear is found fault with.'

In London, with her sparkle, intelligence, gift for light but unthreatening flirtation and physical beauty set off by her wonderful clothes, she found her feet at once and, when they were installed in a house in Charles Street given to them by the Duke, became as popular a hostess as she was a guest. It was not long before she became a close friend of the Prince of Wales, often invited to meet him because he so obviously enjoyed her company.

Almost as soon as it had begun, however, this friendship came to an abrupt halt. In October 1875, only a few weeks after the end of Jennie's first season as a married woman, the Prince set off for a tour of India. With him in his retinue was one of his great friends, Lord 'Sporting Joe' Aylesford. While the two were in India, Randolph's elder brother, Lord Blandford, began an affair with Lady Aylesford. It became so serious that Edith Aylesford wrote to her husband, telling him that she and Blandford planned to elope. The letter arrived when the Prince's party was camping on the borders of Nepal.

The reaction was immediate. The Prince was furious: an elopement could not be kept secret and would probably cause a divorce – and a public scandal could not be tolerated. The intertwining love affairs of the Marlborough House Set were only possible because of complete discretion – after all, he himself had had an affair with Lady Aylesford and no harm done – and now this social *omertà* was about to be broken. Lord Aylesford set off for England in all haste, while the Prince fumed against Blandford from Nepal.

Randolph then stepped in on his brother's side – who was the Prince to pass strictures? What about his own behaviour? Then he said that he, Randolph, had a packet of love letters written by the Prince to Lady Aylesford and that if the Prince did not stop criticising Blandford he would publish them.

Randolph's next step was to visit Princess Alexandra and tell her that if Aylesford sued for divorce he would produce the Prince's letters as evidence in the court. In which case, he told her, according to the Attorney-General the Prince would never accede to the throne.

At the thought of anyone daring to threaten him the Prince became incandescent, and declared that he would not set foot in any house that continued to receive the Churchills – when Jennie and Randolph were guests at a ball where the Prince arrived unexpectedly they had to be quickly smuggled out down the back (servants') stairs so that he did not see them.

With their heir now living openly with a married woman – Blandford and Lady Aylesford were together on the Continent – and a younger son persona non grata with the Prince, the de facto ruler of society, the black shadow cast by the actions of their sons fell over the unwitting heads of the Duke and Duchess of Marlborough. It had become clear that the absence of Churchills, at least for a while, would be the best policy.

Reluctantly, in 1876 the Duke accepted the post of Viceroy to Ireland, which he had previously turned down, including the proviso that Randolph should serve him there as his Private Secretary. Here, until 1880, he provided a home for Randolph and Jennie. Randolph spent much of those years away from Jennie, who took happily to the outdoor, sporting life in Ireland.

Five years after the quarrel, at a London ball, the Prince smiled at Jennie – with whom, after all, he had never had a disagreement

– but would still have nothing to do with Randolph. Gradually, however, Jennie and Randolph – now a brilliant orator in the House of Commons – re-established themselves in society, though the row was not patched up until 1884, when the Prince and Alexandra agreed to attend a dinner party – later known as the 'Reconciliation dinner' – at which the Churchills would be present.

CHAPTER 4

The First Duke Captured

Two years after Jennie Jerome's marriage came that of Consuelo Yznaga, to the heir to the Duke of Manchester. It was a coup that sparked frenzied interest: here was an American girl who had captured a husband from the highest rank in the British peerage! No one, not even Mrs Astor, could climb higher than that.

The future duchess was born in 1853 in New York City, the second of four children of Antonio Yznaga del Valle, a diplomat from an old Cuban family who owned a plantation and sugar mills near Trinidad and a large house in Newport.

The Yznagas may have been rich and connected to several aristocratic Spanish families, but they were yet another family outside Mrs Astor's social circle – and Mrs Yznaga was another mother with whom this rankled. Though Consuelo's blonde-haired beauty, her vivacity and charm, meant that at a junior level her path crossed with the offspring of the established New York families, this was not enough to secure the coveted invitations to the grander balls and dinners.

So, like many other mothers, Mrs Yznaga took Consuelo and her three sisters to France, where they became welcome at the court of the Empress Eugénie and were often invited to the Tuileries for the grand State Balls and Monday-evening musicales. Although only thirteen, Consuelo got to know the Empress well and in the same year, 1866, made an even greater friend, Alva Smith (later Vanderbilt) who, like her, came from the South.

In 1875, when Jennie was marrying into the ducal Churchills, the Yznaga family visited Saratoga Springs. It was a place that was, as the *New York Times* noted on 4 July, 'famous for its flirtations for, after all, people do not come to Saratoga to drink the waters. Miss Nellie, Miss Abbie and Miss Fanny are here to find someone . . . who may fall in love with them and . . . who may be considered eligible'. Consuelo was one who did.

In the mornings, through the heat, the lovely blonde Consuelo was one of the tightly laced young women in sprigged muslin, holding parasols in their kid-gloved hands, who strolled up and down the United States Hotel piazza, eyed by the young men lounging by the railings. At the weekly dances in the hotel's 100-foot ballroom, its parquet floor rubbed to a glassy sheen with cornmeal, she was one of the girls in silk flounces who danced with young men introduced to them under the stern eye of their mother or chaperone.

One of these young men was the twenty-three-year-old George Victor Drogo Montagu (always known as Kim),* Lord Mandeville, the Duke of Manchester's heir. He had left England in bad odour but he had a certain charm, and if he gambled at the Club and went racing at Saratoga's famous track – well, so did a lot of other men. And he was a friend of the Prince of Wales, from whom he received a cable of congratulations on his birthday signed 'Sandringham', the Prince's private code name, which he showed around proudly. To all the mothers there, he would have seemed the catch of the season.

Kim had been ADC to Sir Garnet Wolseley in the Zulu War, and when he fell ill with a lingering fever at Saratoga, it was diagnosed as something he had picked up in Africa. Mrs Yznaga invited this seemingly highly eligible young man, attracted by her daughter, to the Yznaga 'cottage' in Orange, New Jersey, to rest and recuperate. Here he was nursed by Consuelo and her mother, thus neatly bypassing the iron rule of courtship that no young girl should be alone with a man who was not a close relation – the idea that her daughter might become a duchess must have held enormous attraction for Mrs Yznaga.

* Short for Kimbolton, a Manchester title.

As for Kim, already fascinated by this Southern girl, so different from the young women he had met at home, when her father promised him a dowry of £200,000 it was the clincher for the spendthrift viscount. He proposed to Consuelo and was accepted. His family were furious but the couple stood firm and were married in New York's fashionable Grace Church in 1876.

At that time only one other American girl, Consuelo's friend Jennie, had married a British peer, and here was another, not even from the Four Hundred, about to enter the highest rank of the British aristocracy. The papers crowed with delight and the feeling of triumph in the Yznaga family must have been such that all of them would have been prepared to overlook any misgivings as to the unsavoury reputation Kim had already earned.

Every newspaper devoted columns to the wedding details and the route to the church was almost blocked by a cheering, excited crowd. (One of Consuelo's bridesmaids was Minnie Stevens, who with her mother had already been husband-hunting for four years; one of the bridegroom's ushers was Sir Bache Cunard, later to marry Maud Burke.)

The couple arrived in London in May, in time for the season. Consuelo, with her sweet, seductive Southern voice and unforced gaiety, 'took Society completely by storm by her beauty, wit and vivacity,' wrote the Duke of Portland admiringly, 'and it was soon at her very pretty feet'.

Undoubtedly the Yznagas were delighted that Consuelo had made such a sizeable step up the social ladder, but the reality of her life turned out to be very different from that which a future duchess might normally expect. To begin with, her father-in-law, the old Duke, had spent everything he could lay his hands on and his son had copied him, flooding London with what were called 'post-obits' – promises to pay what he owed out of the estate when he succeeded. The Mandevilles could only afford a small house in Mayfair, but Consuelo's looks, originality and bubbling charm meant that 'everyone' came to the small salon she held every Sunday and at first her life seemed set fair.

It did not stay so for long. Consuelo had been brought up with the American reverence for marriage but was quickly disillusioned. Soon she was making excuses for her husband. 'Mandeville's movements are so erratic that I think I had better say he won't come with me on Sunday, nor on the 13th either,' she wrote to the noted hostess Lady Waldegrave.* 'He so often disappoints me that I generally make up my mind to go without him.'

For Kim had returned to his old dissolute ways and louche companions, forming a liaison with a music-hall actress called Bessie Bellwood, a male impersonator with a hoarse, gravelly voice. He spent on her freely, getting through so much money that first year of marriage that his father banished the Mandevilles to Tandragee Castle in County Armagh, the Manchester seat in Ulster.

It was cold, run-down, ill-kept and draughty, and the rainy Irish climate depressed Consuelo even further. All the time, her husband was squandering the fortune she had brought into the marriage but she was determined to do her duty by him. Her son William was born in 1877 and in 1879 she gave birth to twin girls, Mary and Alice.

By 1883, Kim was under such siege from his creditors that the couple decided to go to New York, where they stayed with Alva Vanderbilt in her sumptuous new house at 660 Fifth Avenue. There was a further link between the two friends: Consuelo's brother Fernando had married Alva's sister, Jennie Smith. It was while the Mandevilles were staying with Alva that she gave her famous fancy-dress ball of 1883, ostensibly in honour of Consuelo, that enabled her to storm the icy north face of New York society.

When they returned to England that April, the Mandevilles became more and more estranged, with Kim spending long periods abroad and Consuelo trying to make a life for herself in Ireland and London, where she eventually settled.

The London in which Consuelo had arrived was a brilliant sight during the season. Window boxes were bright with flowers,

* Lady Waldegrave was then married to Chichester Fortescue, a Liberal Minister under Gladstone, but held on to her former title all her life.

striped awnings shaded windows, the dust covers that shrouded furniture and curtains for the rest of the year were removed and holland bags taken off chandeliers. Flowers were sent up from the country, along with hothouse peaches and grapes and whisky in barrels from Scotland.

Every weekday, between eleven and one, the fashionable world congregated by Rotten Row, some to walk and chat, others to watch beautiful women in tight, braided habits riding side-saddle on thoroughbred hacks, sometimes with a cavalier – equally elegant in a frock coat, pearl-grey trousers, boots and tall silk hat – escorting them, sometimes followed by a liveried groom with cockaded hat at a respectful distance. Even dray horses wore straw bonnets trimmed with flowers.

Close by, the children of the hundred or so families who lived nearby in Mayfair played in the Hamilton Gardens, a small strip of Hyde Park then railed off, with governesses – often the daughters of the clergy – knitting on seats while their charges played rounders, bowled hoops, or simply made friends.

On fine afternoons there was a parade of carriages; these ranged from large four-horses barouches with postilions, bewigged coachmen and powdered footmen with plush breeches and flashing shoe buckles to sporty little phaetons and 'sociables' (a cross between a barouche and a victoria, with two facing double seats) like Lord Salisbury's, drawn by his famous 'Salisbury Blacks'. Women in lacy, ruffled dresses could be seen in barouches for which seventeen-hand horses,* difficult to find, were needed. Every evening, near Grosvenor Gate, people lined up to see the Princess of Wales pass, bowing to right and left.

Though the occupants of these equipages were usually protected by leather aprons or hoods if the rain came down, not so the coachmen and footmen, who whatever the weather were not allowed greatcoats from 1 May to 15 October. Other afternoon occupations for society were drives to Hurlingham, Roehampton or Ranelagh, where there were inter-regimental polo matches,

* A hand is four inches, measured at the highest point, the horse's withers, just above its shoulder blades.

watched by women wearing the badges of their husbands' regiments or, if Parliament was sitting, observing the proceedings from the Strangers' Gallery.

It was a small, exclusive world, in which almost everybody knew each other and into which few outsiders managed to penetrate. 'The army, the navy, the diplomatic service, the church or the bar were the only undisputed professions of "Gentlemen",' commented the novelist Elinor Glyn. 'Those who earned money in other ways, whether by professional, literary or artistic ability, or by business interests, were ruled out, and were only seen at hunt balls and charity entertainments.' Elinor knew what she was talking about: her older sister Lucy, despite being married to a Scottish landowning baronet, was not received at court because, to support herself and the child of an earlier union, she had taken up dressmaking and was therefore considered to be 'in trade'.

Footmen, whom only the rich could afford (employers were taxed a guinea for every male servant they employed), were one indicator of the wealth and status of a family, from their height and powdered hair to their gorgeous liveries – Lord Lonsdale's servants wore canary-yellow coats with dark blue facings, white buckskin breeches and tall white beaver hats; Lord Salisbury's footmen were to be seen in sky-blue livery frogged with silver. A 'matching pair' was considered ultra-chic and often given 'suitable' names by their employers – James and John were favourites.

Away from Hyde Park or the grander areas of Mayfair, noise from the street was constant and intrusive. There were the sounds of horses' hooves and wheels, often on cobblestones, organ grinders, the cries of news vendors – especially on Sundays, when cheap weekend editions of newspapers were on offer – of street vendors selling muffins, 'Penny pies – all 'ot!', fresh eggs, lavender or groundsel for canaries, and the shouts of workmen.

Not far away – some as close as Westminster – lived the miserable. London, already the largest city in Europe, was expanding at a huge rate. As well as the move from the land to towns, successive waves of immigrants flooded in, to settle mainly in the East End. As existing houses had degraded or been pulled down to make way for new roads, factories or railways, those that still stood were often divided up into separate dwellings – even by the end of the nineteenth century many families still lived in one room.

This lack of housing meant that slum landlords could put up rents, thus exacerbating the crowded conditions, and afford to disregard necessary repairs; often, if windows were broken, they would not or could not replace them so that rags were stuffed into holes in the glass or paper stretched across them. The filthy conditions, and the overcrowding, made diseases like cholera, diphtheria, tuberculosis and typhoid rampant.

Orphan children, or those of the most impoverished, had to survive as best they could. 'I went barefoot up till about twelve, I should say,' said William Luby, who in 1883 aged nine earned sixpence a week by leading a blind man about, gaining another few pence by selling wax lights. 'We used to buy wax lights at a halfpenny a box and we sold them for a penny.'

The inhabitants were described by the writer Arthur Morrison as 'Dark, silent, uneasy shadows passing and crossing – human vermin in this reeking sink, like goblin exhalations from all that is noxious around. Women with sunken, black-rimmed eyes, whose pallid faces appear and vanish by the light of an occasional gas lamp, and look so like ill-covered skulls that we start at their stare.'

Even the better parts of London were not immune to the tide of human wreckage that seeped westwards. The Embankment, with its gardens, its electric lighting, and where the Salvation Army dispensed soup tickets, became an especial target for the homeless.

'I walked home along the Embankment this morning at two o'clock with the editor of the *Standard*,' wrote Ralph D. Blumenfeld, an American journalist who moved to London in 1894. 'Every bench from Blackfriars to Westminster Bridge was filled with shivering people, all huddled up – men, women and children.' Some had come to London looking for work, others were unemployed. Pickpocketing was rife, with crowds waiting for omnibuses or trains being favourite targets. Watches were removed from chains, purses from pockets.

What everyone noticed about London was the filth, mostly the result of soot. England in the 1880s was a coal-burning economy, with every fire in every house coal-based and factory chimneys pumping out billows of sooty smoke. 'The compartment in which I sat was filled with passengers who were smoking pipes, as is the British habit, and as the smoke and sulphur from the engine fill the tunnel, all the windows have to be closed,' wrote Blumenfeld of a journey on the Underground.

'The atmosphere was a mixture of sulphur, coal dust and foul fumes from the oil lamp above; so that by the time we reached Moorgate Street I was near dead of asphyxiation and heat. I should think these Underground railways must soon be discontinued, for they are a menace to health.'

Domestically, soot deposits meant that furniture had to be cleaned constantly to remove the steady film of greasy soot. On warm days a summer shower could bring soot-laden drops down on anyone walking beneath trees, with the consequent ruin of hat or dress, and the filthy air produced the notorious, dreadful London fogs (the poor in the East End suffered slightly more because the prevalence of west winds pushed this suffocating miasma eastwards).

On some days, these heavy blankets of polluted air were so thick that a person could not see the ground and inhaling was intensely painful. 'The air we breathed scarified where it went, and set up a temporary inflammation,' wrote the London correspondent of one newspaper of the terrible fog of December 1873, when cattle at the Islington Cattle Show were asphyxiated and fifty either died or had to be slaughtered. Seven men fell into the West India Docks and drowned during the week the fog lasted; and the death rate of the elderly and those suffering from lung complaints rose sharply. Cab men shouted their lungs hoarse to avoid crashes, lamps were kept burning all day long, and through the yellow pall a greasy black sediment settled on everything from furniture to lungs.* The only people who profited from fog, at its peak in the 1880s,† were burglars and pickpockets.

Fogs were the only time the noise of London abated. Otherwise, straw laid in front of a grand house helped to muffle some of it and was also a signal of sickness or death. Other exterior signs on a house were those of festivity: the striped awnings that covered doorways leading to dances and the strip of red carpet laid from the road to the doorway so that when carriages, emblazoned with the arms of their owners, drew up, the evening slippers and skirts of the ladies would not be sullied. At most of these houses the host and hostess would be standing at the top of the stairs to greet the guests surging several deep up huge marble staircases, glittering with orders, the family tiara and the family jewels – almost invariably diamonds, though many women were also festooned with great ropes of pearls.

'Mary and I attended Lady Rothschild's ball, arriving at 12.00 o'clock,' wrote Mrs Leiter of one of these entertainments in her daily journal in 1891. 'The Prince and Princess of Wales, the Princesses Victoria and Maud, Duke of Teck, Princess Mary and Princess May came in the Royal suite. Lady Rothschild asked Mary to dance in the Royal Quadrille. The Princess of Wales spoke to Mary and shook hands with her, most friendly. The house is superb, having a court of white marble to the roof and the marble stairway was most grand. The jewels were magnificent, Lady Rothschild wearing a magnificent set of pearls three strands, very large. Mary wore a white lace dress and a diamond swallow in her hair. I wore a blue satin and mauve velvet with my tiara and necklace of diamonds and rubys. We stayed till 3. p.m.'

At these dances, with their quadrilles, polkas and waltzes – though reversing was banned in royal circles – the conservatories that often led off ballrooms were popular for sitting out;

* Fog also clogged up the leaves of plants and trees, inhibiting growth, hence the success of the London plane tree – its shiny leaves were quickly washed clean by rain and its bark peeled regularly, thus was self-cleansing.

† In 1886 there were eighty-six foggy days in London.

comfortable basket chairs half-hidden by tall palms, the heady fragrance of the flowers, and the champagne already drunk made these bowers of romance. Invitations to such balls were by handwritten note; in the 1890s there were twelve postal deliveries a day in London.

A vital part of the London season (roughly from 1 May to the end of July) concerned the bringing-out of that year's crop of debutantes. Now began the strict control of whom they would meet and whom they should marry. Marriage was crucially important, not only for reasons of status, children, an establishment of their own and, hopefully, love: it was the only option for an aristocratic young woman if she were to avoid being dependent on the charity of a brother or other relation after her father died and she had perforce to leave the family home.

Before coming out, a young girl would be trained in how to climb in and out of a carriage gracefully, how to curtsey and how to walk out of a room backwards while holding a long court train – necessary for her presentation at one of the four afternoon Drawing Rooms a year. For this ritual, she wore a low-cut, short-sleeved white dress with a train not less than three yards in length depending from her shoulders, with three ostrich feathers in her hair, worn slightly to the left-hand side of her head, and long white gloves. If the debutante was the daughter of a peer, the Queen leant forward and kissed her; if she was the daughter of a commoner, she kissed the Queen's hand.

Arrival at the Palace, another of the required formalities, presented a spectacle for the crowds. Beautifully dressed women, heavy with jewels and family tiaras, sat in the family state coach, brought out for the occasion, with a bewigged coachman alone in front, seated on a splendid 'hammercloth', and powdered footmen in the family livery glittering with silver or gold lace hanging on to embroidered straps at the back. As they queued to enter the Palace forecourt crowds would peer in through the windows, often making disconcerting comments to each other. Sometimes a hairdresser ran from coach to coach to make last-minute adjustments to his clients' veils and feathers.

Night after night these young girls, dressed in virginal white, made their appearance in ballrooms, under the assessing gaze of the young men whom, it was hoped, they would fairly shortly marry. The young Winston Churchill used to stand in the doorway of a ballroom, rating female looks on the Helen of Troy basis: 'Is this the face that launched a thousand ships?' he would ask a friend standing with him, receiving in answer a murmured: 'Two hundred ships?' as a young woman passed. 'By no means,' Winston would respond. 'A covered sampan or a small gunboat at most.' There was no equivalent of the American belle; in England the beauties were married women and actresses, and by the late 1880s the Professional Beauties had upped the stakes for feminine loveliness.

Proposals during one's first season were seen not only as a route to the desirable state of matrimony but as a benchmark of attractiveness; all girls hoped for several during their first season. 'Anyone who failed to secure a proposal within six months of coming out could only wait for her second season with diminishing chances. After the third there remained nothing but India as a last resort before the spectre of Old Maid became a reality,' wrote Mabell Gore, underlining the assumption that acquiring a husband quickly was essential. Behind her dire prediction, however, hovering like a spectre at a feast, lay something darker, and unspoken – the complex mystery of sex.

For decades the medical profession had been tying itself in knots over female sexual attitudes. Doctors were in no doubt that men needed sex, and indeed might be adversely affected without it. But as the famous Dr William Acton wrote (in *The Functions and Disorders of the Reproductive Organs*, a book widely read in England and reprinted in America), 'The majority of women (happily for society) are not very much troubled with sexual feeling of any kind,' and as late as 1910 the well-known doctor and sex specialist Havelock Ellis was commenting: 'by many, sexual anaesthesia is considered natural in women, some even declaring that any other opinion would be degrading to women'.

But at the same time, many of these (all-male) doctors prophesied that for a woman denied sexual intercourse, hysteria and 'neurasthenia' were the least of the ailments she could suffer. Even an early and fervent proponent of women's rights, Richard Carlile, claimed that 'women who have never had sexual commerce begin to droop when about twenty-five years of age, become pale and languid, a general weakness and irritation . . . takes possession of them . . . their forms degenerate, their features sink, and the peculiar character of the old maid becomes apparent'.

Friends and relations did their best to avert this fate by inviting the girl in her first season on a round of house parties and dinners, where she could polish up her conversational skills and become accustomed to the grown-up world. As Beatrice Webb wrote on coming out in 1876, it was all 'an existence without settled occupation or personal responsibility, having for its end nothing more remote than elaborately expensive opportunities for getting married'.

Now that they were 'out', these young women, who might have romped freely with brothers and male cousins as children, were guarded as if in imminent danger of violent sexual assault or – worse – falling into the arms of some attractive but penniless 'unsuitable'. Although the rules of chaperonage had moved on – a little – from the mid-century, when they were so strict that an unmarried woman under thirty could not go anywhere, or be alone even in her own house with an unrelated man unless there was a married woman or servant there (no unmarried woman, however old, could be a chaperone), they were still fairly comprehensive. Even a married Englishwoman of the upper classes would never have travelled alone or bought a railway ticket – a footman would have done it for her.

As for young girls, they were not allowed to walk down St James's Street as this was overlooked by the windows of gentlemen's clubs (if they were inadvertently taken past them in a vehicle they should cast their eyes down), the north side of Piccadilly (where bachelor chambers abounded) or go to Burlington Arcade, famous for its shops, in the afternoon because of the danger of meeting streetwalkers there. At balls, they were not allowed to sit out a dance with a young man or dance more than three dances with the same one.

To parental eyes, the ever-present danger that a daughter might suffer not so much a fate worse than death but have been in a situation where, with a stretch of the imagination, she could have suffered it, was to be avoided at all costs. To secure the unquestioned legitimacy of a male heir she must be known to be utterly innocent when she went to her marriage bed. Thus an early marriage was considered highly desirable, often for boys as well as girls: what was vital was the production of this heir and if possible a spare, to ensure the continuance of the line and the smooth passing of the estate from one generation to the next.

It was only after marriage that girls, kept in the schoolroom virtually until being presented at court, began to blossom, to make their own friendships and, with a reasonably complaisant husband, perhaps otherwise occupied himself, indulge in a love affair or two.

What was essential was discretion: scandal had to be avoided at any price. So a child of such a liaison – a second daughter, maybe, or a third son – was brought up in the marital nursery, as a child of the house, with no questions asked. 'Never comment on a likeness,' Lady Moncreiffe advised her debutante daughter. It was all very different from the American model of marriage.

Or, as Mary Elizabeth Lucy put it more cynically of another case: 'Sir Edward is a regular made-up old dandy, with a wig, false dyed moustache, false teeth and very crotchety on his legs! But what does that matter? When a man, however old, has a fine house in the country, ditto in London and a fine income, he can always get a wife, and I am sorry to say a young one too if he wishes it [Sir Edward's wife was forty years younger than her husband]. A rich old woman also can get a penniless young man for her husband, for instance that poor Baroness Cheque Book, as an American named the Baroness Burdette Coutts.' (Widely known as the richest heiress in England, the sixty-seven-year-old Angela Burdett-Coutts had shocked polite society by marrying her twenty-nine-year-old secretary, the American-born William Lehman Ashmead Bartlett.)

What was agreed, on both sides of the Atlantic, was the overwhelming desirability of marriage. Age, bad behaviour, the likelihood of infidelity – all were as nothing compared with the horror of being left 'on the shelf'. Few could have mustered the blistering retort of the novelist Marie Corelli when asked why she had remained single. 'I never married because there was no need. I have three pets at home which answer the same purpose as a husband. I have a dog which growls every morning, a parrot which swears all afternoon, and a cat that comes home late at night.'

CHAPTER 5

Living in the Country

What often came as a rude shock to the American heiresses who married into the British aristocracy was just how much of their lives they were expected to spend in the country, rather than in the exciting milieu in which they had first met their husbands.

For it was land that had supported the aristocracy for centuries, from which they drew their wealth and their great houses, on which they led their sporting lives – sporting lives that ruled the social calendar – and land on which lay the village or small market town that marked the nucleus of their greater or lesser fiefdom. In 1873 almost a quarter of England belonged to the great landowners.

Primogeniture had kept these large estates in one piece, aided by the process known as 'strict settlement' that prevented heirs from selling any part of the family estate to pay off debts. Thus the great country house was not so much the property and home of an individual and his family as the seat of a clan that he, as head of the whole family, held in trust for his descendants. It followed – another shock for American girls – that the wife was absolutely subservient to her husband. 'After the Almighty, let your husband reign in your heart,' was the advice given by her father to Lady Cecil Talbot when she married Lord Lothian. 'You have no duty but to obey him. Watch his looks and fulfil all his wishes, conform yourself to his habits and inclinations.'

Unfortunately, these seldom took him in the direction of

creature comforts for his new bride. To an American girl, accustomed to a nice warm house and plenty of hot water when she felt like a bath, the icy corridors and inadequate plumbing of the English country house often came as a hideous shock. Mildred Sherman, from Ohio, who became Lady Camoys, gave up going to dinner at country houses because she couldn't withstand the temperatures in an evening dress (shawls and wraps were never worn at night).

Mary Leiter, on marrying Lord Curzon, was staggered to find that she was expected to bathe in a tin hip bath which was filled with hot water brought up by a housemaid from the boiler in the kitchen. Her sister Marguerite ('Daisy'), who married the Earl of Suffolk and Berkshire, felt the same. She, however, a less yielding character than Mary, insisted on building her own bathroom amid the ancient splendour of Charlton Park, the house built for her husband's ancestor, the 1st Earl, in 1607, even bringing her own bath, a lavish affair with eight taps, from Chicago.

It was all so different from home. Before the Civil War, Americans had been as dirty as Europeans, but by the 1880s, middle-class city dwellers had begun getting water pumped into their houses. The first American bathrooms were largely found in hotel basements (plumbing then seldom extended to the first floor), catering for those who had journeyed across the vast distances of America and so were weary and travel-stained. Soon private houses followed, and by the time the great mansions of the Gilded Age were being built, bathrooms had become a necessity to everyone who could afford them.

This was far from the case in England. Although the most famous writer of the age, Charles Dickens, had an up-to-the-minute bathroom installed in 1851, in which he took a cold shower every morning ('I do sincerely believe that it does me unspeakable service'), he was one of the very few with such an advanced approach. Most people were happy with a daily sponge bath, while in great houses a combination of apathy, disinclination and snobbishness fought successfully against modern plumbing: because the middle classes and nouveaux riches welcomed such things as gas, water closets and piped-in water, the upper classes tended to regard them as – well, middle-class and therefore to be avoided.

Then, too, for some time baths had a flavour of ill-repute. The famous courtesans and actresses – mistresses, in other words, of rich men – were known to spend long hours soaking themselves in their luxurious baths and then anointing their bodies with exotic preparations. And what for? was the unspoken question. When it became known that Cora Pearl and La Païva, celebrated belle époque courtesans in Paris, had respectively a magnificent bronze bath and a bathroom walled in onyx with a silver tub, both furnished with mysterious and delicious oils and unguents with which to prepare their bodies for further sensual delights, there could be only one answer.

So for many years the whole idea of a female removing all her clothes to enjoy bathing in warm, possibly scented (*quelle horreur!*) water had a frisson of forbidden erotic pleasure – many convent-educated girls were ordered to bathe in a shift to avoid the corrupting influence of nakedness. In country houses, however, the lack of bathrooms was due much more to a lethargic contentment with the status quo: there were plenty of servants to cart hot water up to bedrooms, so why bother to install expensive plumbing?

To come from New World steam heat and hot baths to the English equivalent was to experience an unpleasant surprise, although for many American girls the sense of isolation and culture shock was even worse. If a husband did not, or would not, entertain, they might find themselves stuck for weeks or months on end in a large house with few comforts and little to do except gaze at the rain. Life for them felt wretched, and most of them, with their huge dowries handed over to their husbands, could do little about it, a situation that must have accounted for a good many of the unhappier marriages.

A fortunate few, however, still had charge of their own money and thus, to a degree, of their lives. One of these was Anna Murphy, whose solution to boredom and unhappiness was constant travelling. 'What sort of a life do I have to lead to induce me to return any sooner than I can help?' she wrote to her baronet husband on one of her trips abroad.

Anna was one of the four daughters of Daniel Murphy and his wife Anna Geoghan. Daniel had emigrated from Ireland during the potato famine, or Great Starvation (1845–52). Arriving in New York, he had begun work on the transcontinental railway that offered employment to so many Irish labourers, working his way across America until he reached the village (as it then was) of San Francisco, where he opened a hardware store. Then, in 1848, came the Gold Rush, and with Murphy's the only hardware store in town it was the place all the would-be miners went for equipment. Between January 1848 and December 1849, the population of San Francisco increased from 1,000 to 25,000 and Daniel Murphy's business expanded exponentially. Within a few years he had made a fortune. But the Murphys, with their humble beginnings and 'nouveau' money, could not get into society. Mrs Murphy took a route by now beginning to be time-honoured: she took her daughters to Europe in search of husbands, preferably titled.

Charles Wolseley, the 9th baronet, born in 1846, had inherited his title when he was only eight. As a minor, he had been made a Ward in Chancery, and as such his mother was not permitted to go on living at Wolseley Hall, so she took her children abroad, where living was more economical. At eleven, he was brought back to England for formal education, living with his mother at the estate's dower house, Park House.

He did not take to education. His response when she insisted that he go to Oxford University was that he would do so, but he would not study, would not take his degree and would leave when he was twenty-one. He did all three, and the parting words of the Dean of his college to him were: 'I hope to hear anything good of you but I never expect to.'

When Charles attained his majority he had hoped to live at Wolseley Hall, but it needed so much refurbishing and repairing after neglect by its various tenants that when he had completed these he could no longer afford to live there. So he took himself off for long trips abroad, not even returning for his mother's funeral in 1873. When he did return, he lived at Park House (the dower house), where his mother had lived, and spent the next five years working hard at enjoying himself. He shot, he hunted, he raced in point-to-points, and became one of the country's first polo players.

When he lost money betting on races, he let Park House and went abroad again. On his return, he again found that the tenants of Wolseley Hall had let the place go and major repairs were needed. This time, the bill was £4,000 plus another £800 to build new stables. He turned to the solution found by others in his predicament – a pretty American heiress.

Charles had met the Murphys in San Francisco on one of his trips abroad, and now proposed to the prettiest daughter, Anna, with the agreement that her father would settle over $1 million on him. Unfortunately for Charles, after the wedding (in 1883) but before the money had been transferred, Mr Murphy died, and Anna's siblings, feeling that too much of the estate was going to the Wolseleys, contested the will and had the Wolseley portion reduced. Even worse for Charles, it was settled on Anna rather than him.

At first Sir Charles and the new Lady Wolseley were happy, and two little boys were born. But then the familiar drawbacks of life in the English countryside became too much for someone like Anna, accustomed to the lively social scene of the European capitals. Financially independent and with the self-confidence that was her American birthright, she took matters into her own hands – and spent as little time in her new home as possible, largely through extended and highly expensive trips abroad.

By 1899 she was in India, enjoying herself taking photographs, moving around the country, asking her husband to send out some of her clothes and refusing to come home because she 'hadn't seen enough of India yet and didn't have time to pack before the ship sailed'.

Relations between them had begun to deteriorate, so much so that she refused to return for her sons' six-week school holidays, though she continued to sign her letters with the phrase 'The Sweet Wife Wolseley'. But this did not stop her writing that April:

'I cannot see why you wish to make it so great an affair my being away for the holidays instead of suggesting that you will try and fill my place towards the boys for this once . . . with only the past life to face on my return – for I can picture no other – little wonder that I tarry in doing so.'

When she did return, she complained of her husband's indifference, saying that he was too cold, detached, inattentive and unsympathetic ('I don't believe you have once made a kind personal reference to me since I left in one of your letters, as to whether I was well, enjoying myself, or anything about me'), though she hoped the American flag was still flying at Wolseley Hall on the Fourth of July.

As for the wealth that had been supposed to rescue the Wolseley fortunes, this was still firmly in Anna's grasp. Although she sent her husband an allowance to keep up the estate for their elder son Edric, Charles found this inadequate and sold off a few pictures to supplement his income, upon which Anna promptly cut the allowance by half. By now their marriage had become a misery, with Anna's letters bristling with hostility; any hotel room on earth, she assured him, was better than a night under the same roof as him. To survive, Charles sold more and more until, finally, almost everything had gone and, broken and wretched, he was forced to leave the Hall.

In nineteenth-century Britain, politics and land were inextricably mingled: almost three-quarters of the Commons represented landed interests, and so did nearly all the House of Lords, an aristocracy so small that it was almost tribal, with its own nicknames, jokes and expressions. In those old Whig families where the gulf between the two parties still remained, even certain words were differently pronounced. Little Whig children were taught to say 'cawfee' instead of coffee, 'yaller' instead of yellow, 'cowcumber' for cucumber, 'napern' for apron and 'Orspital' and 'orficer' for hospital and officer. To call a chimneypiece a mantelpiece, wrote Mabell Gore, the daughter of Viscount Sudley, 'proclaimed a Tory of the deepest dye'.

It was also strictly hierarchical, with everyone knowing exactly where everyone stood. When Consuelo Vanderbilt married the Duke of Marlborough in 1895 he told her that there were just 200 families whose names and titles she must remember. Precedence was all-important, not just for seating but for the procession in to dinner: one of the four earls she was entertaining at her first big weekend house party reproved her on the second night because she had wrongly given one of the other three precedence over him.

The converse of this was that because gradations of rank were both accepted and well known, there was little jostling for position – competition took other forms – as everyone knew that no matter how hard she tried, a marchioness could never outrank a duchess. At the top, of course, was Queen Victoria, but, honour though it was to serve her, it could not have been called fun. Gloom, cold and formality were the salient characteristics of the court. There was little colour, with the Queen in the mourning she always wore after the death of the Prince Consort in 1861, the conversation frequently of funerals and epitaphs, in which Victoria was keenly interested and, for the last twenty years of her reign, dinner parties conducted in almost total silence. Balmoral, always freezing-cold – the Queen detested fires – was even more hideous for those unlucky enough to be invited. 'We just exist from meal to meal and do our best to kill time,' wrote one of her ladies-in-waiting, Marie Adeane, in 1890. It was not surprising that smart society revolved round the pleasure-loving, genial Prince of Wales.

Another surprise for American brides was the discovery that politics was generally part of daily life – discussed over the dinner table, written about in letters. ('I cannot help thinking you are quite in the wrong when you say so decidedly "Drop the Education Bill",' wrote one wife to her husband before going on to say, 'in less than a week, my darling, we shall be together once more . . .') Spending afternoons in the Strangers' Gallery to listen to important debates or those in which a brother or husband was involved was a recognised entertainment, while the great hostesses were also political enablers.

'Cyril Flower asked us to dine with him at the House of Commons, which we did in the evening,' wrote Mary Theresa Leiter when she and her daughter Mary visited London. 'The guests were Lord and Lady Rayleigh (she is sister of Arthur Balfour), Mr George Wyndham, Mr G. Curzon, St John Brodrick and Lady Hilda his wife, H. H. Asquith, Princesse de Wagram, Mary and I. The dinner was a brilliant one and all were MPs except of course Lord Rayleigh. After dinner we went to Mr Brodrick's Committee Room, where we took our coffee, when all the members were summoned for a Division.'

This intermingling of social life and politics in a way then unknown in America was not merely because the simple geographical reason of lesser distance allowed peers and other landowners to come up to London for parliamentary terms, staying in their own or rented town houses; more that in England 'the ruling class' *was* the ruling class; and it was a matter of hereditary custom that they should be so. As late as 1865 a mere sixty families supplied one third of the House of Lords and one third of the House of Commons, thus one third of the ruling body of an empire that comprised a quarter of the world's population.

In America, by contrast, a large proportion of the 'movers and shakers' were busy opening up the prairies, building railways and establishing mining, stockbroking and real estate businesses anywhere from California to Connecticut – in other words, focusing on the expansion of the country's wealth and economy – while politics per se took place in Washington.

Politics was in fact the ruling social passion of many of the upper-class English. Statesmen met each other at the houses of the leading hostesses, often arriving at a private consensus that would later be ratified in Parliament – and probably to be watched from the gallery that afternoon by the same women at whose houses they had so recently dined.

Once the season was over, they were to be found at carefully arranged country-house parties, where instead of confidential discussions over cigars there were strolls in the shrubbery well away from listening ears; or meetings in a quiet library. Nor did the gossip-writers in England concern themselves with private house parties, so that it was possible for political opponents or ambassadors from arguing countries to have friendly discussions in an atmosphere of privacy and luxury.

Autumn was the best time for these country-house weekends – known then as Saturdays to Mondays (because as in law a 'gentleman' was 'a man who has no occupation', the word 'weekend' implied that weekdays were spent earning a living). There was still late-summer sun, the hunting and shooting seasons had not yet started, debutantes, now 'out', could be asked to leaven the mix, Parliament did not go back until after Christmas – and after the exhaustions of the season, rest in the country was welcome. Besides, there would be plenty of gossip over what had gone on during the balls and dances and close proximities of those three months of gruelling late nights – who had been seen with whom, who had said what to whom, who had got engaged and who hadn't.

Such weekends were, of course, ostensibly nothing to do with politics but all about enjoyment of the company of interesting or like-minded people. Often they were all from the same small set, but as the century drew on, as well as the usual aristocratic contingent there might be a diplomat, one or two well-known beauties, a painter, a writer and a musician, who would entertain the company after dinner.

The hidden agenda, though, was frequently the facilitating or furthering of romances and love affairs. With restaurants largely out of bounds to respectable women – and hotels even more so – there would have been few chances to meet in London but, during a country weekend, riding or walks together or a disappearance for a pre-dinner stroll in the shrubbery were easily manageable.

Assignations were discreetly arranged; any touching in public was taboo, but a man might show his interest in a woman by writing a note that his valet would give to her maid to put on her breakfast tray, perhaps suggesting a walk together before lunch or, if it was a shooting party, that she should stand with him at his 'peg'. Labels with the occupant's name on them slotted into brass holders on bedroom doors not only stopped anyone getting lost in a large, strange house but allowed illicit visits during the night ('children of the mist' was one name for a child sired by someone not the husband).

'For a winter visit you arrived about five o'clock,' wrote the novelist Elinor Glyn of staying with the Prince's favourite, Lady Warwick. 'The entrance hall where you left your furs had trophy heads round it, as had every other hall in this kind of house at that time, because all proper Englishmen (who could afford it) went big-game shooting all over the world, and brought back the heads of every sort of strange animal to adorn their stately houses.'

You would then be taken into the saloon, where your hostess and any other lady guests were to be found. 'They would be wearing tea gowns, of velvet or satin brocade, trimmed with sable,' recalled Elinor. 'They usually had V-necks and elbow-length sleeves. They would be enjoying a substantial tea – muffins, crumpets, cakes, scones with honey or jam and Devonshire cream instead of, as formerly, only slices of thin bread and butter.'

Tea would be removed by footmen. In a grand house, these might be chosen for their matching heights – Lady Warwick's were all six foot – and good looks. The hostess would then take the ladies to their bedrooms, 'made luxurious with sofas heaped with soft down cushions, stands loaded with the newest books near them, white bear hearthrugs, shaded lamps, silk or tapestry hangings, writing tables with pens, paper and stamps'. Behind a screen, tipped against the wall, was a huge, painted tin tub, to be filled with hot water brought up by housemaids every morning. A fire would already have been lit.

Most people arrived by train, often with several changes en route and always accompanied by a mountain of luggage – hat-boxes, trunks containing numerous changes of clothing swathed in tissue paper, guns, shooting sticks, field glasses or fishing rods if for a sporting weekend, as well as personal miscellanea. 'My mother had been born in the era when you took sketching materials, and a great many heavy London Library books, as well as clothes,' wrote Lady Tweedsmuir. 'She usually also had an embroidery frame and, as she was often studying a language, primers were added to everything else.' Once the luggage wagon had arrived – guests went by the faster brougham – trunks would be unpacked by the lady's maid and valet brought by the couple, and clothes hung up on hooks (coat-hangers had not yet been invented).

For breakfast women wore simple morning frocks, changing into slightly more elaborate dresses for luncheon or, if they were going out for a shooting lunch, tweed coats and skirts, followed, in the late afternoon, by a tea gown – the men might change into velvet smoking suits – and, finally, into full fig for dinner. Some houses provided men with buttonholes and ladies with sprays of gardenias or orchids; most had freezing passages along which women in their décolletée evening dresses had to scurry.

On the first night, guests went in to dinner according to rank, with each man 'taking in' (i.e. offering his arm to) a woman. After dinner the new game of bridge* might be played, after which every guest would take a silver candlestick from a tray in the hall and carry it up to his or her room where maid or valet would help them to undress.

As no one could be seen in the same outfit twice, this meant ten or more for a weekend, each with its appropriate accessories – gloves, belts, scarves, wraps, fans and underwear – corsets, shifts and flounced, frilled, lace-trimmed petticoats and jewellery (diamonds to be worn only at night). If royalty were there, this meant tiaras. No one wore make-up.

Life in these houses ran to a series of unwritten rules. The large staff of servants needed for this meant a complex interdependence between family and staff. In a great house, the number of servants was a correlation between how many were required to do its work and how many the owner could afford, the latter in order to display his proper standing. A ratio of three or four servants to each member of the family was quite normal. At Eaton Hall, the Duke of Westminster had fifty indoor servants

* Bridge was first played in London at the Portland Club in 1894. The rules gradually changed and by 1904 the game had developed into Auction Bridge.

and forty gardeners, while Edwin Lee,* second footman to the Honourable Frederick George Wynn, at Glynliven Park, Caernarvonshire, recalled: 'Mr Wynn was a bachelor of some sixty years, living alone, entertaining rarely yet keeping a full establishment [of fifty-one servants) . . . All these people to look after one gentleman.'

Major-domos would remove yesterday's blotting paper from bedroom blotters before curious housemaids had a chance to hold it up to the mirror and perhaps read a love note, a valet would shave his master, iron his shoelaces and could double as a loader in a shooting party, log boys watched an hourglass to know when to run and refill log baskets in the family's rooms, lamp boys kept wicks trimmed and lamps filled, and there might be a night soil man or a spider boy, who had a bunch of feathers tied to a long stick for knocking high-up spiders' webs to the ground.

Followers were generally forbidden and fraternising with someone from the opposite sex within the house meant instant dismissal. 'In Paris we had a housemaid who was a most charming and delightful girl, and she had a child by one of the footmen in the house,' wrote Lady Emily Lytton in October 1892 to her confidant the Rev. Whitwell Elwin. 'Of course the poor girl was sent away, and she went to a wretched lodging in London, where her child was born, and she died, which was the best thing that could happen to her, poor thing.'

It took an American girl, as Lady Grantley, to ignore this brutal policy. 'She created what I believe was a world's precedent for the time, in forgiving and reinstating a kitchen maid who had got into trouble,' wrote her son, the 6th Lord Grantley.

The house itself was divided up in a way that roughly reflected the different lifestyles of its master and mistress – library, dining room, smoking room and billiards room were largely masculine areas, women ruled the drawing room, music room and boudoir, that small private sitting room, decorated in a style that was soft, luxurious and inviting, in which the lady of the house could talk

---

* In Rosina Harris's *Gentlemen's Gentlemen*, Sphere Books, 1976.

freely to her intimate women friends. This separation also meant that a listless or unhappy marriage could be kept going or made bearable. Lord and Lady Howard, for instance, separated but continued to occupy the same house.

Divorce was virtually unthinkable: the husband was entitled to keep not only the children – whom, if the wife had committed adultery, she could be prevented from seeing because of her moral turpitude – but also all the money and property she had brought to the marriage, so that a divorced woman was both ostracised and penniless.*

While the owner of the great house met his agent, saw to the management of the estate or went out shooting, his womenfolk were kept busy. His wife ran the house, conferring with housekeeper and cook over bedrooms and menus for weekend house parties and, with her daughters, took food, medicine and clothing to the poor or sick of the parish. Sometimes she conducted Bible readings as well as organising garden parties for charity and Christmas parties for tenants, servants and families. In some houses there were annual servants' balls, which were extremely popular.

In England women, especially those in the upper classes, were second-class citizens. Sylvia Brett, Lord Esher's daughter, knew from early childhood that 'women were only brought into the world to become the slaves of men. Every morning it was our duty to lace up our brothers' boots.' And, as the anonymous author of *Good Form* (1888), wrote, 'they are brought up to feel that their first duty in life is to get out of the way of their brothers as soon as they possibly can, and marriage is the only possible means within their reach'.

In other words, unlike the mansions of Fifth Avenue or the 'cottages' of Newport, English stately homes were not thought of as impressive backdrops for beautifully gowned women determined to impress with their wealth and social status, but run as the man who owned them thought fit.

---

* It was not until the 1880s that women were able to gain custody of their children and control their own properties.

The only person of whom the head of the house was sometimes afraid was his mother. It was the era when the rule of the dowager was supreme. 'Widowed mothers exacted obedience from sons and daughters, no matter what their age,' wrote Mabell Gore, who became the Countess of Airlie. As for the daughters, their whole upbringing was directed towards finding a husband (of their own class, almost needless to say). Marriage was the only alternative to remaining at home under parental authority, and later being forced out, on the father's death, to dependence on others or a meagre allowance. To this end, accomplishments rather than education were necessary: they learnt French, music, dancing, sketching, deportment, needlework (useful in the long winter evenings) and, perhaps most important of all, how a great house was run. As their social intercourse was limited to those houses considered suitable within reach of the carriage horses, this often meant a fairly isolated childhood and adolescence, largely confined to the house and its gardens. In the year or two before coming out, they might appear at luncheon but were not expected to say anything more than yes or no. It was something no American girl would have stood for.

CHAPTER 6

Mrs Paran Stevens

American society was built on competition. Everything counted, from the size and number of the jewels with which the women were freighted to the smartness of the carriages in which they drove out. Oliver Belmont had chestnut horses with footmen in green livery – well, Mrs Stuyvesant Fish had the rarer colour of strawberry roans.

'I know of no art, profession or work for women more taxing on mental resources than being a leader of society,' said Alva Vanderbilt after years of engaging in that struggle. It was a battle into which Alva and others like her entered with gusto – and none more so than the woman who became known as Mrs Paran Stevens. Though it might seem pointless to us, it was all-engaging to these matriarchs of the Gilded Age.

Their ruthless social ambition was the equivalent of the ferocious, no-holds-barred fights for power in the boardrooms of their men, in whom the early, frontier spirit still lived. Had not the financier Leonard Jerome, cultured patron of the arts though he was, picked up a Gatling gun to defend the office building of the *New York Times*, in which he was a major shareholder, at the time of the New York Draft Riots of 1863? James Gordon Bennett Snr, founder of the *New York Herald*, kept a cache of weapons in his office in case of attack by the angry readers who often gathered outside the building.

Both males and females were descended from the same stock: those who had come to America to make their fortunes, had worked hard, taken chances, gambled on possibilities, survived difficulties and come out on top, but for the women there was only one field open in which to employ these qualities – the social. For the wives of the robber barons (as many of their men were known, with good reason), entry into the élite, exclusive milieu of the chosen was the main purpose of their lives. What made American society so much more competitive than English was that it was instituted by, run by and run for the benefit of women – women who had little else to do.

Hence the battles royal in Newport and New York, the steely concentration, the miseries at social slights, the iron determination to clamber over the top of the stockade into the charmed circle at the centre, the bitter tears if an invitation failed to materialise. Nothing was overlooked, down to the abstraction of cards with famous names on them from the salver on someone's hall table by socially ambitious lady callers to leave out on their own hall tables to impress others.

No aspect of behaviour was too peripheral to be ignored by those wishing to climb to society's upper reaches. Religion, or rather the public practice of it, was also part of the social round, and as competitive as its other rituals. Roughly speaking, the more successful you were in business, the more devout you were on Sunday; and even where you sat in that church was a mark of social status.

As far as the social élite was concerned, there were only five churches in New York City. 'Going to church was a social function,' recalled Elizabeth Drexel. 'Pierpont Morgan took up the collection at St Bartholomew's, the Vanderbilt men roared out the hymns untunefully at St Thomas's.' The most fashionable was the massive Gothic edifice of Grace Church (at the corner of East 10th Street and Broadway), considered so important socially that it was attended not only by its regular congregation but by all those who aspired to enter society – if they could get in.

For so sought after were the 'top' churches that, in a neat compromise between God and Mammon, they were able to sell their pews* at prices only the very rich could afford; indeed, large family pews, the owner's name on a brass plaque on the front, were considered valuable family property that could be handed down through wills. Seats auctioned off at St Bartholomew's in 1872 fetched $321,000, their prices determined by their position, with those on the aisle at the front worth most.

One determined social climber even approached the sexton at Grace Church, offering to pay him handsomely for a list of the most prominent members of the congregation, and when asked why she wanted them, said that she was about to enter society by giving a smart dinner and dance and wished to ask only the best people (the sexton turned down her offer in horror). Another tried to buy the stained-glass windows behind the altar of Calvary Church (on 21st Street) for a huge sum to decorate her dining room, with the same result.

Although awkward subjects like the corrosive effects of great riches were avoided by tactful vicars, morality was emphasised. The passage of time could sterilise fortunes dubiously acquired (three generations washed it white as snow), so that while a father, or preferably a grandfather, might have been known for sharp practice here and there, probity was essential for the son if he was to be an upright member of the congregation or belong to clubs like the Union and the Knickerbocker.

And once the hours of planning, the strategic and tactical manoeuvres, the swallowed snubs and the cruel struggle had succeeded, what then? A life that seems to us, looking back on it, both comic and tragic in its stultifying boredom. The rules, the rituals, the stilted patterns into which the day fell for those who had reached the sunlit uplands of social success were all-important and, to those determined to maintain their position, unavoidable.

Possibly the most relentless social climber of all was Marietta Reed – better known as Mrs Paran Stevens – the tall, good-looking daughter of a grocer from Lowell, Massachusetts. She literally

* There was also an annual rental of 6 to 8 per cent of the purchase price.

forced her way into New York society through sheer persistence, the lavish and unscrupulous use of the fortune her husband had left her, a skin so thick insults bounced harmlessly off it, a legendary temper and a judicious marriage for her daughter. Nothing, from her son's happiness to countless lawsuits and adverse publicity, was allowed to stand in the way of her climb to the top.

This began with her marriage. It was said that she had met her future husband, Paran Stevens, a rich widower who owned a chain of hotels, when she was working as a chambermaid in one of them. Stevens was quickly taken with this pretty, lively brunette and in 1851 they married. At forty-nine, Stevens was more than twice the age of his bride (her birth date is given as 'circa 1834'). Marietta's first step on the road to her ultimate goals, wealth and social eminence, had been taken.

Nine years later, Paran Stevens built the hotel by which he became best known and which hugely increased his fortune: the Fifth Avenue Hotel. Having, to general derision at the time, bought its site in 1848 for a mere $5,000, he proceeded to raise this impressive building on the entire block between 23rd Street and 24th Street, at the south-west corner of Madison Square. Its address was 200 Fifth Avenue and it quickly became known for its luxury and elegance, attracting exactly the sort of clientele that he and Marietta had hoped for.

Then, in 1860, came a huge and unexpected boost to the Stevens' fortunes: when the nineteen-year-old Prince of Wales made his spectacularly successful visit to America (of its triumph the Prince's governor, General Bruce, wrote: 'exaggeration is impossible'), he came to stay at the Fifth Avenue. There could have been no greater imprimatur of excellence for the hotel.

Naturally, Marietta Stevens made it her business to ensure that HRH was comfortable and happy there and a friendly acquaintanceship was formed, Marietta even presenting her small daughter Minnie to the Prince.

As her husband's business expanded to include more hotels and his wealth grew, Mrs Stevens decided it was time to tackle the icy peaks of New York high society. Without family connections, exceptional beauty or an introduction from someone within the circle, and hampered by the story of her past in domestic service, Mrs Stevens realised that her strongest suit was her husband's wealth – and whatever ingenuity she could summon to her aid.

She began her assault by giving musical evenings – musicales, as they were called. It was a wise choice: in early New York, an interest in and appreciation of classical music was a stepping stone towards social acceptability; by 1879 the Academy of Music was the musical centre of the city. Never mind that much of the stage was blocked from view by its huge pillars or that the seating was too close, its eighteen white and gold boxes with their red velvet cushions were filled by all those considered in the social swim. In practice, this meant the Knickerbockers, who would only sell or hand down a box to someone in their own circle.

One of the newly rich, William Henry Vanderbilt, was extremely fond of opera, but his attempts to buy a box were rejected time and again; even when he offered the vast sum of $30,000 for a box for one season only (that of 1880) it was refused. For William Henry this was too much: he had had enough of being thwarted, as had some of his rich friends. None of them was accustomed to being frustrated; all of them had the determination to do something about it. Twenty-two of them, including several Vanderbilts, J. P. Morgan and an Astor (all of whom had been excluded from the Academy), contributed a minimum of $10,000 each (this sum would secure the donor a box) to build their own opera house, bigger, better and grander. They called it the Metropolitan Opera House.

Behind its yellow-brick façade the 'Met's' interior was sumptuous. It was done up in a rich plum colour, with plenty of gilt and three tiers of boxes known as the Golden Horseshoe. On Monday nights carriages, their doors emblazoned with newly bought coats of arms, driven by coachmen with cockaded hats, would draw up at its entrance at 1411 Broadway. At the front of each box would sit two beautifully gowned and bejewelled women, with their men behind. In the intervals, the velvet curtains at the back of these boxes would be drawn aside and the party would repair to the salons behind, some massed with flowers, some hung with satins and brocades. The Vanderbilts acquired five of these boxes.

Not everyone approved of the change. When Anna Robinson, from one of New York's old families, was invited to the Met's opening in October 1883 she was delighted, and thought 'the opera was lovely apart from seeing the new building. Seinbrick is excellent & Canpanini was just as good as ever. Nilsson sat in a box very near us, & looked beautiful, just as handsome as ever. I only hope someone will ask us to see her. The house is enormous, and after one has looked at it for a little while I think one likes the shape of the auditorium, but the decoration is so ugly, the whole building one colour, a dingy coffee color that they will surely have to change. It is so absolutely unlike the other house.'

Monday was the day society went to the opera. The day Mrs Paran Stevens chose for her musical entertainments was Sunday. It was a clever choice as there was no competition for it; Sunday evenings were traditionally a time when the sobriety of the day was concluded by evenings spent in the family. Although breaking this custom was a matter for disapproval, Mrs Stevens did not care. When told by one friend,* 'You don't know what people say about your Sunday evenings, they call it Sabbath-breaking,' she replied with magnificent scorn: 'Do they indeed? They say. *What* do they say? Then *let* them say.'

She was aided in her efforts by her sister, Fanny Reed, a well-known and popular singer often in demand for musical evenings – Fanny had moved her patrician audience to tears when she sang 'The Battle Hymn of the Republic' at Newport in 1860. Indeed, so popular was Fanny that some said she had sung her sister into society, so much so that when she left to live in Paris one Knickerbocker matron, Maria Daly, observed acidly of another musical evening: 'Mrs Fifth-Avenue-hotel was there, of course, with her sister. I would rather dispense with the music than have to take Mrs Stevens with it.'

---

* Frederick Martin, brother of Bradley Martin.

Marietta Stevens also served her guests champagne, just coming into fashion then but still somewhat of an innovation. A cruel portrait of her is drawn in Edith Wharton's 1920s novel *The Age of Innocence*: 'a tremendous black-wigged and red-plumed lady in overflowing furs' who gives Sunday-night musical soirées because, she says, 'it's the day New York doesn't know what to do with itself'.

Marietta Stevens's soirées became popular among many Knickerbocker males, bored by spending the long Sunday evenings in the unaccustomedly close embrace of domesticity . . . but the all-important wives were angered by this so-called desecration of the Sabbath. When the widow Mary Mason Jones, from an old New York family (with whom Marietta would one day become entangled), moved into her Marble Row mansion in 1869, she announced: 'This is one house Mrs Stevens will never enter.' It was a veto that echoed round the exclusive social circles in which Mrs Jones moved, and would entertain in her grand new house.

For Mary Mason Jones believed in sumptuousness. Her box in the Park Theatre was considered the most luxurious: she had had it upholstered in blue silk and all the metalwork replaced by silver rails and fittings, and when in 1854 she inherited two blocks of land from her father, the banker John Mason, she planned buildings like no other. Mason had bought up several acres of undeveloped, rocky terrain in 1823 for approximately $10 a city lot, a bargain that would prove immensely fruitful when the land was eventually carved into sixteen city blocks in what would become known as Midtown.

Mason's will was tied up in the courts for fifteen years, but once the property was hers outright, Mary Mason Jones set to work improving it. Far-sightedly, she took no notice of the fact that her inheritance was more than twenty blocks above the northern fringe of society, stretching from Fifth Avenue to Park Avenue, between 57th and 58th Streets, and in 1867, with the architect Robert Mook, she put her ideas into the building of this part of Fifth Avenue.

Instead of the usual brownstones, the accepted hallmark of the Knickerbocker society to which she belonged, her scheme was based on the exuberant architecture of Paris, Fontainebleau and the country palaces of France, and carried out in white marble. For herself, there was a massive white marble château on Fifth Avenue and East 57th Street. When the project was completed, these isolated mansions, like nothing the city had ever seen before, were immediately given the name Marble Row. Mrs Jones ensconced herself in No. 1 East 57th Street and waited for society to come to her. And it did.*

Decades later the *New York Times* would say: 'Mrs Jones built the series of residences and introduced French tendencies in the architecture. Her innovation has been credited by some as ending the fashion of "brown stone fronts" as the home hallmark of "society".'

The impact of this building was such that Mary Mason Jones's great-niece, Edith Wharton, featured a portrait of her, too, in *The Age of Innocence*. Here she is depicted as Mrs Manson Mingott, the shrewd social leader who constructed her lavish mansion daringly north of the affluent residential district. As for the mansion itself, Mrs Mingott 'put the crowning touch to her audacity by building a large house of cream-coloured stone (when brown sandstone seemed as much the only wear as a frock coat in the afternoon)'. The description of the 'wilderness' that followed was equally true to life.

'It was her habit to sit in a window of her sitting-room on the ground floor,' wrote Edith, 'as if watching calmly for life and fashion to flow northward to her solitary doors. She seemed in no hurry to have them come, for her patience was equalled by her confidence. She was sure that presently the hoardings, the quarries, the one-storey saloons, the wooden green-houses in ragged gardens, and the rocks from which goats surveyed the scene, would vanish before the advance of residences as stately as her own – perhaps (for she was an impartial woman) even statelier.' And as society had come to Mary Jones's door, so it did in the Wharton novel.

* Her foresight and success were such that they gave rise to the saying 'keeping up with the Joneses'.

*

Perhaps Mrs Stevens herself could have lived with the veiled disapproval emanating from New York's old-established families, but by 1871, when her pretty daughter Minnie was eighteen and the time had come for her to be presented to society, society made it clear that it would turn its collective back. Although she kept a carriage at the ready to whisk Minnie from party to party so that she could be seen in all the 'right' places, this had little effect. A season at Newport was tried, where a young man called Fred May from Baltimore wooed Minnie, until Mrs Stevens intimated to him that she had a higher fate in mind for her daughter. For in Mrs Stevens's determination to reach the top, her children were co-opted as stepping stones.

The death of Paran Stevens in 1872 left Marietta a wealthy widow and her daughter an heiress. Now there was nothing to hold her back. Briskly, she withdrew the beautiful Minnie from the longing gaze of several swains and the pair set off for Europe – and, they hoped, a titled husband.

Minnie's looks were of the kind then most in fashion: she had dark hair growing rather low on a broad forehead, well-marked dark brows and brilliant grey-blue eyes. She also had taste, chic and plenty of money. But it seems that Mrs Stevens exaggerated the wealth that Minnie would inherit as there was an embarrassing incident when the most suitable *parti* cried off at the last moment, citing the disparity between what he had been told her dowry would be and the actuality – four times less. 'How galling for a girl to be put in that position!' wrote a friend from New York, where the story was current, to Lady Waldegrave in England.

All the same, the pretty Minnie received a number of proposals, but both she and her mother hoped for an even grander match than the various French counts and second sons who offered. After trawling Europe unsuccessfully for several years they moved to England and, to make the most of the princely connection, Cowes, where the Prince of Wales invariably spent most of August, although Marietta did not much care for the sea, declaring that she 'preferred terra cotta'. At Cowes the friendship with the Prince was renewed and the Prince, who found the chic, style, wealth, superb clothes and general sparkle of American girls entrancing, was glad to welcome another of these charmers.

Finally, when Minnie was twenty-five, which at that time meant she was almost an old maid, when there were no other grander takers she decided to go for the most persistent of her suitors, Captain Arthur Paget, a regular soldier and the grandson of the Marquess of Anglesey, who had earlier courted her in Newport at her mother's house, the Villa Marietta. Although he had originally pursued Minnie largely for practical reasons – as a younger son, Paget was far from affluent – he soon fell in love with her. 'When I first asked you to marry me,' he said, 'my proposal came from my head. *Now* it comes from my heart!'

For the Stevenses, part of Paget's appeal was his close friendship with the Prince of Wales. Much of this centred on the turf, as Paget owned numerous racehorses and would place bets on favoured horses for the Prince, who could not be seen to gamble. Now the Prince did his best to encourage the match, largely to help his friend. When Minnie accepted him, the Prince wrote to her: 'Long ago I hoped that Arthur would find favour in your eyes, and now that all is so happily settled, I cannot tell you how I rejoice that he is to be your future husband.'

As entertaining the Prince was always expensive, Minnie's inheritance was doubly welcome: one estimate of her dowry reckoned she had brought £200,000 to the match, with her mother contributing a further annual $20,000. Marietta also organised the wedding, which took place at St Peter's, Eaton Square on 27 July 1878. The day before, as the papers reported, the Prince 'condescended to pay a visit' to offer his best wishes, and gave Minnie a gold serpent bracelet set with sapphires, diamonds and rubies as a wedding present; a year later, he became godfather to the couple's son.

Married to one of the Prince of Wales's great friends, Minnie was now installed in the highest echelon of English society, the Marlborough House Set, as the group round the Prince were known – and her mother had risen with her. When the Prince visited Marietta the day after Minnie's wedding to congratulate her, this put the final seal on her position. Back in New York, as a friend of the Prince of Wales, Marietta had now, at long last, achieved her objective: she was 'in society', a fact noted publicly when Caroline Belmont, one of its leaders, called on her.

To keep hold of her place within the magic circle Marietta Stevens needed money, and plenty of it; all her life this need for money, representing as it did her only strength in the society to which she had been born an outsider, remained with her. At the same time, she spent to the hilt, as a means of impressing those around her and maintaining her position as an exquisitely dressed social leader.

It was for this reason, undoubtedly, that after her husband Paran's death and although he had left her $1 million and the sole use of both the New York and Newport houses during her lifetime, she instituted legal proceedings against his estate and endeavoured to have two of the three trustees (the third was herself) who managed his properties removed, so that she could be the sole arbiter of its disposition.

'Collecting dollars wherever she could' was how newspapers saw this. The verdict for the first case was announced when she was on the way back from a visit to her daughter in England, whither she had gone to try and procure Minnie's signature on a document that would give her more control over the estate but had failed, as Arthur Paget had objected.

Her attempt to overturn the will was the first of many further lawsuits. 'Her denunciation of those who opposed her was both vigorous and bitter,' said the *Boston Evening Transcript*: this, coupled with her conviction that she was always right, meant that she took no notice of her numerous defeats and that most of these cases made front-page news. Her lawsuits involved anything from a dispute with tenants to the firing of her French chef; another featured fisticuffs and the bribing of a witness, another the alleged assaulting of the tenant of an art gallery, from which she had to be removed by police.

It is also likely that she managed to bring her son's engagement to an end to benefit herself financially.

Harry Stevens, a handsome and charming young man of

twenty-one, had fallen in love with Edith Jones, then a quiet young woman from an old, upper-crust family. In 1880 he spent the summer with Edith's family in Maine, accompanied them to the South of France the following year – where Edith's father died – and after the early period of mourning was over resumed his courtship of Edith at Newport in the summer of 1882.

Here the couple's engagement was announced in the *Newport Daily News* with, unusually, the future bridegroom's name ahead of that of Edith – a fairly definite pointer to the fact that the announcement was placed by Marietta Stevens (about whom there were several other stories in the same issue of the paper) rather than by Edith's family. For to be thus publicly linked with the patrician Jones family could do Marietta nothing but good, augmenting as it did her social credentials.

However, although nothing could take away from the benefit brought by the engagement, from Marietta's point of view there were compelling reasons why the marriage itself should not take place; and a few months later, in late October, the society magazine *Town Topics* reported that the wedding had been postponed 'indefinitely'. Quite apart from the fact that most of the Jones family thought that Marietta would make a poisonous mother-in-law, those closest to Edith believed that the couple were still in love and that 'Mrs S. was at the bottom of it all'.

What is undoubted was her financial motive. Under the terms of her husband's will, Marietta was in control of her son's assets (amounting to more than $1 million) and received the income from them 'until he married or reached the age of twenty-five'. Determined to keep her hands on the money as long as possible, she had already sought (unsuccessfully) legal means to divert part of her son's trust to herself; his marriage would put it out of her reach completely.

Unlike the remnants of 'old' New York society, who curled up with embarrassment at publicity, Mrs Stevens enjoyed it, believing that it kept her firmly in the public eye. She had also learnt, to some extent, how to manage it. Since the entire Jones family would have shunned contact with a newspaper, it was clearly Marietta who managed to make it appear that the hapless

Edith had caused the break-up. *Town Topics* stated that 'the only reason for the breaking of the engagement . . . is an alleged preponderance of intellectuality on the part of the intended bride. Miss Jones is an ambitious authoress and it is said that, in the eyes of Mr Stevens, ambition is a grievous fault.' (Later the magazine remarked that he had keenly felt the breaking of this engagement.)

Shortly afterwards, Mrs Jones took Edith away to the South of France; and in 1885 Edith married Teddy Wharton in Newport. Few were deceived, and Mrs Stevens was less popular than ever. 'Mrs Stevens is such a universal favourite among all Newportians that when it was heard that her jewels had again been stolen the propriety of clothing the town in black and hanging all suspicious characters to the lamp posts was seriously considered,' said *Town Topics* sarcastically (the jewels were later found under her pillows).

Harry Stevens died a few months later at his mother's home in Newport. A few days after his death, she took the highly unusual step of commissioning an autopsy by three top New York doctors; the results – the cause of death was 'a cancerous stomach tumour' – appearing on newspaper front pages.

This deliberate revelation of something so private in the midst of grief displayed, as perhaps nothing else could, her determination to manipulate events for her own benefit: what she wanted was to make it clear that Harry had not died of a broken heart – and above all that she herself had not played any part in the affair.

After the requisite mourning period, she resumed her life as a respected member of the society she had fought so hard to enter. Her daughter Minnie came to visit her at Newport but without her husband because, according to The Saunterer, the acid-tongued gossip columnist of *Town Topics*, 'it is pretty well known that she is not averse to strong language, and her son-in-law has come in for a share of it on occasions'.

Town Topics was a society magazine with a difference. As it punched far above its weight, this rates an explanation. Founded from the ashes of a failing social journal, by 1887 it was a sophisticated weekly that reached most subscribers on a Thursday morning, to be opened with a mixture of excitement and dread. It was run by Colonel William d'Alton Mann, a Civil War veteran who had made and lost a fortune. The Colonel was a Father Christmas-like figure with thick white hair and whiskers, a large red nose, sparkling blue eyes and a genial and gregarious nature, who would invite his employees to lunch at Delmonico's, giving sugar lumps to the horses he passed en route.

Benevolent as he may have appeared, under the Colonel's editorship the magazine was anything but. Taking it rapidly upmarket, he quickly built up an unparalleled network of informers, from telegraph operators to caterers, from bandsmen to those in the smart set with a grudge against one of their number. Then, in pungent, witty and usually mocking prose, these revelations would emerge under the title 'Saunterings', written by the Colonel under the pseudonym The Saunterer, and occupying the first twelve or fourteen pages.

These jottings, as the Colonel liked to call them, went in both for the sharp dig and the scabrous innuendo. Thanks to Mann's no-holds-barred remarks, in four years the circulation rose from 5,000 to 63,000. 'Mr Drexel's head is gradually assuming the smoothness and polish that is so familiar on a billiard ball.' 'Lady Sarah* is humpy, pudgy and homely, and no chicken.' 'I observe that the Misses Paton are gaining materially in weight since their mother's death.' A hat in magenta 'makes [Lillie Langtry] look ghastly'. 'The Marquis [of Queensberry] looks exactly, with his red face and black side-whiskers, like a butler in a small family . . .'

When Mann remarked: 'To save the sinner by rebuking the sin is an achievement over which the angels rejoice,' readers could be sure that one of their number was in for some merciless exposé. It did not matter if the name was left out: in that small group who all knew each other identification was easy. Innuendo was constant: 'I venture to predict a startling sensation in a pending Newport divorce suit . . . The evidence involves a detailed account

* The Duke of Marlborough's daughter, Lady Sarah Spencer-Churchill.

of a supper party for six, and its sequel, which will probably plunge two more happy households into most serious trouble.'

'Seldom does a brunette make a pretty bride, and Miss Maria Arnot Haver was no exception,' was a typical offering, as were 'Miss Van Alen suffers from some kind of throat trouble – she cannot go more than half an hour without a drink,' and 'Mr Henry Sloane has been looked on as a complaisant husband who wears his horns too publicly,' while 'Mr Bend's Wall Street career has been marked by many picturesque ups and downs.'

As Blanche Oelrichs later remarked: '*Town Topics* . . . played an enormous part in everyone's life. Climbing matrons were driven to despair by its jibes; indiscreet young married couples went in terror of its insinuations; hardy financiers whose pile concealed a more than ordinary toll of ruined persons hastened to try and buy off the editor.'*

Marietta Stevens was a favourite target, although unlike many she was indifferent to its jibes. With a social life that was all in all to her, she quickly resumed attendance at fashionable weddings and receptions and gave musicales and she entertained visiting English nobility. One such visit, in 1887, caused a scandal, although Marietta, being Marietta, fought back indignantly.

In her Newport mansion she had entertained the Duke of Marlborough, cited when he was Lord Blandford as one of four co-respondents in the sensational divorce trial of Lady Colin Campbell, described by the newspapers as 'the filthiest case ever reported'. One newspaper, it was said, gave the trial only 1,258 fewer words than were in the entire New Testament.

The beautiful, witty, Irish-born Gertrude Blood had married Lord Colin Campbell, a brother-in-law of Princess Louise, Queen Victoria's fourth daughter, and the fifth son of the Duke of Argyll, whom she had met while visiting friends in Scotland. They married in 1881, after the wedding had been twice postponed because of his health. Her father, Colonel Blood, suspected that Lord Colin was suffering from a venereal disease and the Duke also opposed the match, though not because of any such

* This was the literal truth.

suspicion – he simply thought his son was marrying below his station in life.

Once married, it turned out that Lord Colin did indeed have a venereal disease and had infected Gertrude. She was granted a judicial separation from Lord Colin in 1884 on the grounds of cruelty, that he had knowingly infected her. Both parties then filed for divorce, Lord Colin accusing his wife of adultery with four men, one of whom was Lord Blandford (already a notorious adulterer with an illegitimate child or two to his credit).

Gertrude lost her suit. As the suffragette leader Christabel Pankhurst was to write later: 'According to man-made law a wife who is even once unfaithful to her husband has done him an injury which entitles him to divorce her . . . On the other hand, a man who consorts with prostitutes, and does this over and over again throughout his married life, has, according to man-made law, been acting only in accordance with human nature, and nobody can punish him for that.'

With the scandal of the attempted divorce Lady Colin was ostracised by the society she had longed to enter but her talent, cleverness and wit made her popular in literary and artistic circles – Shaw saw her as 'a goddess' and she posed for Whistler's painting *Harmony in White and Ivory*. Lord Blandford (now Duke of Marlborough) took himself to America where Marietta, ever on the lookout for assistance up the ladder, promptly invited him to stay at her Newport home, for which she was castigated by the press, then almost always astride its moral high horse.

Marietta simply rose above it. Here she is in 1891, as recorded by The Saunterer, who encountered her on a visit to Madison Square Garden. 'With her glasses raised to her eyes, her nose *en l'air*, and a lovely aspect of serene unconsciousness of the existence or propinquity of anybody else, Mrs Stevens' look, bearing and movements made up a vision and a lesson.'

A final triumph came in 1893, when she bought the marble house built by Edith Wharton's aunt, Mary Jones – the woman who had declared in 1869: 'This is one house Mrs Stevens will never enter' – redecorated it and moved in. Here her quest to become a social leader succeeded. Her ballroom would see the city's most prominent names, just as it had during Mary Mason Jones's time, and in March 1893 it was the scene of a 'salon concert' by the entire sixty-member Boston Symphony Orchestra.

A month later Marietta Stevens scored an even greater social coup. In 1890s New York nothing caught the attention of society like a title, and when the Duke and Duchess of Veragua (a Caribbean duchy) with their retinue were in New York, she was the hostess who managed to give a reception for them, receiving her guests in her second-floor ballroom. Her invitations were accepted by around 150 of the 'best' names in New York society. It was, perhaps, the apogee of her entire career as a social climber: she had hauled herself up the slopes, inch by painful inch, until she now breathed the rarefied air at the summit.

Two years later the intensity of her feelings, especially where anything to do with money was concerned, took its toll. In March 1895 she received the news that the Victoria Hotel, one of the prime Stevens properties, had failed. As by this time whatever she did or did not do was news, on 2 April *The Times* ran the headline 'Mrs Paran Stevens Prostrated', stating that since last week, 'Mrs Stevens had been unable to leave her house, at Fifty-seventh Street and Fifth Avenue. Acquaintances who called have been informed that she caught cold at a musicale, and that the probabilities of serious developments were so near at hand that she could not receive visitors.'

The doors to the mansion were closed and, continued the paper, 'The butler refused to take cards or to give any information, except that Mrs Stevens was suffering from a very severe cold.' The truth was that her shock at the news of the hotel's collapse and therefore the huge drop in her income was such that she had suffered a massive stroke. She was sixty-one.

A telegram was sent to Minnie Paget, who boarded the first available steamship leaving from Liverpool for New York, but Marietta died on 3 April while Minnie was still at sea. Her body lay for days in a room with drawn curtains on the third floor of the mansion.

The following day the *New York Times* wrote: 'To persons familiar with the peculiarly nervous and excitable temperament of Mrs Paran Stevens, and to all who knew of the shock that the failure of the Victoria Hotel was to her, the sudden announcement of her death yesterday afternoon was not a surprise.' Even in reporting her death, the newspaper did not hold back concerning her peculiarities. 'No woman in New York society was better known than Mrs Paran Stevens, despite certain personal idiosyncrasies that all her friends thoroughly understood.' Prime among these was her filthy temper and the expression of it in what was called 'strong language'.

She left $1.5 million, most of it to her daughter Minnie, who also received her emerald and diamond tiara, collar, pendant and brooches. Her sister Fanny, to whom she owed much of her social rise, received $3,000 a year for life. The Marble Row house with its cluttered rooms stuffed with French furniture where she had entertained so lavishly was sold. But she had achieved her goal: for many years she was at the heart of New York society. One obituary described her as 'an ambitious woman, eager for social prestige [who] stamped out everything that stood in the pathway of her ambition'. It was an extraordinarily accurate summary.

CHAPTER 7

Alva

Alva Vanderbilt, sexy, aggressive, iron-willed, was the supreme embodiment of both husband-hunter and social climber, first pulling her family into the higher echelons of American society through strategic moves and then forcing her daughter into marriage with a high-ranking nobleman whom she herself had tracked down and marked as quarry, to ensure and maintain her own high-status position.

She was born on 17 January 1853 to Murray Forbes Smith and his wife Phoebe, the seventh of nine children of whom four died in infancy. As plantation-owners the family had been comfortably off, living in one of the grandest houses in Mobile, Alabama, with large, high-ceilinged rooms, tall casement windows and a hint of the Renaissance in its architecture – something that would influence her strongly in later life, as did also the fact that, like all well-off Southern families, the Erskine Smiths were slave-owners. As a five-year-old she would be taken for a weekly visit to her godmother, where she played with the small son of the house and the little black slave boys. 'I never [in my life] played with girls,' she wrote; and as a young adult, she invariably got on better with men than women.

She grew up strong-willed, plump and pugnacious – as a child she loved screaming matches and a good fight and her personality was so forceful that she invariably won them; and she was rebellious from the start, always determined to go her own way and do what she wanted. As she herself wrote in her unpublished autobiography: 'There was a force in me that seemed to compel me to do what I wanted to do regardless of what might happen afterwards . . . I have known this condition often during my life.' She shared the same ruthless ambition and determination to succeed as had brought their millions to the power brokers of Wall Street and the railway magnates. All she lacked was their wealth.

When the family moved to New York in 1859, they brought their slaves with them, including Alva's favourite, Monroe Crawford – who had been given to her mother as a wedding present by her father – whom she bossed unmercifully. 'It was a case of absolute control on my part,' she told Sara Bard Field, the writer and poet to whom she dictated her memoirs in 1917. By the age of six, so deeply engrained was her sense of dominance over those she considered her inferiors, and her attitude to them, that it remained with her all her life.

The Smiths' Southern extraction might have made it easier for them to slip into New York society, Southerners having a certain social cachet; but the Civil War turned feelings against them. The Smith children and their mother travelled frequently in Europe. As Southerners, this was politic during the Civil War (1861–5), so that Alva was largely educated there. She was an obstreperous child and adolescent, rebelling against the highly regimented and constricted life of a girl and frequently fighting, with girls and boys alike. Often, when she went too far, she was whipped by her mother, but it made no difference to her behaviour.

When Abraham Lincoln was assassinated in 1865, the Smiths put black bombazine bows in their windows to avoid attack. But this was not enough to stem the rising tide of hostility towards Southerners and Alva's father, who had lost most of his money through the war, decided to remove his family. The smart house on Fifth Avenue was sold and from 1866 Murray Forbes Smith conducted his business from Liverpool (the main English port for cotton from the Southern states).

That summer, when Alva was thirteen, the family took a house in Newport, not then the citadel of prestige it was to become but merely the favoured summer resort of many Southern plantation-owners. Again, Alva's upbringing was different in one respect from many of those around her and must have accounted for much of her later social confidence. 'Southern children were never shoved off into nurseries but were always part of the family and allowed to see company . . . I sat always next to my father and stayed in the room when the women left, to hear discussions.'

Another Southern family there were the Yznagas; before the Civil War Mr Yznaga, a Cuban, had owned a plantation in Louisiana worked by his 300 slaves.

From Newport the Smiths went to Paris, where they rented an apartment on the Champs-Elysées. They were soon welcomed by the imperial court of Napoleon III and his glamorous Empress, Eugénie.

France, largely through Paris, affected the teenage Alva strongly. She loved its art, its architecture, its history, its sophistication; her education proceeded with French and German governesses, visits to the great châteaux, sketching expeditions to Versailles and a year at a French school.

In 1869, by which time feelings against Southerners had simmered down, Murray Forbes Smith decided to take his family back to New York. The sixteen-year-old Alva was desolate. 'I was broken-hearted that I must leave France,' she wrote. 'I was in sympathy with everything there. This musical language had become mine. I loved its art, people, customs. America struck me in contrast . . . as crude and raw.'

The America to which the Smiths returned had changed enormously. The huge number of new millionaires had sent expenditure on houses, servants, clothes and all the outward trappings of wealth soaring, while Mrs Astor, with her major-domo Ward McAllister, now ruled and regulated a society built on exclusion and exclusiveness – and the Smiths, who did not know Mrs Astor, were not in it. Just at this moment, Murray Forbes Smith's business began to fail and the family had to move away from Fifth Avenue to ever smaller houses. Then, in 1871, came a shattering blow for Alva: her mother died at only forty-eight.

Her father's business continued to haemorrhage money and the responsibility of four daughters exacerbated his worries.

Alva decided the only thing to do was to put herself on the marriage market for two years. Fortunately, her social circle was younger than that ruled by Mrs Astor and, although neither the Smiths nor the Yznagas were within the magic Astor Four Hundred, their looks and personalities ensured that Alva and Consuelo Yznaga were welcome in this younger group – which also contained many of the children of Four Hundred families. Entering it, though, was not always easy and it is to Alva's credit that, motherless and poor, she managed it – again, her determined character must have had much to do with this. She was not beautiful, but she had the freshness of youth, a well-rounded figure, vivacity and complete self-confidence.

Another member of this group was William Kissam Vanderbilt, always known as Willie K, grandson of the famous Commodore who had founded the family's railroad fortune. One day at a party Alva's friend Consuelo Yznaga introduced them, and fostered Alva's chances by bringing Willie K several times to the Smith house. He was handsome, charming, like Alva had been educated in Europe and spoke fluent French – and was potentially very rich.

For Alva, with the shadow of permanent genteel poverty and even bankruptcy hanging over her and her family, Willie K must have seemed heaven-sent. She already knew what it was to be poor; and she was adamant that this was not for her and that a rich husband was a necessity. Although not pretty – one of her friends described her as 'having the face of an intelligent Pekinese' – she was sexy and above all determined. It is unlikely that she loved Willie; as Sara Bard Field wrote to her lover,* 'Alva's terrible marriage to Mr Vanderbilt with its sordid selling of her unloving self but with its truly noble desire to save her Father was . . . a pathetic mixture of good and bad.'

To Willie K, Alva's wit, vitality, attractiveness, ease of manner and drive must have seemed just what he needed in a wife and the interest in Europe and its culture they shared must have been

* The married Charles Erskine Scott Wood, author, civil liberties advocate, artist and soldier.

another bond. While the Smiths had simply slid out of society, there had been an active raising of barricades against the Vanderbilts by Mrs Astor. To overcome them would be a mammoth task and Willie K, just as anxious to achieve acceptability as Alva, must have believed (correctly) that in Alva, well educated, steeped in the sophisticated culture of Europe and without the black mark of Mrs Astor's disapproval, he had found the woman to do this.

Perhaps, also, Willie K was attracted by the forceful streak already visible in the youthful Alva as echoing the vigour and determination so evident in his own family – the Commodore still behaved and swore as in the days when he founded the beginnings of his immense fortune as a tough sixteen-year-old ferrying passengers between Staten Island and Manhattan. It is likely that the Commodore also recognised these qualities in Alva, for he took to her from the beginning.

Willie and Alva married in 1875, when Alva was twenty-two. Already her gift for planning how to attain her ends was visible: she had realised that publicity was essential for social success – the papers described the crowds at her wedding – and she was the first New York bride to issue admission cards to guests, thus turning the exclusion principle that had hitherto hindered her to her advantage.

For the first few years Alva was busy giving birth to her three children – Consuelo, named after her friend Consuelo Yznaga, who became the little girl's godmother, then William Kissam and Harold Stirling – and running the large Vanderbilt house on Long Island. Then came the next step. When the Commodore died in 1877, both his sons spent some of their huge inheritance – his will had disclosed that he was the richest man in America, with a fortune of $100 million – on equally huge and ostentatious houses on Fifth Avenue. William Henry's was enormous but in the classic brownstone tradition, whereas the one built by Willie K – or rather, by Alva – was anything but discreet.

For it, she formed what was virtually a partnership with the architect Richard Morris Hunt, who loved France and its architecture as much as she did. Sited at 660 Fifth Avenue, it was nothing less than a French château (it was based on the sixteenth-century Château de Blois), built in pale limestone, with spires, tall chimneys, deep windows, balconies, gargoyles, flying buttresses and an ornate, extravagant frontage.

It had a central atrium rising to the roof of coloured glass with balconies on all four sides, and was packed with treasures: the walls and floor of the hall were marble, there were carvings, statues, oriental rugs, paintings and porcelain everywhere. There were Renaissance mantelpieces, Flemish tapestries, bronzes made for Marie Antoinette, stained glass and Rembrandt portraits. The newel post of the grand staircase – the statue of a female slave – was in bronze overlaid with gold, and even Alva's boudoir, its walls hung with dark blue silk, was twenty-six feet long. It had a sixty-foot hall, a large stone staircase, library walls clad in sixteenth-century French Renaissance panelling, a Louis Quinze-style salon with a ceiling painted with mythological scenes, a two-storey banqueting hall with marble caryatids and a musicians' gallery and a stained-glass window depicting the Field of the Cloth of Gold. Nothing like it had ever been seen in New York before.

Alva also managed to persuade her father-in-law to acquire a knowledge of the arts and to invest in them and to display his family's wealth in houses that reflected this. Soon two other Vanderbilts were building grand houses on Fifth Avenue (by the 1880s the area of Fifth Avenue north of 50th Street was known as 'Vanderbilt Alley').

But Alva was not only ambitious; she was a strategist, with a cool, analytical intelligence that could work out a coherent plan of campaign – a campaign to achieve not only acceptance but social dominance. In 1882 she and her husband were invited to a Patriarchs' Ball, with another to come in early 1883. So far, so good – but for Alva, not good enough. There remained Mrs Astor.

Her opportunity to overcome the resistance of this *grande dame* came in the spring of 1883. She and Willie K had planned to give a housewarming party for the opening of their new house, now finally completed, and Alva decided on a fancy-dress ball, something New York had not seen for a long time. She let it be known that the ball would be like no other in terms of display and extravagance, and sent out 1,600 invitations. The bait, and final note of reassurance to those who might have hesitated, was that the ball was in honour of her friend and bridesmaid Consuelo Yznaga, who had married Lord Mandeville, the Duke of Manchester's heir. And as Alva knew, even the most diehard Astor adherents were unlikely to refuse to meet a future duchess.

Even the date was cleverly picked: this sumptuous affair would take place on 26 March, the first Monday after Easter, so that it would be the first real entertainment after the low weeks of Lent for a city craving amusement and already agog to see the interior of No. 660. In addition, Monday held a particular significance in that it was traditionally the day Mrs Astor was 'At Home'. Not, as Alva pointed out to her friends, that this mattered, as Alva did not know Mrs Astor: after all, Mrs Astor had never called on Alva, so Alva could not possibly call on Mrs Astor – protocol demanded that the senior or longer-established family made the first call. Alva, the newcomer, was therefore correct in not inviting New York's queen to the ball – except that Mrs Astor was, and always expected to be, invited everywhere, though whether or not she accepted was another matter entirely.

One story has it that, as Alva knew, Mrs Astor's adored debutante daughter Carrie, with a group of her friends, had been religiously practising their 'Star Quadrille'* in order to shine at Alva's ball. Suddenly, Mrs Astor realised that no invitation had come; she let this be known among her circle. In response, Alva allowed it to filter out that as Carrie's mother had never officially recognised the existence of Mrs William K. Vanderbilt, Mrs William K. Vanderbilt could not invite Carrie to her ball.

Shortly afterwards, a footman in the blue Astor livery delivered a card to 660 Fifth Avenue after which, even more expeditiously,

* Quadrilles were square dances of five movements, danced in costumes designed round a theme; they needed weeks of organisation and rehearsals and were popular at society balls.

an invitation was sent up the Avenue to No. 840, the Astor home. The coup had succeeded; with the receiving of that one small piece of pasteboard, Alva was officially on the Astor calling list. She had arrived.

Such crowds gathered outside the Vanderbilt mansion long before the hour the ball was to begin that they held up the carriages of the guests. For the ball, the huge ground-floor rooms were full of gilded baskets of roses, 6,000 of them, each of which had cost $2 – twice as much, as Alva informed everyone, as Mrs Astor paid for hers. Up the grand staircase walked the guests, into a vast room decorated with palms, giant ferns and orchids, where Alva and Consuelo received them side by side, Alva a Venetian princess of the Renaissance in a Worth gown with a gold embroidered bodice and a blue and gold embroidered train, Consuelo Mandeville in a black velvet dress copied from a Van Dyck painting of Princesse de Croy.

There too was Mrs Astor, in blue velvet hung about with endless diamonds – tiara, earrings, strings of diamonds round her neck, brooches, stomacher, numerous bracelets round the wrists of her white gloves – escorted by Ward McAllister as Count de la Mole (the lover of Marguerite de Valois) in a suit of purple velvet slashed with scarlet silk.

At midnight the 100 dancers, who had been practising their quadrilles for weeks, went down the stairs and through to the Louis XV salon with its Gobelin tapestries, carved walnut wainscoting and ceiling decorated with the union of Cupid and Psyche. The most spectacular of these dances was the 'hobby horse' quadrille, for which the dancers were costumed as if they were riding horses – each hobby horse had a real leather hide and flowing mane and tail. After the quadrilles came the dancing. This continued until six in the morning, when Alva led a Virginia Reel as a sign that the party had finished.

The ball had cost over $250,000, but to the Vanderbilts it was worth every cent. Soon afterwards, Willie K was admitted to membership of New York's most exclusive clubs: the Coaching Club, the Metropolitan, the Knickerbocker, Union, Racquet and Tennis, Turf and Field and the New York Yacht Club. That winter the Vanderbilts were invited to Mrs Astor's traditional winter ball. It is hardly surprising that Alva had a photograph taken of herself in her ball costume.

The ball, talked about for years afterwards, set a benchmark. The publicity-conscious Alva was the first hostess both to allow reporters to wander round the house early on the day of the ball and to enable a full report of it to be syndicated to newspapers around America through the *New York World*, so that citizens everywhere marvelled at its lavishness and what it cost.

But one ball did not a social leader make, and Alva's plans were long-term. They included her children, notably her daughter Consuelo, now six. Consuelo's education was rigorously supervised; by the time she was eight she could read and write in French, German and English. French was spoken at home and she had a German governess; during lessons she sat with a steel rod strapped to her back to ensure the necessary elegance of deportment. It was a time when children were supposed to be seen and not heard, but even then Alva was known as a ferocious disciplinarian, frequently punishing her children with a riding whip. Yet at Idle Hour, the Vanderbilt house on Long Island, there was plenty of fun, exercise and freedom.

When William Henry Vanderbilt, Alva's father-in-law, died at an unexpectedly early age in 1885, it was found he had succeeded in doubling the family fortune to $200 million – and Willie K inherited $50 million of this. Now he and Alva were stratospherically rich and little Consuelo, aged nine, had become one of the world's richest heiresses.

Willie K celebrated by ordering himself a yacht. The *Alva*, a 285-foot steam yacht, was launched in 1886. The walls of the cabins and staterooms were panelled in mahogany, the teak decks covered in oriental carpets, the dining room held a piano, there was a library with a fireplace and a crew of fifty-five. From then on the family would often cruise to Europe in the spring, taking with them friends, governesses, tutors and a French chef; other voyages took them to the West Indies, Turkey, North Africa and Egypt. Often these cruises ended at Nice, and the party would continue to Paris.

Alva, characteristically, celebrated the Vanderbilts' sudden new wealth by building a house, this time in Newport, now the essential summer destination for New York's smartest. This was the sumptuous Marble House, so called because this was the main building material. Much of it was shipped over from Italy – because of its weight, a special dock had to be built to unload it. The house was Alva's from the start, given to her by Willie as a thirty-ninth birthday present, perhaps as a conscience-salver.

For by now Alva and Willie K were getting on badly. During the early years of their marriage youth, sex and their joint, overpowering ambition to enter and conquer the society that meant everything to them had made them a team. With their acceptance by Mrs Astor and their sudden, huge wealth this 'glue' no longer held them together. Later Willie K was to talk of Alva as a 'virago' – and she certainly had a violent temper and an over-riding conviction of her own rightness – while she found his continued infidelities difficult to turn a blind eye to in the way that other women of her circle did. For whatever happened, scandal must not emerge.

As many of these men, like Willie K, had yachts, ignoring what happened out of sight at sea was not too difficult – as Alva knew. As she wrote later: 'Colonel Astor's yachting parties were public scandals. He would take women of every class and kind, even chambermaids out of the hotels of the coastwise cities where the yacht put in, to amuse himself and the men of his party on these trips.' Yet Mrs Astor, *grande dame* of New York society, did not see what she did not wish to see, and did not hear what she did not wish to hear. New York might be full of gossip about the wild, disreputable parties given by her husband on board his yacht, but if anyone dared to ask about him she would reply calmly that he was having a delightful cruise – 'the sea air is so good for him' – while regretting that she could not accompany him as she was such a bad sailor. Alva, however, was not one to sit down under either a real, or imagined, slight.

Later, after she became involved in the battle for female suffrage, she wrote bitterly of the double standard: 'the husband, stepping over the confining threshold of his home whose respectability he left in the hands of his discarded wife, like a young colt in a meadow kicked up his heels and was off for a romp in the wide world . . . and met his obligations as a husband and father by signing generous checks'.

It was certainly true in Alva's case. The start of their differences was believed to be in the winter of 1888 when Alva's best friend Consuelo Yznaga, now Lady Mandeville, came with her husband for a long visit to Alva and Willie K in New York. Willie K's penchant for Lady Mandeville, a beauty with pale-gold hair and melting dark eyes, became so obvious that Alva had row after row with him, so much so that her father-in-law had to step in. To avoid the chance of this happening again, and word leaking out, the senior Vanderbilt arranged with Consuelo Mandeville that she would never return to America – and she never did.

Willie K now spent more and more time on his yacht, it was said with various young women, while Alva threw herself into the furnishing of the Marble House and, increasingly, the grooming of her daughter. Consuelo had led an isolated life, being educated largely at home, under her mother's eye and thumb, a subordination that increased as the years passed.

By 1890, when Consuelo was sixteen, Alva had banned all contact with the opposite sex. Not for Consuelo the innocent and well-chaperoned picnics with her friends and their brothers that Alva had enjoyed as a girl, in case her fancy was taken by one of the boys. Alva had decided that her daughter was to make the most brilliant marriage possible and that, irrespective of her child's feelings she, Alva, would decide with whom that match would be. So Consuelo spent the day studying while everything, from the furniture and bibelots in her room – she was forbidden to put out anything of her own – to her clothes, was chosen by her mother. Even her ideas were censored. 'I don't ask *you* to think, *I* do the thinking, you do as you are told,' Alva once snapped to her daughter.

But Consuelo still had eyes and ears and she realised what was going on between Alva and Willie. 'I had reached an age when the continual disagreements between my parents had become a matter of deep concern to me,' she wrote of that time. They still cruised together – perhaps in an effort to keep the marriage going – but in 1892 the *Alva* was sunk, run down by a steamer off Nantucket Shoals during a heavy fog (fortunately with no loss of life).

Willie K's immediate reaction was to order another, even more splendid yacht, the *Valiant.* It was built in England, by Lair Brothers, and the following year, 1893, Willie sailed her across the Atlantic to Newport, to pick up his family and friends for a round-the-world cruise. Consuelo believed it was a desperate last effort to 'avoid the rupture which I felt could not be long delayed'. Their guests included several bachelors, ostensibly to amuse the seventeen-year-old Consuelo, on the verge of making her début.

One was Winthrop Rutherfurd, a rich and handsome twenty-nine-year-old considered one of the most eligible single men in New York. Another was Oliver Belmont, an open admirer of Alva's. Often, she had sat beside him on the box of his coach, with its four famous bay horses (Sandringham, Rockingham, Hurlingham and Buckingham) at New York's annual and very public Coaching Parade.

He was the son of the financier August Belmont, a man whose Jewish ancestry was redeemed in the eyes of smart New York by his marriage to a society woman of unimpeachable background. Oliver, a smallish man with a high colour, was passionate about horses, coaches and their turnout. His coachmen wore maroon coats with scarlet piping and silver buttons, and black satin knee breeches with silver-buckled shoes, and all his carriages were painted maroon with a scarlet stripe on the wheels. When he himself drove one of his coaches he was decked out in a green coat with brass buttons, scarlet waistcoat and pearl-coloured bell-crown hat* with lilies of the valley in his buttonhole.

Oliver had also married a socialite, but when, on their honeymoon in Paris, her mother and two sisters had moved in and refused to leave, he had walked out angrily – and with another

* A bell-crown hat was a top hat wider at the top of the hat than where the hat meets the wearer's head.

woman. The divorce that followed and subsequent birth to his wife of a daughter whom he refused to acknowledge did nothing for his reputation. His parents were mortified, but women tended to find him attractive, liking 'his face rutted with lines – from the hopes and disillusions of his life as a lover, I suspected,' wrote Blanche Oelrichs, 'for certainly he was a romantic man'. With no job, he spent his life amusing himself and was a racing friend of Willie K's.

The *Valiant* set off in late November, with a total of eighty-five people on board, arriving in Bombay on Christmas Day; then, with the *Valiant* sailing round to meet them, the party had a ten-day train journey to Calcutta. Here, unexpectedly, Alva and Willie were invited to stay at Government House (Calcutta was then the capital of British India) by the Viceroy, Lord Lansdowne.

For Alva it was a transformative experience, setting her a social goal with which nothing and nobody would be allowed to interfere. Her weapon would be her unwitting daughter.

During Lord Lansdowne's viceroyalty the British Raj was at the height of its splendour and the Viceroy and Vicereine lived in far greater magnificence than the Queen they represented: they were attended by a host of servants in red and gold liveries, the viceregal band played at dinner, top-booted bodyguards with scarlet coats and huge black, blue and gold turbans lined the stairs for parties. Regal pomp and ceremony were everywhere. At evening parties they sat on a 'throne' – a sofa on a dais with their feet on a tiger skin – and on official occasions were bowed and curtsied to.

Even to Alva, accustomed to the external trappings of wealth, this was an eye-opener. When the Vicereine told Alva that she had a nephew – the young Duke of Marlborough – the right age for marriage, Alva's plans crystallised, though for the moment she kept them to herself. Consuelo, she determined, would marry either the Duke or his cousin, Lord Lansdowne's heir. That neither she nor Consuelo had met either of them was, to Alva, irrelevant.

After the Vanderbilts had stayed with the Viceroy in Government House, the *Valiant*'s cruise had continued to Ceylon and then back to the Mediterranean via Alexandria. During this, the final fracture in the Vanderbilt marriage occurred and when the yacht reached Nice, Consuelo was told that her parents' marriage was over. Alva took Consuelo to Paris, as she had often done before, installing the two of them in twelve large first-floor rooms in the Hotel Continentale and, in characteristic Alva fashion, having the furniture ripped out so that she could furnish it herself to her own liking. Willie K, mutteringly, paid the bills.

In Paris the unsuspecting Consuelo enjoyed driving with her mother in the Bois de Boulogne, walking under the chestnuts in the Champs-Elysées and going to museums, churches, lectures at the Sorbonne and classical matinées at the *Théâtre Français*. Here Alva furthered her plan for her daughter's marriage by commissioning a portrait of Consuelo, specifically requesting that the background be not the painter's usual red velvet but a classical eighteenth-century landscape *à la* Gainsborough, as seen in many English family portraits, so that it would fit seamlessly into a stately home – although Consuelo, naturally, did not realise this.

Here, also, Consuelo made her début, at a *bal blanc* (a debutantes' ball at which everyone wore white), attracting several admirers; by the end of June, five of them had – unsuccessfully – asked Alva for her hand. But Alva had already made up her mind: Consuelo would marry the Duke of Marlborough.

What Alva did not know was that on the *Valiant* cruise Consuelo and Winthrop Rutherfurd had fallen in love.

CHAPTER 8

Newport

It was in Newport that the seventeen-year-old Consuelo Vanderbilt was kept a prisoner by her mother Alva in her enormous 'cottage', the Marble House, until she agreed to marry the man of her mother's choice. This captivity was probably the most extreme example of maternal husband-hunting, in a setting that represented the extreme of social exclusivity.

For by the 1880s this small town on the north-east of Rhode Island had become the testing ground for those who wanted to get into society. If you couldn't make it in Newport, you wouldn't make it in New York.

There was still a pretence of bucolic, country living, rather in the fashion of Marie Antoinette playing at being a milkmaid. But the 'cottages' of the rich, jostling each other along Bellevue Avenue, had ballrooms and stables, Paris chefs cooked the dinners in the great marble dining rooms, and the daily round was as formal as anything at a European court. It was a long way from the rum-distilling for which the town had originally been known.

Then, Newport had been the centre of the infamous 'triangle trade': rum shipped to Africa in exchange for slaves, slaves despatched to the West Indies to cull the sugar canes, and the sugar then sent to Newport to make the rum. Through this, by the beginning of the eighteenth century it was a fashionable resort for wealthy Southern and West Indian planters, so much so that it had become almost a Southern colony. Also making them feel welcome was the produce of its twenty-two distilleries, its famous rum. As tensions grew between the North and the South, Southerners felt more at home here than in the richer, more Yankee resort of Saratoga Springs.

Throughout the 1870s Saratoga, noted for its spa, had been the place to go. Its season began on 1 July, when everyone (who could afford it) went for a cure, and it was, according to Cornelius Vanderbilt Jnr, 'where Broadway and Fifth Avenue met'. Sporting men enjoyed it because there was trotting and flat racing, in July and August respectively. It was masculine in tone. 'Nowhere do women seem so much like appendages,' said the author Mary Gay Humphreys, describing the place.

The truly smart stayed in the old United States Hotel, with its black walnut staircases, red-carpeted floors and long verandahs on which guests would sit lazily in wicker rocking chairs. In the round wooden bath houses with their five-foot-deep pools, the clear, warm water bubbled like champagne; male visitors, who bathed in the nude, could have tall frosted mint juleps floated out to them on cork trays. Every morning people would check the hotel register to see who had arrived.

It was also where illicit liaisons were condoned – millionaires with beautiful 'secretaries' or 'distant cousins' settled in one of the colony of hotel cottages. Many of the demi-monde, flashing with diamonds and bright with paint, descended on Saratoga, justifying its racy reputation. Gradually the old smart set found themselves being swamped by the moneyed louche.

The catalyst for the change in Newport from an unpretentious seaside resort of white clapboard houses, their lawns bordered by blue hydrangeas, to a social centre dominated by huge cliff-top palaces was, as in New York, Ward McAllister. He was one of Newport's earliest aficionados, having summered there as a child with his family like other Southerners. After the steamy heat of Savannah, Georgia (where the McAllisters lived), Newport's fresh sea breezes, meadows full of clover and daisies and gardens where roses, clematis and carnations grew profusely were a delicious change. In the late 1850s he bought Bayside Farm on the island, where he intended to live for nine months of the year, wintering in the West Indies.

Here he would entertain New York friends during the summer months to simple dinners and picnics (partly owing to her health, his wife seldom made appearances at any of his entertainments). It was simplicity with a twist: the farm had a cellar for claret and an attic for madeira,* some of the latter seventy or eighty years old and well preserved thanks to the cold Rhode Island winters. As he sipped it, McAllister would tell the company how many times the bottles had crossed the Atlantic before the wine had been mellowed to perfection.

From the start McAllister saw Newport as a place where the feminine element was strongest: here business, politics and religion were banned as topics of polite conversation. Soon he was organising dinners and picnics for friends and, sometimes, others. As he put it in his autobiography: 'Riding on the Avenue on a lovely summer's day, I would be stopped by a beautiful woman, in gorgeous array, looking so fascinating that if she were to ask you to attempt the impossible, you would at least make the effort.' Fortunately, what she invariably wanted was not the impossible but one of his famous picnics. 'I will do your bidding,' he would reply, and a date would be fixed and he would jot down: 'Monday 1 p.m., meet at Narragansett Avenue, bring *filet de boeuf piqué*.'

After that it was a question of waylaying every carriage known to contain friends – all the smart world went driving in the late morning – and assigning to those who could come the bringing of a certain dish plus a bottle of champagne. For single young men, it was a bottle of champagne and a bunch of grapes or a quart of ice cream. McAllister would then hire servants and musicians for the day, get a carpenter to make and lay a dancing platform, order flowers, arrange for people on the outlying roads to point the way to his farm and generally organise everything down to, as he said, the last salt spoon. Once he even hired a

* Madeira, a wine that can stand rough seas, was a favourite drink with the officers of sailing ships.

flock of Southdown sheep and some cattle for half a day to add verisimilitude to his 'farming life'.

Such 'picnics' might have been called 'rural', but they had all the ersatz simplicity of the Petit Trianon. For, as McAllister pointed out: 'These little parties were then, and are now, the stepping stones to our best New York society. Now, do not for a moment imagine that all were indiscriminately asked to these little fêtes. On the contrary, if you were not of the inner circle, and were a newcomer, it took the combined efforts of all your friends' backing and pushing to procure an invitation for you.

'For years, whole families sat on the stool of probation, awaiting trial and acceptance, and many were then rejected, but once received, you were put on intimate footing with all. To acquire such intimacy in a great city like New York would have taken you a lifetime.'

With the opening of Newport's summer season of 1871, the year when the new structure of American society was being launched, came nine 'Cliff Cottages'– an experiment in luxurious rental properties – with an exclusive hotel nearby. 'The grounds are tastefully laid out, each family having separate grounds and flower-beds, and which are kept in order by the association,' commented the *New York Times*. 'Stables are provided also, with servants' apartments at the hotel. Surely it is a novel idea.'

Novel it might have been, but it soon caught on. By the 1880s the truly smart, led by the queens, went to Newport in the summer; six weeks there was essential if you wished to keep, or improve, your place in society. Conversely, not to do so showed that one's status was insecure. People would even travel to Europe in order to have a realistic-sounding excuse for not being in Newport for the season if they were still on the fringes and not certain of acceptance. One way of finding this out was to be invited onto someone's yacht for a week or so, thus 'testing the waters'.

Anyone unwise enough to take a villa without the certain knowledge that they were 'in' would suffer the humiliation of being omitted from the splendid balls and dinners that took place almost every night. They could not take part in bathing parties on Bailey's Beach, nor were their men allowed to join the

Reading Room or the Club, with its bronze owls on the gateposts. They could arrive on the Casino lawn on Bellevue Avenue and be ignored while the 'rubber plants' – as the ordinary townsfolk were known – peered at their discomfiture through hedges. They usually left after a month of such treatment.

The sea might be sparkling, the copper beeches glowing in the sunshine, but the refreshing sea breezes brought no sense of holiday relaxation; rather, the rules of etiquette were even more stringent here.

For some the day began with riding, changing at around mid-morning from riding habit to day dress, or with a visit to the Horse Shoe Piazza at the Casino (signing in here was a sign to your friends that you had arrived in Newport). Some women would sit listening to Mullaly's orchestra, in clothes that swished and rustled if they moved or gestured – countless petticoats, of satin, lace or taffeta, embroidered, flounced, decorated with seed pearls or cupid's bows in gold, enormous feather hats, parasols to match every dress, eighty or ninety different dresses for a season. 'You will see at a reception in Newport more Worth dresses than anywhere else in America, except in New York during the height of the season,' commented one newspaper. Sometimes the prettiest girls would seek a quiet corner 'to listen to the music', demurely embroidering while they waited for swains to gather round them, with whom they would take turns to promenade.

On fine days the destination would be Bailey's Beach, a crescent of coarse grey sand reserved exclusively for the élite and for them the 'only' beach out of the half-dozen-odd suitable for bathing. But even the drive to Bailey's, at the southern end of Bellevue Avenue, required the right clothes. 'When I was seventeen my skirts almost touched the ground; it was considered immodest to wear them shorter,' wrote Consuelo Vanderbilt of 1894.

'My dresses had high, tight whalebone collars. A corset laced my waist to the eighteen inches fashion decreed. An enormous hat adorned with flowers, feathers and ribbons was fastened to my hair with long steel pins, and a veil covered my face. Tight gloves pinched my hands and I carried a parasol. Thus attired I went to Bailey's beach for a morning bathe.'

The veil that Consuelo mentioned was not just a coquettish adornment. To be considered a beauty a perfect complexion was essential, which meant the skin had to be defended against the ravages of sun, wind and sea air. A parasol was merely a second line of defence; a heavy veil, sometimes even made of wool, was the most popular answer. Occasionally one of the more dashing women would wear something even stronger: a mask made of fine chamois leather, often with embroidered lips and eyes.

Bailey's had a watchman in a gold-laced uniform who knew every carriage by sight and would allow no one else in unless accompanied by a member or with a note from one of the great hostesses; everyone else had to go to Easton's, used by the townspeople. Women bathers wore full-skirted costumes and long black stockings, often wading into the water holding their parasols. At midday, when a red flag was run up, they beat a hasty retreat: it was now the turn of the gentlemen, who as always bathed nude.

A few played the new game of tennis, the women in pleated skirts, black stockings and white tennis shoes, with sailor hats to which were attached the inevitable double veils to protect them from the sun. Later, bicycling was to become the craze, with even a bicycle fête (in 1894) when forty or fifty of the social cream set off for a picnic destination – followed, naturally, by their carriages in case of fatigue or accident. Others visited the Worth boutique, conveniently sited on Bellevue Avenue, for a little light shopping.

Then came luncheon, perhaps on a yacht for which smart clothes were essential – though only married women could wear jewels in the daytime – followed, possibly, by a short visit to the polo field after which came the all-important rite of calling. This, along with the other immutable patterns into which the day fell, was, to those determined to maintain their position, unavoidable. 'I could never comprehend why we should spend every glorious summer afternoon at Newport showering the colony with our calling cards when we had already nodded and spoken to our friends several times since breakfast,' wrote Consuelo's cousin, Cornelius Vanderbilt IV, son of the redoubtable Grace.

'Yet punctually on the dot of three Mother expected my father, sister and me to join the splendid dress parade of carriages on Bellevue Avenue. How vividly I can recall the tedium of those occasions when, proceeding at a snail's pace in a shiny black victoria and clutching our hateful card cases in spotless white gloves, we accompanied Mother on this sacred ritual . . . for two hours in the velvet-upholstered carriage we were not allowed to lounge, or slump, or cross our legs. My cards, at the age of nine, read: "Master Cornelius Vanderbilt, Junr"'.

Children, for whom this was supposedly a summer holiday, were taught never to laugh or cry too loud, always to stand when a lady entered the room, never to sit down in a carriage until all the ladies were seated, and only to speak when spoken to.

Other lessons quickly absorbed from their parents were those of snobbishness. One girl, a scion of two of the oldest Knickerbocker families, wrote in her journal of a seamstress who came to their home to mend carpets: 'I don't like to have her use our forks and drink out of our cups . . . I try to pick out a nicked cup for her to use so that we can recognise and avoid it.' Another felt humiliated because she was the only one at a formal luncheon without a personal servant to carve for her.

When calling, it was important never to overtake the carriage of a social superior (in the same way that you must not out-dress, out-jewel or out-entertain her). These rules of exclusion even extended to marking invisible boundaries on the ground itself: although the cottagers could wander in the town, the townspeople were not allowed in Bellevue Avenue. Only during Tennis Tournament week did the two sets mingle. The 'outsiders' could also attend the Tennis Club Ball – and did – which ended the season although, again, there was no mingling.

In the late afternoon, for the privileged, there was the equivalent of the European evening stroll up and down the boulevards. Carriages of all sorts, from dog-carts to four-in-hands, drove up and down Bellevue Avenue in a double line, passing and repassing each other; the custom was to make a ceremonious bow the first time you passed a friend, to smile the second time and to look away the third.

It was as necessary then to be well turned out on wheels as to have a fine house. The grandest equipage was that belonging to Mrs August Belmont, drawn by four horses, on two of which rode postilions in short jackets, tight breeches and velvet jockey caps. In these vehicles sat women dressed to the nines in satin-striped dresses fitting smoothly over tight-laced corsets, flower-trimmed bonnets and the ubiquitous parasol, this time in fringed silk or velvet.

Fashionable young men drove dog carts, with two horses in tandem; older men drove showy phaetons with the best horses they could find and a groom with folded arms behind. A handsome pair of horses would draw a 'sociable', in which four people could converse easily while leaning back on cushioned seats under a sheltering canopy, the women in picture hats and organdie dresses, the men in white flannels and peaked sailor hats. It was as much a promenade of Newport society as a visit to the Casino.

Edith Jones (later Wharton) remembered seeing a young woman staying with the Jones family appear for the afternoon drive in a white silk dress with a broad black satin stripe and a huge hat wreathed in crimson roses, hung with a green veil against the sun. She was escorted by Edith's brother Harry, dressed equally smartly in a frock coat, a tall hat and pearl-grey trousers. After tea and gossip, it was time to change for the evening, perhaps for dinner on another yacht, perhaps for a grand dinner in one of the 'cottages', perhaps for a dance or ball.

'Newport is like an enormous and brilliant garden in which are palatial homes,' commented Price Collier. 'We have summer resorts in and out of France, all over Europe in fact, but no one place where the wealth and fashion of a nation focus themselves as here.

'When an American family gets money enough to afford an attack on the citadel of Society, they begin at Newport. Here congregate what are called "society people" from New York especially, but from Washington, Philadelphia, Boston and

Chicago as well, and for two months in the summer the most highly polished American kettle boils and bubbles and steams upon the Newport hob.'

Nothing was too expensive or too grand for those summering in this little town. On the Vanderbilt lawns ices were eaten under the shade of Japanese umbrellas, with feet upon Turkey rugs. Tapestries were brought from New York drawing rooms along with silk sheets that could be changed twice daily, 100 pounds of lobster would arrive in basement kitchens on party days. There were fancy-dress balls galore, dinners on gold plate for 100 overlooking the distant sea dotted with white sails and the Newport shore, glowing in the last bright rays of the sun setting behind the Narragansett Hills. Once, a butler who was sacked got his revenge by painstakingly unscrewing the whole of a gold dinner service into 300 separate pieces and leaving them mixed in a heap on the dining-room table. As there was a dinner party that night a wire had to be sent to Tiffany's, who despatched two men from New York to put the service together again in time for dinner.

In this society designed by women for women, a husband – provided he paid the bills and turned up dutifully at important dinner parties – was scarcely needed. Even Newport's most eligible widower, James Van Alen, a man with an impeccable Knickerbocker background and a passion for all things English, from copper warming pans and oak settles to pewter tankards and expressions like 'Prithee' – once, he even brought over a man from England at vast expense to teach the members of the Coaching Club how a coaching horn should be blown – had to toe the line laid down by the female half of society.

When he invited a pretty young woman whom he had met at Narragansett, to which he had sailed on his yacht, to stay for the weekend, he was quickly made to feel he had gone too far. The reason? She was not part of 'the circle'. Every single woman of the twenty-odd who had been coming to his luncheon party on Saturday now found that, somehow, it had become impossible – a headache here, a slight cough there, friends arriving unexpectedly – and a number of their husbands called off too.

Eventually, the desperate Van Alen asked his daughter to act as hostess. She agreed, but only on condition he paid her $5,000 – and if he wished her to talk to his pretty guest, he would have to make it $10,000. With no alternative, he had to agree. She took the cheque and told him it would get her some earrings she had seen in Tiffany's. The luncheon party took place but the guest was left in no doubt that she was unwelcome and departed the following morning, saying the sea air did not agree with her.

Another who broke the rules was the colourful and popular James Gordon Bennett Jnr, publisher of the *New York Herald* and a noted sportsman who had introduced polo to the United States (he also funded Stanley's expedition to find Livingstone). Frequently drunk, he would pursue one of his favourite hobbies by driving a coach and four at breakneck speed through the streets of New York, often in the small hours and sometimes in the nude.

His real prowess was as a yachtsman, something greatly admired by Newporters; in 1866 he had won the first trans-oceanic yacht race, between three American yachts, the *Vesta*, the *Fleetwing* and his own *Henrietta*. On another of his yachts, the 300-foot *Lysistrata*, he kept a milk cow in a fan-cooled stall, a Turkish bath, a company of actors and a luxury car – later he sponsored motor racing.

For years he had summered at The Elms, a house facing the Casino. Then, at the age of thirty-six, he became engaged to the socialite Caroline May, an engagement that ended in scandal when he arrived late and drunk at a party at her family house and then urinated into a fireplace in full view of his hosts. Caroline was so shattered that she broke off the engagement at once; the next day her brother attacked Bennett with a horsewhip and challenged him to a duel – fortunately both men were such bad shots that they missed each other completely. This time, Bennett realised he had gone too far and sailed for Europe. The Elms remained empty for years until he judged, accurately, that sufficient time had passed for his return to be welcomed.

Some found the relentless Newport social round tedious in the extreme. 'To take a meal with them was to look dullness squarely in the eye,' wrote Blanche Oelrichs, daughter of one of society's leaders, of the small 'informal' lunches McAllister organised in Newport.

Men, in particular, chafed at its restrictiveness and some managed to escape from it on their yachts. 'Father's boredom on these expeditions [the afternoon ritual of calling] matched my own,' wrote Cornelius Vanderbilt IV. 'However, he soon developed the habit of disappearing to his boats or club just before the calling hour began. Mother left several of his cards, anyway, with the corner turned down to indicate that he was in Newport and available for parties, a favour for which he did not thank her.'

The yacht to which the nine-year-old Cornelius's father disappeared was one of the most luxurious in the world. The 233-foot *North Star* was gleaming white, with a thirty-foot dining room, cabin walls hung with silk, velvet-rope handrails, Irish linen sheets, a well-stocked wine room and a library.

Yachts also served another purpose. They provided the perfect hideaway for the clandestine affair: out at sea, there were no prying eyes and no one could prove what did or didn't go on. As both husbands and wives, for their different reasons, did not wish to upset the status quo, even when some magnate had added a boatload of chorus girls to the crew both he and his wife could maintain the convenient fiction that he was merely taking a short cruise for his health.

As in New York, there were never enough men. Many husbands only came from their offices at weekends, often in their own private train; others simply remained in New York or took off in their yachts. Sometimes there were so many absentees that there was a serious shortage of men for dinner or dancing. When extra were needed, the young officers from the Naval Training Station were invited. 'Can you let me have five bridge players for tomorrow at Mrs Hamilton Twombly's?' would run a typical call to the Commanding Officer. Or 'Will you send a dozen dancing men for Mrs Oliver Belmont's ball?' Although, naturally, they had to be of good family, they were still outsiders, and certainly nowhere near their hosts in wealth, so as one woman put it:

'They always wore their uniforms, so that no one wasted any time on them.'

Magnificent as were the yachts, it was the 'cottages', stretching the length of Bellevue Avenue along the cliffs and over Ochre Point, for which Newport became (and remained) best known – houses like White Lodge, a villa with a Nile-green ballroom, Elm Court, with three entrances (copied from those at Buckingham Palace), built by a coal baron, and the Frederick Vanderbilts' Rough Point, a grey stone 'Tudor' house with lawns running down to the cliff edge and a Gothic hall. These Newport mansions had stained-glass windows by Tiffany, mosaic floors, panelled walls, furniture of bronze, white holly, red cherry or black walnut.

The best known and grandest of these huge mansions was The Breakers. In 1885 Cornelius Vanderbilt II had bought an estate at Newport's Ochre Point that included a three-storey brick and frame house as a holiday home for his family. When the house burnt down seven years later, his wife Alice took charge of the rebuilding. What emerged was a palace (no wood was used in its construction as Cornelius insisted the building should be fireproof). Instead it was almost entirely marble.

The Breakers had seventy rooms (thirty-three of them to house the necessary number of servants).* Twenty-six horses lived in the outlying stables, together with their grooms and the twelve gardeners who looked after the eleven acres of garden. Its massive double staircase had bronze and gold balustrades, the white and gold music room with its tapestry panels and the morning room were designed and built in France, taken apart for shipping, and reassembled at Newport; weekly crates of treasures – fireplaces, columns, tapestries, pictures and mantelpieces – came from the houses of European noblemen; in the bathrooms with their marble tubs and solid silver taps were not only hot and cold running water but hot and cold running salt water, and the

* In 1895, the 2,229 servants living in Newport (a town of less than 20,000) made up over 10 per cent of the population. Over half of them had emigrated from Europe.

kitchen was so large that Mrs Vanderbilt could give a dinner party for 200. At a cost of $5 million it was far and away the most impressive house in Newport, and Alice Vanderbilt surged ahead towards the leadership of society.

At the same time, Cornelius's brother Willie K was building the Marble House, designed by Richard Morris Hunt and masterminded by his wife Alva, in hot competition with her sister-in-law Alice, with whom no love was lost. It was finally finished in 1892.

At $2 million to build, with another $9 million spent on its interior, it outdid Alice's creation (hence the term 'vanderbuilding' for this form of social competitiveness). It was inspired by the Sun King's Grand Trianon at Versailles. Two sweeps of drive rose towards its portico, held by four Doric columns the height of the entire two-storey house; its fifty rooms needed a staff of thirty-six servants. The hall and staircase were built of yellow marble, the dining room of red; the walls of the Gold Room were covered in gold leaf applied by hand. Over Alva's bedroom door, cherubs clasped shields featuring the initial A.

Luncheons were formally served in the huge red marble dining room (the Salon of Hercules at Versailles), where the high-backed bronze chairs were so heavy that footmen had to move them in to the table. Anna Robinson, a fellow socialite, wrote of their housewarming party: 'It was a superb affair and I was very glad I went. The house is gorgeous of course but too ornate it seems to me to live in everyday particularly the dining room which is only suitable for a banquet . . . the bedrooms are very pretty but simple & you could feel perfectly comfortable in them at once. While downstairs I should think one must be educated up to the surroundings.' It was here that Alva held their daughter Consuelo's coming-out ball on 28 August 1895 – and here that Consuelo was imprisoned until she bowed to her mother's will.

After the Vanderbilts' world cruise, Alva had taken Consuelo to London, where she made use of her friends for introductions, one of which resulted in a dinner party where Consuelo met the Duke of Marlborough for the first time. Neither made much impression on the other.

Meanwhile, Willie K, a keen racing man, rushed to London to see the Derby and then returned to Paris for the *Grand Prix*, on which he won 40,000 francs. Almost immediately afterwards he was introduced to a glamorous member of the demi-monde, Nellie Neustretter, an adventuress from Topeka, Kansas, known for her beauty and its effect on men. Instantly, Willie K gave her his winnings, following this by setting her up in a pied-à-terre in Paris with a dozen servants and giving her a superb carriage (grander than Alva's), a Deauville villa and an allowance of $200,000 a year.

'Willie is running round the town with this cocotte as publicly as possible, with the express design, as he loudly says, of humiliating his own wife, with whom he quarrelled latterly in a very bitter fashion,' commented *Town Topics* gleefully, as stories trickled back of the pair's visits to Les Ambassadeurs (the most expensive restaurant in Paris) and the Café de la Mort, done up in black, with coffin-shaped tables and waiters dressed as undertakers' men.

This gave Alva her chance. Although gossip sheets had long alleged that Willie was unfaithful, she now had more concrete evidence. She filed for divorce, citing adultery in her suit, thus breaking the greatest social taboo of the Astor circle into which she had so painfully climbed. Even the word 'divorce' was taboo and ladies usually left the room if it was uttered.

Alva's behaviour was the challenging of an unwritten rule: rich society men assumed that they could have anything they wanted, including women who weren't their wives, in return for which the wives, the beneficiaries of the husbands' great wealth, were supposed to accept this and look the other way. Alva's lawyer did his best to talk her out of suing but the more he tried, the more she became convinced that the only reason for this was his fear that other fed-up society wives would follow her lead – and what would happen then to the world as everyone knew it?

It is possible that Willie's fling with Nellie was planned because Willie, too, was determined to escape from the marriage – and also to hide his true interest. Among the women he was rumoured to have seen on the side was Consuelo Yznaga. Alva never discussed this, but that same year she dropped her old friend permanently from her life, a breach promptly broadcast by *Town Topics*.

After the summer in London, Alva and Consuelo returned to New York, where the divorce (in March 1895) had rendered Alva an outcast. The Vanderbilts cut their ties with her, a torrent of unsavoury press rained upon the family (one newspaper deemed the split 'the biggest divorce case that America has ever known' – it was splashed across eight columns in the *World*) and the judgement of those in her circle was swift and harsh. 'When I walked into church on a Sunday soon after obtaining my divorce, not a single one of my old friends would recognise me,' recorded Alva. 'They walked by me with cold stares or insolent looks. They gathered in little groups to make it evident they were speaking of their disapprobation of my conduct.'

But she was still enormously wealthy. She owned the Marble House outright – she had refused Willie K's offer of 660 Fifth Avenue and Idle House because of 'unpleasant memories' – and had received a sum of $10 million plus an income of around $100,000 a year and sole custody of their children. Not one to suffer in silence, she broadcast the tales of Willie's infidelities to some effect and her social grip was such that she still received invitations to parties – but only the hostess would deign to talk to her.* She claimed that other women, upon seeing her enter the room, would file out in silence, although 'the men would talk to me even though they did not approve of my actions but they did not wish their womenfolk to notice me'. This ostracism was particularly hard on Consuelo, who could not now have a New York début and hardly went out at all.

---

* When a sister-in-law, Jessie Sloane, who had made no secret of her passion for a brother of Alva's admirer August Belmont and had abandoned her husband and two daughters, was divorced, she was cast out of society for good. Her daughters were brought up never to know, or even to mention, their mother.

By now Alva had discovered that Consuelo was in love with Winthrop Rutherfurd; earlier, when he was one of a group on a cycling expedition, he and Consuelo had managed to outpace their respective mothers – and Winthrop hurriedly proposed. Although they kept their engagement secret Alva realised from Consuelo's sudden happiness what had happened and laid her plans accordingly. She took her daughter to Europe; Winthrop followed them to Paris, but when he called at their hotel he was refused admittance.

From then on, Consuelo was guarded. Alva intercepted and destroyed Winthrop's letters to Consuelo and those from Consuelo to him, so that her daughter did not even know that her suitor was trying desperately to contact her – or even that he was in the same country.

For Alva's decision that the Duke of Marlborough would be Consuelo's future husband had never wavered. So determined was she to bring this off that while in Paris she took the opportunity of ordering Consuelo's wedding dress, telling Worth to send it when the engagement was announced. This done, she took Consuelo to London. Here, with friends in common, she knew it was only a question of a short time before they met the Duke again.

From the Duke's point of view, a rich marriage was essential. By the 1870s the Marlboroughs had found themselves in such financial trouble that they had had to sell pictures and most of the family jewellery at auction, raising £10,000. Then came the sale of the wonderful 18,000-volume Sunderland library, a Raphael, a Van Dyck and finally the jewel of the collection, Rubens' *Rubens, His Wife Helena Fourment, and their Son Peter Paul.** But the sums raised were still not enough to cover either the family's debts or the maintenance of the ducal palace and by 1892 the Spencer-Churchills were almost broke.

Consuelo's second encounter with the Duke took place at a ball, when he invited Consuelo and Alva to join a small house

* Now in the Metropolitan Museum of Art in New York.

party at Blenheim. The day after their arrival he took Consuelo out on her own for a drive around some of the villages on his estate. Alva, who had dropped her strict chaperonage of her daughter for any meeting with the Duke, followed this up by inviting him to Newport for the ball she was going to give for Consuelo in August.

At the news of the ball, the society papers were agog. Who would come to it and who would stay away? What would happen when the different branches of the Vanderbilts met? Would the boycott of Alva still continue?

The Duke, as Alva had guessed, proved too much of a draw for anyone to resist, and her invitations were all eagerly accepted. Consuelo, seeing the inexorable approach of a fate she dreaded, was in despair. As Alva was determined that nothing would interfere with her plan – let alone the fact that her daughter was in love with someone else and did not wish to marry the man her mother had selected – Consuelo was kept a prisoner in the Marble House.

The porter was under orders not to let her out alone, her mother and her governess were always with her and when friends called they were told she was not at home. She was unable to write a letter because she had no means of buying a stamp or posting it and all the letters that arrived for her were taken straight to Alva, who destroyed them. Equally powerful as a prison wall was the psychological factor that she had been brought up from babyhood with the habit of total subordination to someone whose will was law.

It was not long before Newport society, aware of Alva's treatment of her daughter, echoed with the phrase: 'A marble palace is the right place for a woman with a marble heart.'

Consuelo held out against the prospect before her as long as she could but, after five months without word from her lover, and unable to reach him, with her mother raging, screaming and shouting that either she would have a fatal heart attack or that she would 'shoot Winthrop Rutherfurd' and threatening that therefore she would be arrested, imprisoned and hanged, she cracked, and agreed to accept Marlborough when he proposed.

She was barely eighteen, completely isolated, utterly miserable and brought up to be subservient to her mother in all things.*

When the Duke arrived in Newport as part of an American tour he was entertained by several of its notables, with others crowding to watch where possible. But the highlight was Alva's ball, planned so that she would outdo any previous entertainment in both taste and lavishness.

She succeeded. The grounds were lit by thousands of tiny lights, a host of servants wore livery in the style of Louis XIV, there were nine French chefs, three orchestras and the tables were decorated with pink hollyhocks among which swarmed tiny hummingbirds. In the yellow marble hall, a bronze drinking fountain held pink lotus plants, above which hovered artificial butterflies.

Even the cotillion favours, previously chosen by Alva in Paris – Louis XIV fans, etchings, gold watch-cases – were so splendid that guests actually stole them from one another. Alva wore white satin with a court train and a dazzle of diamonds; beside her stood Consuelo in white satin and tulle. It was a triumph – except that there was no offer of marriage from the Duke.

The parties and dinners went on . . . and on . . . and on – and still nothing. Finally, the evening before he was due to leave, the Duke proposed. Alva, determined to waste no time in clinching the matter, announced the engagement the following day, even ordering her servants to spread the good news with the words 'Go out and tell everyone you know.'

The magazine *Town Topics*, under no illusions, remarked on the 'short but decisive campaign of General Alva', while Consuelo's twelve-year-old brother told her: 'He is only marrying you for your money.' Consuelo burst into tears, perhaps because it was true. After some hard bargaining, the eventual settlement to the Duke was $2.5 million in share stock on which 4 per cent gave him an annual income of $100,000.

The wedding was also choreographed by the dominating Alva

* Or, as Alva put it in her autobiography with breathtaking disingenuousness: 'I threw them together and an engagement resulted.'

who, on the grounds that Consuelo had 'no taste', did not let her daughter choose either her bridesmaids or her trousseau, and refused to ask any of her Vanderbilt relations.

For weeks beforehand there was constant press attention, with the daily doings of the couple retailed to a fascinated audience. The publicity-conscious Alva sent some of Consuelo's trousseau underwear to *Vogue*, which to Consuelo's squirming embarrassment ran a feature on her bridal corset with solid-gold clasps, her rose-embroidered corset covers, her pink, lace-trimmed drawers and her silk nightgowns. 'It is not too much to say that the future of female underclothing will be momentously affected by the light which the public has lately received,' wrote The Saunterer in a caustic paragraph about Alva's pursuit of publicity.

The couple were married at the end of November 1895 in St Thomas's Episcopal Church on Fifth Avenue, Consuelo spending the morning of her wedding in tears alone in her room, with a footman posted at the door – Alva was taking no chances. As soon as Alva had left the house for the church Willie K arrived to escort his daughter there. They were half an hour late, owing to efforts to try and conceal the signs of her red-eyed weeping. A huge and excited crowd waited outside, following the carriage to the church and then back to Alva's house on 72nd Street, where the wedding breakfast took place, with Mrs Astor as guest of honour – Alva had not forgotten her priorities.

Other guests were sensitive to the faint aura of scandal that hung like a mist in the church, as one of them noted: 'It was the most peculiar thing to see Mr & Mrs Vanderbilt quite near each other listening to the choir sing the hymn "O perfect love".'

With her daughter's marriage into the highest rank of the British aristocracy, Alva managed to overcome the disgrace of her divorce. Her place regained in society, she married Oliver Belmont the following year, a wedding attended neither by the Vanderbilt clan, who had stood by Willie K, nor the Belmonts – perhaps because they disapproved of Oliver's treatment of his first wife and his behaviour in settling so much of his fortune on his second, a woman already hugely rich.

For not only did Alva's alimony continue after her marriage

but her new husband settled on her both his estate of Grey Crag and his enormous Newport 'cottage' Belcourt – also designed by her favourite architect, Richard Morris Hunt, this time based on the Louis XIII hunting lodge at Versailles. Virtually the whole of the ground floor was devoted to Belmont's collection of carriages and his prized horses – he was known for his skill as a four-in-hand carriage-driver – its huge Gothic rooms with their stained-glass windows emblazoned with the Belmont coat of arms. True to form, Alva lost no time in making alterations, converting Oliver's carriage room into a banqueting hall and transforming a study into her boudoir, complete with eighteenth-century French panelling.

That year, a society reporter wrote of Newport: 'Never before have the lines between the smart set and the others been more closely drawn. A few women seem to lead the concourse like sheep and there is an almost riotous struggle of getting in and keeping other people out.'

CHAPTER 9

The 'Marrying Wilsons'

One of the most spectacular entries into New York society was that of the Wilsons. They were exactly the sort of people that the Knickerbockers wanted to keep out, with their new money, no particular pretensions to family background, and the added drawback that Richard Wilson was the subject of unpleasant rumour. But as so often, success in husband-hunting allowed them to leapfrog their way into the heart of New York society, so much so that a favourite joke of the time was: 'Why did the Diamond Match Company fail?' 'Because Mrs Richard T. Wilson beat them at making matches.'

The father of the 'marrying Wilsons' was Richard Thornton Wilson, born in Habersham County, Georgia, in about 1829. The son of a poor Scottish tanner and shoemaker, the twenty-year-old Richard left home after the death of his father with forty dollars in gold and a mule. He first found work as a clerk in a store, then became a travelling salesman. One evening, exhausted by life on the road, he fell asleep on the doorstep of a store belonging to a man called Ebenezer Johnston, the owner of a 700-acre estate and a number of slaves. Ebenezer took him on and was soon impressed by his ability and hard work, and in 1852 Richard married Ebenezer's eldest daughter Melissa. Their children, May, Orme, Belle, Richard and Grace, were born respectively in 1855, 1860, 1864, 1866 and 1871.

Richard, at six foot six, was a handsome giant of a man with plenty of Southern charm who was said to be the model for Rhett Butler, the glamorous Southern black sheep of a hero in *Gone with the Wind*. Hard work, enterprise, an unswerving determination to succeed and perfect manners took him up the ladder until, during the Civil War, he was appointed Commissary General of the Confederate Army by Jefferson Davis, where his fortune was said to have begun by selling cotton blankets to the Confederate Army while charging them for wool.

At the time England's sympathies lay with the South, thanks largely to the lucrative cotton trade they shared, so to England Richard moved in 1864, accompanied by his family, chiefly as an agent to dispose of the South's cotton crop – though some said to sell Confederate supplies to foreign governments. When the Civil War ended he brought his family back to America, this time to the Union, along with a fortune of $500,000. Always with an eye to the main chance, he began buying up derelict railways in the devastated South to refurbish or sell later at a large profit, amassing another fortune in doing so.

The Wilsons settled in a brownstone house at 812 Fifth Avenue, between what is now 63rd and 64th Street – then very much the unfashionable part of Fifth Avenue, with much of the land north of 59th Street still a rocky, hilly area dotted with wooden farmhouses and squatter settlements. Later they moved into the much grander house of the disgraced Tammany Hall supremo, Boss Tweed,* on Fifth Avenue and 43rd Street, a much smarter neighbourhood.

Here, despite all Melissa's efforts, the family remained outside the charmed circle of society until the eldest Wilson daughter, May, struck gold, in the form of Ogden Goelet. Ogden, although a scion of one of the oldest New York families, lacked confidence: he was serious-minded, shortish, not very rich, and shy. When he was sent to recuperate from a long illness in a small New England town, Mrs Wilson seized her opportunity. Cannily, she rented a nearby house and got her daughters to read to him during his long hours of enforced idleness.

---

* Boss Tweed, the corrupt politician who drained the city of New York of millions, was arrested in 1873.

To this young man with little faith in his attraction to women, May's warmth and generous open-heartedness must have had an irresistible appeal. Natural flirtatiousness – Southern belles were accustomed to have admirers competing with each other for their favours – only added to the allure, and May was clearly not afraid to step up this attitude until it would almost seem that she was making most of the running.

'I never liked you so well, or wished more to be with you, than last night,' she wrote, 'and yet you left me – heedless of my entreaties, left me with a man too prone to say sweet nothings, which some think mean so much, or so little.

'I am convinced you have no jealousy – I shall really be awfully disappointed if I do not see you tomorrow, and prefer of course seeing you in the evening. Forget the other girl and I will do the same with the other man.'

He did, and they married in 1877; to make their union even sweeter, Richard settled $75,000 on the young couple. Then, unexpectedly, Ogden's rich but parsimonious uncle died, leaving his nephew $25 million. Soon afterwards, Ogden's father died – and also left Ogden $25 million. Ogden and May, already socially secure, were now among the richest in their set.

Five years later May's brother Orme achieved an even more stunning coup, marrying into the most exclusive of all the New York families. His bride was Caroline (Carrie) Schermerhorn Astor, the youngest daughter of William Backhouse Astor and his wife, *the* Mrs Astor. Carrie, a slender – she had an enviable twenty-two-inch waist – sweet-natured girl with a wistful, heart-shaped face that many thought plain, could be said to have been born into the purple; and certainly her mother, though dominating, treated her like a little princess. Carrie and Orme had known each other since both had attended the same New York children's dancing class and Carrie had fallen in love with him when she was sixteen, to the horror of her mother, who regarded the Wilson family as outside those 'one knew' socially, an attitude enhanced by her awareness of Richard Wilson's shady past. She made it clear to Carrie that such a match was out of the question.

Carrie, like so many girls completely subservient to their mothers, did not openly revolt. But her misery was such that she became pale, depressed and ill. Although uncalculated, this was the best thing she could have done. Mrs Astor, although socially implacable, was a kind-hearted mother who adored her daughter. She became worried and unhappy at seeing Carrie so wretched, and one day – or so she told her friends – seeing the young couple emerge from church hand in hand, thought they seemed so much in love that 'I felt I could not stand in the way of their happiness any longer'. She did, however, make them wait for two or three years, considered nothing unusual at a time when long engagements were the fashion; partly, perhaps, to ensure that the feelings of her daughter, still so young, had not changed.

It was not until 1884, when Orme was twenty-four and Carrie twenty-three, that they were finally married in the Astor mansion, even its chandeliers hung with pink roses and not a society 'name' missing from the thousand-odd guests seated in the house's art gallery. The Astors had insisted on Richard Wilson putting up $500,000 as a settlement, at that moment a severe strain on the family's finances, but as the strength of the Wilson clan was that they all worked towards the common good, this hefty price was considered well worth it in terms of the step up it gave them. Carrie's father gave her what was described as a 'full set of diamond jewels' and threw in 'a handsome residence on Fifth-avenue'. Richard Wilson completely furnished the new house, then added 'a full table service of silver knives, forks, and spoons'.

Now, the Wilsons were connected through marriage to two of the most important, respected, socially impeccable and richest families in New York. It was the start of the legend of the 'marrying Wilsons'.

As she grew up, the youngest Wilson, Grace, slim and honey-blonde with fine, aristocratic features, became a favourite of Mrs Astor. Thirteen at the time of her brother's wedding, she was developing into a beauty, and, what was probably more important to this doyenne of society, her demeanour was one of distinction and refinement – in fact, a worthy addition to the Astor family circle. When a debutante she was even, honour of honours, asked by Mrs Astor to lead a cotillion at her exclusive annual ball. This approval would stand Grace in good stead in years to come.

Grace was always close to her sister May and May's husband Ogden, most of whose fortune came from real estate. The Goelets lived at 608 Fifth Avenue, at the corner of 49th Street, where their two children, Mary (May) and Robert (Bobby), were born in 1878 and 1881 respectively. May, who like Grace had spent many summers in Europe, collected paintings; Ogden joined the Fine Arts Society and was one of the founder members who bought shares in the Metropolitan Opera House.

The only small cloud on the horizon was Ogden's health: his physique was frail and he suffered from chronic asthma. Like many of his peers, he was a keen yachtsman – also, his asthma was less troublesome at sea – and owned a superb and beautiful schooner, *The Norseman*, built for him and launched in 1881.

Gradually both Goelets became disenchanted with the society into which they had the unquestioned right of entrée. The competitive splashing around of money in an attempt to upgrade status or popularity had become insufferable to them, and they set off to cruise round Europe in *The Norseman* with their children, now seven and five, governess and tutor. They were joined the following year by the second Wilson daughter, May's sister Belle, on the lookout for a husband of the right sort. She would soon find one.

When the party arrived at Cowes for the regatta that August, the spectacular beauty of *The Norseman* at once caught the eye of the yacht-loving Prince of Wales. He invited himself on board for a closer look and stayed to tea, returning twice that week, once for a luncheon party in his honour and again for tea.

With the Prince of Wales's open interest in *The Norseman* and its passengers, it was not long before the Goelets had a circle of acquaintances – and Belle had found her man. On the yacht of the 14th Earl of Pembroke, she met his diplomat younger brother Michael (Mungo) Herbert and the two fell in love. The wedding in 1888 of Mungo and Belle saw the start of a successful and happy marriage – and another triumph for the Wilson family, this time one that took them into the heart of the British aristocracy. His family welcomed her warmly, his sister Lady de Grey writing to Belle that: 'Now Mungo has got the wish of his heart I have nothing left to wish for, and my gratitude towards the person who has brought us such happiness is beyond expression.'

As did all in their exclusive social set, the Goelets were accustomed to spend summer weeks in Newport, where Ogden Goelet commissioned Ochre Court, second only to The Breakers in size and built at a cost of $4.5 million in 1892. Like the next two largest houses, Belcourt Castle and Marble House, it was designed by Richard Morris Hunt. In this château-like building of grey granite with its sheet-copper roof, gilded magnificence and ballroom that would hold 1,000, crowded near other grand mansions, the family spent eight summer weeks, looked after by twenty-seven house servants, eight coachmen and grooms and twelve gardeners. But May soon tired of the running of such a large establishment, and Ogden was becoming increasingly unwell, needing a nurse's care and living mainly on hothouse grapes.

So the Goelets turned again to the sea, leasing a large steam yacht, *The White Ladye*, from Lily Langtry (the former favourite of the Prince of Wales who had, by 1881, become an actress) and set off in her for the winter season of 1895–6. Also on board was the dazzling Grace, at twenty-five the youngest of the 'marrying Wilsons' sisters. It was a happy family party, only shadowed by Ogden's steadily declining health.

Grace Wilson was beautiful, distinguished-looking and extremely well educated: she spoke flawless French and good German, she knew all the great operas and she was used to the sophisticated, cosmopolitan life of European capitals as she had spent most summers abroad since the age of eleven. She had been engaged to Cecil Baring, the son of Lord Revelstoke, who had lost most of his fortune in the crash of 1893. Some said that Lord Revelstoke demanded such a high dowry that Richard Wilson had refused.

By 1895 she had a new admirer, the shy, twenty-two-year-old 'Neily' Vanderbilt (Cornelius Vanderbilt III), the eldest son of Cornelius Vanderbilt II. Neily was just under six foot tall and extremely good-looking, with square-cut features, thick, curly brown hair and dark blue eyes. He was shy and hardworking, but had recurrent bouts of rheumatism. In 1892, his older brother Bill had died of typhoid at the age of twenty, while the two were sharing a room together at Yale. In 1893 Neily had been sent on a world cruise in a chartered yacht – packed with fresh produce from the family farms in Rhode Island – to gain some European polish.

He returned much fitter, aged twenty-one, in time for his sister Gertrude's coming-out ball in Newport in the summer of 1895. It was a lavish affair: the favours – gold cigarette cases and fans – distributed to all the guests cost $10,000. For the ball the twenty-four-year-old Grace, surrounded by admirers, looked her best in a deeply décolletée white chiffon dress embroidered with pearls; round her waist was a chain of diamonds from which hung a small ivory fan. Neily was dazzled, and it showed; to anyone watching, it was obvious that he was hopelessly in love with Grace – and overnight the Vanderbilts began to disapprove of her.

She was older than their son, too sophisticated, and she had perhaps been too open in her search for a wealthy husband who could raise her socially: one American onlooker, Jay Burden (later to marry Neily's sister Gertrude), had written of Grace 'raking the Solent for dukes' when the Goelet yacht was at Cowes. One of her potential targets, or so the Vanderbilts believed, had been Neily's older brother Bill, to whom it was said she had been secretly engaged, and there was also the broken Baring engagement. In short, the Vanderbilt clan looked on Grace as an adventuress, out for what she could get and determined above all to make a rich marriage.

Sometime in the autumn of 1895, Neily's mother Alice paid a social call on Mrs Wilson, during which she enquired casually if the family were remaining in New York for the winter or, as many did, going abroad. When she heard that they were staying,

Neily was quickly despatched on a European holiday. When the Wilsons learnt about this, they were so angered that Grace, too, was sent to Europe where, inevitably, the couple met.

'There is *nothing* the girl would not do,' wrote Gertrude in her diary, claiming that Grace was at least twenty-seven and had 'unbounded experience. Been engaged several times. Tried hard to marry a rich man. Ran after Jack Astor to such an extent that all New York talked about it. Is so diplomatic that even the men are deadly afraid of her. There is nothing she would stop at.'

To her brother she wrote a frantic plea: 'Please, please don't announce your engagement now. You may think because I do not say much that I don't really care for you. You may think too that I am as narrow as the others and that I don't understand your point of view. That is not so. I care so much for you that if I were not absolutely sure that you would not be happy I would take your side against the family. I am not narrow and I know how hard your position is and how desperate you feel, but you are not going to do yourself any good by announcing it, and you certainly are going to do Miss Wilson harm. A man may say he does not care what the world says but for a girl it is different – a slight is a hard thing to stand and you will find it is so when it places someone you care for in an awkward position.

'When you are sure of their feelings it is not such a hard thing to wait. You are positive you won't change, you are positive she won't change, why can't you wait? You will say your position is a hard one. Yes but not as hard as it will be if you announce this engagement. What could be my object in saying all this if I did not care for you. The family have not asked me to speak to you.

'It's four years ago tonight you came to New York and found Willie dying. He died and you instead of taking his place . . . what are you about to do?'

Grace's sister Belle wrote from Constantinople to her: 'I am still waiting, every nerve on edge, for further developments . . . I feel, with your love for Neily and his undoubted and much-tried affection for you, things must some day be right. But the misery you have been through!'

Battle ranks had been drawn up. The Vanderbilts used every

weapon in their arsenal to part the two; Neily's father Cornelius II threatened to disinherit him, while the scandal of this feud within the world's wealthiest family swirled outwards through friends and acquaintances to anyone who had heard of them – even the Prince of Wales, who knew Grace, asked to be kept informed of developments. When, in June 1896, Richard Wilson announced that the couple were to be married that month, Cornelius II responded with: 'The engagement of Cornelius Vanderbilt Jnr to Miss Wilson is against his father's expressed wishes.'

So sharply divided was New York society on the question that only a third of those invited to the wedding accepted, the rest fearing the displeasure of the powerful Vanderbilt family. The matter was solved when, the day before the proposed wedding, a statement was issued by Neily's father that his son was confined to bed suffering from rheumatism and the wedding was cancelled.

It provoked the comment from one woman of their circle to another: 'I wager you that as soon as that boy is well enough he'll be whisked off to Newport and there'll be no match this summer at least.' To which her friend replied: 'My dear, you do not know the Wilsons.'

The last speaker was right. When Neily, who had been ill, learnt what his father had said, there was a violent confrontation – Neily did not intend to abandon Grace. Shortly after this, Cornelius II collapsed with a stroke so severe that he was confined to a wheelchair unable to speak, a catastrophe blamed on Neily by his family. 'He knows it is his behaviour that gave Papa his stroke,' wrote Gertrude in her diary. After this she, like almost all his family, cut him off completely.

Neily stuck to his word. He and Grace were married in a small and simple ceremony at her parents' house in August 1896. Wisely, after it they left to spend some months abroad. Once there, his ill-health surfaced again.

Without Vanderbilt backing, the newlyweds had to economise – a relative term, as Grace's father gave her a trust fund of half a million dollars that brought in an income of $25,000 a year (a sum she was used to spending on clothes alone). Neily, who had written to his father asking if he could see him in the hope of healing the breach, was flatly turned down. Neither Grace nor Neily could understand the reason for his family's disapproval of Grace: if Neily's mother had had any question in her mind concerning Grace, why had she invited this beautiful and well-behaved debutante time and again to her balls and dinners when she had three (then) unmarried sons in the house? But when Cornelius Vanderbilt II had his stroke, it was immediately put down by the Vanderbilt family to Neily's obduracy in marrying Grace.

The rift in the Vanderbilt family seemed impossible to overcome. When Cornelius Vanderbilt II died in 1899, in a will dated the day originally planned for Neily and Grace's marriage, he left the major part of his fortune – $42 million – to his second son, Alfred, while Neily, his erstwhile heir, was left a mere $500,000 and the income from $1 million in trust funds. Alfred settled $6 million on Neily (largely in order to avoid any potential litigation over the will), but the rupture remained: when they met, the brothers did not speak but only nodded at each other. Even Grace's first child did not bring them closer, Neily's mother Alice referring to it as 'that Wilson baby'. None of the Vanderbilts attended the baby boy's christening.

Meanwhile, at the end of 1896 Ogden Goelet took delivery of yet another beautiful new yacht, *The Mayflower*, designed in Glasgow by the man who had built the Prince of Wales's racing yacht, *Britannia*. The following year the Goelets rented Wimborne House in Arlington Street for their daughter May's first London season. Petite and dark, with an excellent figure, she had grown into a charming and accomplished young woman who could read and write in several languages and whose dusting of European sophistication did not hide her youthful high spirits and the warmth of her nature – her family relationships had all been close and loving. She viewed the coming season, during which the family friendship formed with the Prince of Wales would stand her in good stead, with excitement.

'On Sunday the Prince dined with us,' she wrote on 1 June

1897, 'and I'm happy to say it all went off most successfully – you have no idea of what a struggle it was though – Everyone we could think of to ask was going out of town, either to Waddesdon or some other Rothschild's . . . After dinner we had Melba to sing and the Prince was simply delighted. I have rarely seen him in such good spirits. He let everyone go at a quarter to one and he stayed till 1:15. He told Mamma it had all been most beautifully done and I don't think he could have been bored otherwise he would never have stayed so late.'

The family's entry into the inner circle of British society was made even clearer by the invitation to the most exclusive event of 1897, the Duchess of Devonshire's Jubilee Ball on 2 July – an invitation to which confirmed that you were absolutely among the chosen. It was fancy dress or, as the Duchess decreed, 'allegorical or historical costume before 1815', with five 'courts' that individuals could join. May went as Scheherazade, the *Arabian Nights* storyteller, in a Worth gown of golden gauze embroidered with precious stones and a flower-bedecked headdress topped with a large white ostrich plume.

Devonshire House, which stood between Stratton Street and Berkeley Street, facing on to Piccadilly, with views over Green Park, had a large courtyard in front so that carriages could arrive and depart quickly, avoiding congestion. Across the stone floor of the pillared entrance hall glass doors led to the inner hall, from which a curving marble staircase with a crystal handrail led up to the first floor. Here yellow and white silk brocade covered the walls, the gilded furniture was upholstered in dark blue, the light from the myriad candles in the brilliant crystal chandeliers gleamed off heavy polished mahogany doors, huge mirrors and superb paintings. For the party, the large garden was lit by 12,000 lamps and supper was in a marquee carpeted in crimson, with blue and gold walls hung with tapestries and mirrors.

The United States was well represented: nine other heiresses who had married into the nobility were there, from the Countess of Essex as Berenice Queen of Palestine, with a wonderful art nouveau crown shaped like a peacock's tail, to Mrs Arthur Paget (née Minnie Stevens) as Cleopatra in white and gold, so ablaze with diamonds, rubies and emeralds that when she entered people gasped in astonishment. Jewels were everywhere – many of the 700 guests had their own jewels reset to match their costumes. The Duke of Marlborough's Louis XV suit of pale gold velvet was thickly embroidered in silver, pearls and diamonds, all sewn on by hand, while his wife the slender Consuelo disguised her seven-month pregnancy in an eighteenth-century pale green satin gown garlanded with roses. Jennie Churchill, as the Empress Theodora, wore embroidered mauve satin by Worth.

Also there was the young Duke of Roxburghe, dressed as a Yeoman of the Guard, in a scarlet and gold tunic above scarlet breeches and stockings, with a white ruff emphasising his good-looking face. This 8th Duke, six foot four, the handsome eldest son of seven children, was called Kelso (the Earl of Kelso was one of the Roxburghe subsidiary titles) by his family and Bumble by his friends. With an estate of 60,418 acres bringing in over £50,000 a year, he was also rich.

But the man with whom May's name became linked was another duke, Kim, as the son of Consuelo Yznaga the half-American 9th Duke of Manchester, who had followed May round the ballroom wherever possible. Then aged twenty – he had succeeded at fifteen – he had already established a reputation as a notorious spendthrift. In fact, he was following in some well-defined family footsteps: the previous two dukes had frittered away much of the family fortune and he was on the lookout for a wealthy bride. May, pretty, charming, hugely rich and petite – he himself was on the short side – seemed an ideal target. Consuelo, now forty-four and the widowed Duchess of Manchester, agreed and, whether or not the rumour was put about by them, it was soon believed in London that May was engaged to the profligate Duke.

To Ogden who, in common with his class and kind, had always avoided publicity, this bruiting-about of his daughter's name in connection with a man of whom he thoroughly disapproved was intolerable. A denial by Kim, on which Ogden had insisted, did something to calm the outraged American headlines ('England's poorest Duke after our richest heiress!'), but Ogden, as always, felt safer at sea. The Goelets left Wimborne House and anchored at Cowes in the *Mayflower* for the August regatta.

They were only able to enjoy it for a few days. Ogden had been growing steadily worse and when, finally, his liver ceased to function he died, on 27 August, on his beloved yacht, his family clustered round him. 'It was a tragic ending of one of the most sensational social successes ever made by an American in England,' recorded one newspaper. 'The Prince of Wales had been his guest at Cowes for the third time, and his American host had already made plans for other important social entertainments. Some of Mr Goelet's friends think his daughter's determination to marry the young Duke of Manchester may possibly have hastened the father's end. He felt very strongly about it, but as was cabled at the time of the suit of the young English nobleman he was supposed to be favoured by Mrs Goelet.' Unsurprisingly, perhaps – May Goelet was, after all, one of the 'marrying Wilsons'.

Ogden's body was transported back across the Atlantic in his yacht for the funeral service in Newport in September. He had left $10 million dollars to his wife and – where an English girl with a brother might have expected much the smaller sum – May and Bobby were treated equally. Each received $20 million, the only difference being that May's was to be held in trust for her, gathering interest, until she reached twenty-five, when the whole sum would be hers absolutely.

When the Goelets returned to Europe May was a golden target for every man who felt a rich wife was one of life's essentials. 'How I should hate to be May Goelet,' commented Daisy, Princess of Pless, 'all those odious little Frenchmen and dozens of others crowding round her millions. An English duke does not crowd around – he merely accepts a millionairess.'

May, however, was a girl with plenty of emotional common sense. She had been brought up in a close and warm family environment and she had the example of a loving marriage before her in the shape of the two women to whom she was closest, her mother and her favourite aunt Belle. She wanted the same for herself and she was prepared to wait until she got it. Flattering though it might be to receive all these proposals, she was well aware that part of her attraction was her potential dowry.

'I must give an account of my proposals,' she wrote to her aunt Grace. 'Well, first Lord Shaftesbury popped almost as soon as he returned to London. He came one afternoon. Mamma happened to leave the room for a few minutes and off he went – like a pistol. I told him it was quite ridiculous as he had only known me three weeks and he couldn't possibly know his own mind.' She added shrewdly that she knew nothing of him or his past.

The same letter brings a mention of the Duke of Roxburghe. '[He is] the man everyone says I am engaged to,' wrote May. They met at a dinner party – 'he never goes to balls' – and the following night at another, given by May's countrywoman Lady Curzon. 'Such a nice dinner,' though she added: 'Lord Castlereagh took me in (the Londonderry boy) and we talked together afterwards so I didn't have a chance of saying a word to the Duke.'

To a girl with her head as well screwed on as May, the twenty-four-year-old Charley Londonderry's looks and charm were no threat:* he was already married. Of the Duke, who had been commissioned into the Royal Horse Guards and served throughout the South African (Boer) War of 1899–1901, all she was able to observe was that he seemed shy and well read, with charming manners. But there was not then any striking of sparks nor, on the part of the Duke, the pursuit that May was used to.

Although May's immense wealth meant that she would always be a matrimonial target, her friends had begun to feel that it was time she got married. She was twenty-five – that dread age which to the Victorians was the cusp between fresh young girlhood and old maid-dom – and most of those in her circle had been married for several years. Even the King told her that it was time to settle down and, indeed, tried to arrange a match for her with Captain George Holford, owner of Dorchester House on Park Lane and two estates in the country. For May, who had a keen sense of her priorities, this was not enough. 'Unfortunately, the dear man has no title, though a very good position [he was the brother-in-law

* He was the model for the glamorous Sebastian in Vita Sackville-West's *The Edwardians*.

of Lord Grey] – and I am sure he would make a very good husband.' To someone else, was the unspoken corollary.

For May knew exactly what she wanted. With her money and looks, only a duke would do. And within a year, during which she and Roxburghe gradually got to know one another better, she had got one. The Duke of Roxburghe was handsome, brave, a conscientious landlord and rich enough himself not to have pursued May for her money – though it was undoubtedly welcome. When, in July 1903, Mrs Goelet returned to New York, May, significantly, was left behind – but with her aunt Grace to chaperone her as they stayed at Claridge's. Soon the Duke of Roxburghe arrived there too, and their families were told of their engagement. It was announced by the Dowager Duchess in Scotland and Mrs Goelet in Ochre House simultaneously, on 1 September. They were married in New York, the Duchess having first presented May with the family emeralds.

May brought with her to Floors Castle not only her magnificent $20 million dowry but some wonderful French furniture and a set of superb tapestries. Like May, they fitted perfectly into Floors. From the start, she enjoyed the panoply, and the grand treatment: when she and her husband returned from their honeymoon to his family seat on the Scottish Borders, they were greeted at Floors Castle by 100 torch-bearers and a band of pipers. She redecorated the castle in deluxe American style and settled down to a happy life growing carnations and doing good works among the villagers. The only problem was her failure to produce an heir. After ten childless years, the Duke and Duchess went to visit a specialist in Vienna, promising him £1,000 if he could help them conceive, and double that if the child was a boy. The doctor apparently did nothing more to earn his fee than advise the Duchess to give up sugar, but the Marquess of Bowmont was born a year later, in 1913. His birth was marked by a chain of bonfires along the Borders of Scotland, lit by jubilant tenants, relieved that the Goelet money would stay in the Roxburghe family.

Several years after his father had died in 1899, Neily managed to persuade his mother Alice to allow them to visit her with their son Cornelius Vanderbilt IV, and the breach was officially healed. But Grace had neither forgotten nor forgiven the behaviour of her husband's parents, and when she finally greeted her mother-in-law, even her son realised that 'her smile was as the flash of sun on a glacier'. Alice Vanderbilt and her husband were, after all, the only people who had ever tried to halt the advance of the 'marrying Wilsons'.

CHAPTER 10

The Call of Europe

Many of the 'buccaneers' wound up as the brides of European noblemen, if only for the reason that Americans were naturally drawn towards Europe. Some were either immigrant or only a generation or two away from immigrant, with families or relations there; and, living in a continent where great distances were a part of life, travel seemed normal. The wealthy among the old New York families, very conscious of their Dutch or British ancestry, frequently visited Europe to renew links and enjoy its culture and horizons.

Then there were the buildings: a few decades earlier, Washington Irving's tales and travel narratives induced the first of many generations of American sightseers to visit the great aristocratic houses and castles of the Old World. Later, the impact these had on the rich of New York and Newport was reflected in the building of vast French châteaux along Fifth Avenue or Newport's Ochre Point.

Despite the fear of absence – out of sight was out of mind in the new model of New York high society – many Americans travelled to Europe to spend a few out-of-season months there. Europe was believed to impart polish and knowledge of culture: in 1866, according to the American fashion bible, *Godey's Lady's Book*, 50,000 Americans travelled to Europe. They went in clipper ships, often with livestock aboard, and steamers, and all of them suffered horribly from seasickness, not helped by engine fumes, the vibration of the screw and poor ventilation.

Although these newly wealthy were firmly republican in outlook, they were fascinated by the traditions, the sense of centuries behind various established customs, the sophistication of people who knew exactly who they were and how to behave in any given set of circumstances. With the War of Independence now far enough away in time to be overlooked, their own society had taken its lead from that of England: Ward McAllister, its self-appointed arbiter, had largely shaped the Patriarchs' Balls on the model of Almack's Assembly Rooms in London's King Street, and English fashions (for men), customs and etiquette were the model for New York. Besides, several summers in Europe meant an excellent education for their daughters, who would learn to speak good French and possibly Italian or German as well, and become familiar with artistic and musical masterpieces, all of which would make them more desirable brides – many to the young aristocrats impoverished by the fall of the Second Empire, who flocked round them like hungry sharks.

Although travel was so often undertaken, there was little of the relaxation usually associated with sea voyages. Even on the ocean, etiquette ruled. No woman, whatever her age or station in life, would venture on crossing the Atlantic without placing herself in the captain's special charge, or under the escort of some male passenger. Such precautions even extended to the mundane business of tidying the cabin: if a woman were married, or with some male relation, she could be waited on by a male steward, otherwise not.

Then there was the question of safety. July and August, potential passengers were informed, were considered the safest and least stormy months to cross the Atlantic. June had southbound icebergs and heavy fogs – on some voyages the wind whistled through the rigging and the foghorn blew all night. The rest of the advice administered to ocean travellers was largely concerned with seasickness; it is impossible for anyone born after stabilisers were invented for ships or in the age of air travel to comprehend the duration and virulence of this horrible condition.

'After the most terrific, terrible and dreadful sea voyage of my life (& I have crossed the Atlantic five times, and from Marseilles to Alexandria, Egypt twice),' wrote Mary Theresa Leiter, mother of the future Lady Curzon, on a tour of Europe, from Bergen in 1881. 'Oh, if I could communicate to mankind a warning to never under any circumstances venture upon the North Sea. We left the mouth of the Humber at six o'clock on Tuesday morning, & from that hour until Wednesday night Mary & I suffered such tortures as only are known to people who traverse the North Sea.'

With no stabilisers, ships rolled tremendously, so passengers were advised to try and get a cabin near the centre of the ship, as there was less motion there. By sail, a crossing took ten days or more and, judging by the tone of a book of advice on ocean travel, would involve several days of prostrating nausea. 'It is quite impossible to prevent. Whatever you do, get up on deck.' If prostrated, then 'hang a strip of cloth with pockets beside your bed, to aid undressing if you are too ill to move'.

The rather gloomy conclusion by the writer of this popular booklet of advice was to dress well, because 'I have always felt that a body washed ashore in good clothes would receive more respect and kinder care than if dressed in those only fit for the rag bag.'

Later, journeys were by steamer; these often had sails as well, and took around nine or ten days. Conditions were fairly primitive: as late as 1870 the Cunard liner *Tarifa* had no baths and only two toilets. All the same, when they arrived in port, the passengers would give three cheers for the captain and crew.

Once arrived, they found a glamorous, exciting milieu, made more so by the young noblemen with whom the American girls danced and flirted: men who were accustomed to pay romantic homage to women in a way their brothers and cousins at home would have thought at best insincere or at worst unmanly. That they were also keenly aware of the value of the dollar in restoring their faded fortunes did not go unnoticed but, sometimes, the thought of an ancient title outweighed more practical considerations – besides, it was always something to flaunt back home.

The epitome of this mingling of European high-society glamour and American hard cash was the match between Anna Gould and Boni de Castellane.

Anna Gould was the daughter of the robber-baron Jay Gould, immensely wealthy and castigated as unscrupulous even in his own time. Like many of his contemporaries, he bought up or bribed officials and legislators, his ice-cold objectivity, utter determination and speed of action enabling him to outwit competitors and build up a huge fortune. Even Commodore Vanderbilt, once a sworn foe, later an ally, described him as 'the smartest man in America'.

Anna, the fifth of his six children and the younger of his two daughters, was born in 1875 and brought up amid every luxury. Her pleasant, vivacious manner concealed an iron will, doubtless inherited from her father, that made her determined to get her own way in everything she wanted to. She was not a beauty: she was short, with a sallow complexion, hairy arms, a prominent nose and thick, caterpillar-like eyebrows, although she was slender, with tiny hands and feet and black eyes. Against these drawbacks, over which lay the vague aroma of her father's unsavoury doings, was the allure of the huge fortune she had inherited from him – both her parents had died before she was eighteen.

When she was nineteen a thirty-seven-year-old financier called Oliver Harriman, a well-to-do friend of her brother's, proposed to her, a match approved by both families. She accepted immediately and set off to Paris in March 1894 to buy a luxurious trousseau. Here she stayed with the singer Fanny Reed, the sister of Mrs Paran Stevens, who was a Gould family friend. Fanny had settled in Paris, where she entertained widely and gave musical evenings. On one of these, Anna met the twenty-seven-year-old Paul Ernest Boniface, Comte de Castellane, the eldest son of the Marquis de Castellane. 'It was soon apparent that she found me a pleasant companion,' he reflected complacently, 'and I confess that I found her an interesting study.'

'Boni', as he was always known, was slim, elegant, good-looking, charming, a dandy to his fingertips, wildly extravagant, very conscious of his ancient lineage and what he felt was owed to him on account of it – a life untouched by gainful toil and buttressed by the best that money could buy. Although his parents lived in a broken-down château, Boni had servants galore (and almost as many mistresses), his toenails were painted pink, and he was always douched in scent – all on credit. He was, in short, what the average upright, rather puritan American citizen would think of as an effete foreign fortune-hunter.

Anna was dazzled by his worldly, hand-kissing charm, his title, by the hinterland of sophisticated European glamour that seemed to stretch behind him. 'I paid assiduous court to her,' wrote Boni. 'I passed under her windows on horseback, I wrote to her several times, I sent her Persian lilac. Her feet trod on a carpet of flowers.' He added, with breathtaking disingenuity: 'I can honestly affirm that Miss Gould's fortune played a secondary part in her attraction for me.'

A more complete opposite to poor Mr Harriman could not have been found, and Anna briskly broke off her engagement and remained in Paris, on the excuse that George and Helen Gould, her older brother and sister, were coming over – by the terms of her father's will, George had to approve any marriage she wished to make while she was still a minor. The three went yachting round England, returning to Paris in the spring of 1894, when Boni continued his courtship of Anna. Whether or not George thought Boni would be a good match, he certainly did not then disapprove.

With her father's scandalous reputation hanging over her and minus the looks that might have gained her an entrée, Anna had no hope of achieving the social eminence she wished for at home unless she married a title.

The Gould siblings returned to New York in the autumn, followed by Boni. Now so close to a fortune, he could not give up the chase merely because he was penniless, so he borrowed enough money from his bankers to fund the voyage. In New York, he stayed with a friend, to whom he explained the situation – and from whom he borrowed more money. Nor was he discouraged when Anna told him she would never marry him, merely answering: 'My dear lady, you forget that I have not asked you to marry me.' Anna went scarlet – but from then on, he believed, began to consider him as a husband.

Helen Gould was the only one who realised he was a fortune-hunter, but as she had already meddled in family affairs with a dire effect, her opinion was disregarded. Anna could not make up her mind. 'I don't like foreigners and I won't live out of America,' she said at one point. Hoping to make Anna jealous and thus speed things up, Boni and his friend departed for Newport, where the pair gave a highly successful dinner dance and Boni's title ensured that they were fêted by everyone. But still, nothing, although he was asked with his friend to stay at Lyndhurst, Helen's country house, then at George Gould's Georgian Court, both of which Boni found intensely dull and badly decorated. Meanwhile he was running out of other people's money and soon the game would be up.

Finally, in the spring of 1895, he was considered to have courted Anna for a sufficient length of time. His probation was over and he could now propose. When he did, she accepted at once: 'a real live count ought to be a passport for them [the Gould family] into the innermost of the inner circles, which privilege they so much crave,' said the New York *World*, showing a lively appreciation of the truth that the simplest way for a family to elevate itself into the top level of New York society was through the strategic marriage of a daughter.

Boni, aware that his fiancée lacked not only looks and polish but chic, described Anna as possessing 'what is always delightful to a man, possibilities'. As his family was facing financial ruin, it was not hard to see what these possibilities were. However, he did not hesitate, even though shaken by Anna's response – which could, and indeed was, a disclaimer to a business deal – when he suggested she took his family's religion, Catholicism. 'I will never become a Catholic,' said nineteen-year-old Anna, with a steeliness worthy of her father, 'because if I were to do so, I should not be able to divorce you, and if I were not happy I would not remain your wife for a moment longer than was necessary.'

They married in March 1895. Every detail of the preparations, the presents, the decorations in the church, what Anna might have included in her trousseau, was discussed in the press, conscious of what its readers wanted. Anna was given a brooch by her sister with the famous Esterhazy diamond at the centre, surrounded by eleven other diamonds; from her parents' collection she was given a ten-strand collar of pearls, held together by crosswise bars of diamonds; the bridegroom's parents gave her a five-rope pearl necklace, to which was attached a huge emerald that dated back to 1763.

Anna's capital (her share of the Gould fortune) was $12 million – but this was untouchable, as her father's will had tied all the capital up in a single trust, with each child living off the income of their share, in Anna's case almost $750,000 a year.

When the de Castellane family left for France on the steamship *Bretagne*, seen off by the Goulds, there were over 500 people on the pier, all intent on having a good look at them. A crowd of about a hundred fashionably dressed women boarded the ship to watch the final farewells and followed them round the deck, staring and commenting audibly on the appearances of the women of the party.

In Paris, the young de Castellanes rented the mansion of a fellow aristocrat while the house – the palace – they wanted was being built where the Avenue Malakoff met the Avenue Foch. It was a counterpart of the Petit Trianon, in pinkish stone, with carved balustrades, newel posts of silvered bronze, inlaid wood floors and a marble and gold ballroom – and the money for it had to come out of Anna's income.

This did not stop Boni spending. Now that he had credit again he bought some priceless Gobelin tapestries, in such haste that the dealer's floor was covered in the banknotes he pulled out of his pockets ('I wanted to feel they were mine *that very instant!*'). He bought a dinner service of rare green Sèvres, Chinese vases, fine furniture and silver soup plates, he staged a magnificent fête in the nearby Bois de Boulogne to celebrate the birth of their first son, for which he ordered 80,000 Venetian glass lamps and scarlet livery for the sixty footmen needed.

The de Castellanes went yachting, they went to Moscow, they

went to Deauville. For Anna it was a new and exciting world. Guided by Boni's taste, impeccable eye and backed by her own lavish fortune, she blossomed into one of the best-dressed women in Paris, renowned for her stylishness – something that must have gladdened her heart and done much for her social confidence. It looked as though her choice had been the right one.

Unfortunately Boni's impeccable eye for a pretty lady had not deserted him with marriage, and even more unfortunately there were plenty ready to tell Anna about them. Although she did not mind his spending her money, she did mind his infidelities.

At first it had seemed as if Boni was settling down. In the summer of 1898 he was elected to the Chambre des Députés, to the great delight of his family, who were very conscious of their responsibilities as aristocrats and patriots (he celebrated at a dinner where almost everyone got deplorably drunk). Although Boni too took his new role seriously he did not let it impinge on his way of life and, still spending only on Anna's credit, he was threatened with bankruptcy. The de Castellane debts were enormous: almost four million francs in connection with the building of their new house, six and a half million in mortgages, over four million to suppliers and banks – and Boni owed over nine million to dealers in antiques and fine arts.

Anna, alone in a strange land with a husband antipathetic to all the values with which she had been brought up, wrote to her brother George to ask his advice. He told her they must come to America, as he could not prescribe at a distance. It was not a happy homecoming as the rumours of Boni's huge debts and unfaithfulnesses had preceded them. (When showing Elsa Maxwell, the American professional hostess, round the de Castellanes' Paris house, he came to their bedroom and remarked laconically: 'La chambre expiatoire.') Now dressed with French chic in dark skirt, Persian lamb jacket and boa and muff of marten (Boni's long blue overcoat was, typically, lined with silver fox), Anna waited by the rail, peering through the mist to see if her family had come to meet her. When she saw a woman waving a handkerchief her face lit up – until she realised it was not for her but a fellow passenger. After this had happened a second time, she burst into tears.

When they at last saw George and he learnt what they owed, he told them the answer was to raise a loan to pay off these pressing debts as the trust could not be touched. This in turn meant raising the money from the rest of the family. George also appointed himself Anna's trustee, which meant that all debts would now be referred to him, and cut down her income to $20,000 a month – a sum she often spent on dresses alone – putting the surplus into a fund to pay off the debts. It was estimated this would take ten years.

The de Castellanes went back to Paris. Anna by now was enjoying the position in French society which Boni's name had brought her, and her own hard-earned reputation for elegance, all of which needed more money than George's trusteeship allowed. No longer a minor, she went to her lawyers and got this reversed, with the immediate result that Boni went back to his big spending – and also to his mistresses.

The result could have been predicted. By the end of 1905 Anna had become so fed up with Boni's liaisons, extravagance and general way of life that even he had become aware that the end of the marriage was in sight. Gossip to this effect was swirling round Paris, but perhaps what finally made him realise his days were numbered was when at a dinner party he was asked casually how he had spent the day and replied, 'Oh, I've been to the *Chambre* [*des Députés*],' to evoke from Anna the response: 'I don't think so. I think he prefers a different kind of *chambre*'.

But he could not have foretold the coup, worthy of her father at his most ruthless and quick-witted, with which Anna would deal the final blow.

The morning of the day it happened he and Anna strolled together for a short time in the Bois de Boulogne, as they quite often did. Their conversation was cheerful and amicable, so that when Boni left their house, the Palais Rose, ostensibly to go to the Palais Bourbon on state business (he was an ardent royalist and missed no opportunity of putting this forward), he believed that all was well and even that Anna might be softening towards him.

When he returned that evening the house was dark. He went

in, felt for the light switch and – nothing. He felt for a familiar piece of furniture – nothing. Anna had organised enough removal men and servants to strip the entire house of its furniture and furnishings in four hours, and had also seen that the electricity and telephone were cut off.

When Boni finally saw a dim light he made for it. It was a solitary candle, beside which was sitting an elderly priest, who told him that Anna and the children had gone and so had everything in the house. 'She will never return,' he said gently.

Anna had also been in touch with George and one of his lawyers had come to Paris to see her. The next day Boni was served with an application for judicial separation, and the wheels for a divorce were set in motion. It took place in 1906 amid much washing of dirty linen. 'A scion of an ancient race, a man of rank and title, which, indeed, induced his wife to marry him . . . now stands unmasked as one of the most noxious blackguards that infest the earth and constitute malicious parodies on human nature,' thundered the *New York Times*, the very paper that had so avidly chronicled his doings when he visited America.

The difficulty was dealing with the debts Boni had run up, some for women's clothing and jewellery that Anna had never ordered, although the largest amount was, as usual, to the dealers in art and antiques. Eventually, these were settled for thirty cents in the dollar.

Anna, clearly anxious to be fair, or perhaps with the remnants of the love she had once felt, gave Boni a pay-off of around a quarter of a million dollars, as well as an annual income of $30,000 from her share of the estate. Two years later, she married Boni's cousin the Prince de Sagan. In this case, not even the press could feel a sense of outrage: the Prince was almost as rich as Anna.

CHAPTER 11

Virginia

The beautiful young Virginia Bonynge, heiress to millions, and the blond and handsome Lord Deerhurst, heir to the Earl of Coventry, married on 10 March 1894, the brilliant sunshine seeming a symbol of this gilded young couple's future happiness. Among the wedding guests was royalty, in the shape of Virginia's faithful friend, Princess Christian (sister of the Prince of Wales) and her daughter Princess Victoria of Schleswig-Holstein, as well as several Americans, titled and otherwise, and their husbands: the Earl and Countess of Essex, Lord Deerhurst's cousin the Earl of Craven, his American Countess and her mother Mrs Bradley Martin, Lord and Lady Burton, General and Mrs Byron. The wedding presents were numerous and magnificent. The bridegroom's parents gave a service of silver plate, a pearl necklace, and a pearl and diamond bracelet. Charles Bonynge presented his daughter with a diamond tiara, a diamond bracelet, a silver tea and coffee service and a handsome cheque. Virginia's parents had got their wish: Virginia was now a member of Britain's aristocracy.

But it was a marriage that almost did not happen, thanks to her mother Rodie's 'scandalous' background and the bitter rivalry between two immensely wealthy men. Her story has all the elements of a Gilded Age fairy tale: a beautiful girl whose humble origins should have ensured that she only met the peer she married in the most menial capacity, let alone become best friend of the King's sister. It is also an example of the kind of ferocious feud typical of the no-holds-barred life of early mining communities, and the equally ruthless social climbing of their womenfolk.

As in all good fairy stories Virginia, our heroine, was the child of a poor couple. Her father, William Daniel, born in London in 1838, had emigrated to America, where he became a gardener. Then, possibly because of the passing of the Homestead Act in 1862,* he decided to try his hand at farming. In March 1865 he married the seventeen-year-old Rodie Stephens, born in Sacramento, the Californian capital. The couple bought 160 acres of farmland,† hoping to put down roots and, in October 1866, their daughter Virginia was born.

But Daniel could not make a living out of the farm. He decided to turn to the mines, where fortunes were still being made from gold-mining,‡ taking his small family with him. Once in California, Daniel went to work as a miner. It was a tough, rough, gun-happy community, where shootings were regular occurrences. 'I haven't time nor space to chronicle one tenth part of them,' wrote one young miner, Daniel A. Jenks, in his diary. In one episode that he recounts a murder and lynching take place in just fifteen minutes 'before the breakfast bell could ring in the camp!'

Another time, two card players jumped up to fire their guns at each other simultaneously; both missed, killing innocent bystanders at adjoining tables, but were acquitted on a verdict of 'Accidental Death'. Murderers filled all the offices, wrote Jenks. 'The judges, sheriffs and other officers of the law are all the most desperate of all and the city police is a gang of highwaymen and thiefs.' In March 1851 he notes with wonderment the arrival of 'a real live Yankee woman, with her husband and babe', to

* This allowed 160 acres of unoccupied land to be sold to each homesteader on payment of a nominal fee.

† Known as a quarter section. Land was surveyed, sold or awarded in square grid sections of 640 acres, which could be broken down, still in squares, to the smallest (quarter-quarter) size of forty acres.

‡ Gold was first discovered there in 1848; 1849 saw the Gold Rush as thousands piled in as miners.

establish a boarding house. 'All want to see the woman and kiss the baby.'

Behaviour had not changed much in the decade between Jenks's diary and the Daniels' arrival. One day, so the story was put about many years later, William Daniel was involved in a fracas, in which he killed a man. He was not executed but was sentenced to life imprisonment in San Quentin, the state prison.

Soon after he was imprisoned, along came another man seeking his fortune in gold: a thirty-year-old Irishman called Charles William Bonynge. As a trooper, he had been one of the Six Hundred in the Charge of the Light Brigade, and had come out to America shortly afterwards. At first he put his experience as a cavalryman to good use by working in a livery stable in San Francisco, where he began speculating on the stock market with tips given him by some of those who hired horses or vehicles from him.

When he had built up a certain amount of capital he went to Virginia City, where he first worked in the mines and dealt in mine shares as a 'kerbside broker', then in the 1860s set up as a stockbroker. Here he met Rodie Daniel, fell in love with her and, eventually, persuaded her to divorce her convict husband and marry him (in 1869), promising to bring up four-year-old Virginia as his own child.

By now Bonynge had made a huge fortune; meanwhile, so the story goes, Daniel was eating his heart out in a prison cell, ignorant of the fact both that his wife had divorced him and married another man, and that his daughter, last seen by him as a baby, was being brought up by the couple as the child of both of them. The Bonynges moved to San Francisco, where Bonynge became broker to the Bonanza King John William Mackay – the other party in the bitter feud that later developed.

Mackay was an Irishman, born in Dublin in 1831 and taken to New York City when his family emigrated in 1840. Two years after they arrived, his father died and he had to leave school and find work. After two or three jobs, he was drawn by the prospect of doing well in the California Gold Rush and went there in 1851. He was strong, determined, tough and twenty, and with his possessions in a knapsack on his back set off across the Rockies for California. It was a journey both arduous and extremely dangerous, partly from the threat of hostile Indians ('Short naps, with my hand on my six-shooter . . . quiet my nerves,' wrote one traveller that year), but chiefly from dehydration, lack of food and above all the infectious diseases that plagued travellers, such as cholera. With thousands travelling along the same watercourses these diseases, carried by the bodily waste of those ahead, were swept downstream to infect those following – and drinking from the same streams.

Once in California, Mackay worked in the diggings for eight years. Unlike many of the other miners, he did not carry firearms but relied on his ready fists. In 1859, a rich seam of silver, known as the Comstock Lode, was discovered in Nevada. Silver was then considered the equal of gold for coinage and the US government bought it all (later this wealth financed much of the Union side in the Civil War when it broke out two years later), so was equally attractive to miners. With his savings, Mackay moved in 1860 to Nevada's rapidly expanding Virginia City, then a town of flimsy wooden huts, some held vertical only by perpendicular wooden props, that had sprung up overnight on the eastern slopes of Mount Davidson, where the Comstock Lode had been discovered. Beneath the town, 6,200 feet up the mountain, amid the stunted cedars and yellow-flowering sage, ran the intricate tunnels and shafts of the new mines.

Mackay, determined not to continue as an ordinary miner, sank his money into forming a mine-contracting business, servicing various mines by organising the driving and shoring-up of tunnels, and taking shares in them in lieu of cash payment. It was a far-sighted move: as the mines expanded,* so his shares rose in value and gradually he became a rich man.

About three years after he arrived in Nevada, Mackay met a pretty, dark-haired young woman with deep blue eyes called Marie-Louise Bryant, well educated and musical. Her mother was French, her father Daniel Hungerford had been a barber in

* By 1876, Nevada produced over half of all the precious metals in the US.

New York before serving in the Army of the Potomac in the Civil War (after which he always called himself Colonel Hungerford). Her parents, taking their daughter with them, had emigrated to Downieville, California, where, at fifteen Louise, as she now called herself, had married a doctor called Edmond Bryant. Both Bryants were drawn by the possibilities in the rapid growth of Virginia City, so Bryant took his wife and small daughter Eva there. Once in Virginia City he set up a clinic, but the temptations of the pharmacy cupboard proved too much and in 1863 he died of alcohol and drug abuse. Twenty-year-old Louise was now stranded with her small daughter in a shanty town surrounded by rough miners, penniless and alone. To earn a pittance, she sewed and took in washing, but it must have been a nightmare.

Her unenviable position became known to Virginia City's Catholic priest, himself a former miner, a kindly man who determined to do something for the young widow. Knowing of John Mackay's good heart, he got Mackay to raise a cash subscription for her among the miners, which Mackay took round to her one evening after work – he was by now the superintendent of a mine. Soon he was visiting her constantly, visits that quickly turned into courtship.

They married in 1867. Louise was twenty-four and Mackay, at just thirty-six, a millionaire. Thanks to the wealth now pouring out of it, Virginia City was no longer a collection of shacks: as well as the numerous brothels, saloons and prostitutes inseparable from a mining boom town,* there were brick and stone houses, an opera house, a library, three theatres, four churches, three daily newspapers, a 100-room hotel and restaurants serving French cuisine.

From the start Louise had social aspirations. One description of her tells of her attending the local opera in a striped silk dress with her hair done in the newest fashion and a small square of velvet tied flat on her head. She had already seen a way of living that inspired her with the desire to become a social leader, houses with crystal chandeliers, Italian fireplaces and a butler

* The population increased from 4,000 in 1862 to over 15,000 in 1863.

and footmen. But although her husband was interested in art and literature, he was absorbed by his work in the mine, with other men, many of them much rougher, and with no interest in social life for the sake of social life.

By 1869 Louise had had enough of Virginia City. The life of a mining town, with its emphasis on saloon life and gambling, did not suit her. What she wanted was to live surrounded by the amenities of the civilised life of which she had caught a glimpse. When she said that she was suffering from 'a nervous affliction', her doctor tactfully advised a recuperative trip to Europe, and consultation with a famous specialist there. Soon after her first son by Mackay was born, in 1870, she left for Paris.

Mackay, who adored her and could deny her nothing, was wretched, but could not leave his business. His knowledge of mining had led him to believe that much deeper in the mountain lay a huge tranche of silver ore, and he was in the midst of complicated negotiations to ensure the legal ownership of the various small Comstock mines above it, earlier bought by three other Irishmen with whom he had formed a partnership. The following year, with the necessary paperwork tied up, he went to Paris to try and persuade his wife to return.

Then came one of the most extraordinary stories in mining history. Mackay's instinct had been right. In March 1873 a huge mass of almost solid gold and silver ore was found at more than 1,200 feet deep, so enormous that it became known as the Big Bonanza; Mackay and his partners were quickly christened the Bonanza Kings.

There was instant turmoil in the mining world. The Bonanza shares, originally sold at $5, shot up, at one point reaching $710 a share, the markets fluctuated and in 1873 the federal government de-monetised silver – thus lowering its value – largely because of the flood of silver now pouring into international markets from the silver mines of Virginia City. Mackay and his partners became four of the wealthiest men in America – and Louise agreed to return, provided they left Virginia City.

The Mackays now settled in San Francisco, where their second son was born in 1874 and where John Mackay had begun to employ a broker to handle his business affairs. This broker was Charles Bonynge, who with his wife, daughter and stepdaughter Virginia was now living in San Francisco. It was to be a fateful crossing of paths, although at the time relations were cordial enough.

Louise, who had hoped to establish herself socially in San Francisco, was not happy. Despite her husband's enormous wealth, she was snubbed by its old aristocratic families, who would not accept her because of her past as washerwoman and seamstress in a mining camp. She suggested settling in New York for the sake of their children as the education was better there, and where Mackay could visit her. Here, where her background was, she hoped, unknown, she might be more successful in her social ambitions.

But it was the same story in New York, where the barriers were still up against 'new money'. With the same determination to climb the social ladder as the husband-hunting mothers of desirable heiresses, she decided that France was the answer; and in 1876 settled at 9 rue du Tilsit, Paris, from which she decided to make her assault on Parisian society. But first, the preparations: encouraged by Mackay, who liked her to spend if it made her happy, there was the refurbishing of the house and the ordering of a Tiffany silver service of 1,250 pieces that took two years to make, and the buying of clothes and, above all, jewels.

These became justly famous. She had a wonderful set of sapphires: bracelet, ring, diadem, earrings and two-row necklace of large square sapphires and diamonds from which depended a sapphire pendant the size of a pigeon's egg. There were pearls (then more expensive than diamonds), in bracelets, necklaces and diadems, a parure of turquoises and diamonds, a necklace of pointed diamond leaves, there were black pearls, pink pearls, rubies, brooches and hair ornaments, all kept in a metal chest lined with red velvet. Thus adorned, exquisitely dressed, immensely rich, and beautiful, she began to entertain.

Then came what she hoped would be the event that not only allowed her full entrée into French society but would place her squarely on its pinnacle: in the autumn of 1877 she and Mackay, who had come over for a visit, gave a reception for General Ulysses S. Grant, who had finished his second term as President of the United States that March and was making a two-year world tour. It was a glittering affair: even the menus for the dinner were framed in gold instead of the usual silver and at the reception for 1,000 that followed, musicians from the Opéra had been engaged.

But what rocked Paris was the story circulating round the city the following day. It was said that the Bonanza Queen, as Louise was called, wanted to have the Arc de Triomphe, opposite her house, illuminated in honour of the General, and when this was refused by the municipal authorities, she was supposed to have retorted that she could buy it and light it up whenever she chose. This seeming arrogance over one of their most treasured monuments so angered the Parisians that, once again, the doors of high society slammed.

In San Francisco, Mackay had returned gladly to the demanding routines of the mining world, but gradually things were changing. The magnificent lode of silver was beginning to run out and silver itself was down in value. In 1881 he decided to move into another new field, the cable/telegraph business, and in 1884 formed the Commercial Cable Company – largely to fight Jay Gould and the Western Union Telegraph Company. He laid two transatlantic cables, forcing the price for messages down to twenty-five cents a word and thus undercutting Gould. A rate war followed for two years until Jay Gould finally gave up, saying of his rival: 'If he needs another million he will just go into his silver mines and dig it out.'

While her husband was away Louise, now forty, suffered a further social misfortune. While staying in the French countryside she had decided to have her portrait painted by the most celebrated artist in Paris, Jean-Louis-Ernest Meissonier, who came down from Paris to paint her. After several sittings the plan was for him to take it back to Paris to finish, with the aid of a model seated in Louise's pose. Before he left, Louise made some critical comments on it, at which the internationally celebrated Meissonier took offence, and decided that the portrait would not be a pleasing likeness of her but one that would depict her as elderly and plain. According to one of Louise's friends later, he deliberately copied the stand-in model's large and ugly hands and heavy make-up worn to disguise lines.

When the picture, its price an astronomical $14,000, was brought to the ever-supportive Mackay, both Mackays saw it as a disaster. The story goes that Mackay immediately threw it on the fire. Unfortunately, Louise had agreed to its being exhibited before it was handed over to her, so that *le tout Paris* was able to see what one paper* described as 'the irreparable ravages of years'. Or as another correspondent pointed out, Meissonier, famous for detail, had 'marked all the wrinkles, showed the paint and powder, spoilt the ear, exaggerated the imperfection of the fingers, etc.'. The gossip about the affair, and the ridicule of Louise Mackay and her flaunted millions, raged round Paris. (It also did for Meissonier, as other critics described it as a revenge caricature.)

However, Louise was not deterred in the pursuit of her goal of social eminence. Although Mackay hoped that his family would return with him to San Francisco, Louise had other plans. It was time to conquer London. Saying that she wanted to have her sons schooled in England and learn English customs, she persuaded Mackay that a move to London was necessary. Here he bought for them a palatial house opposite Kensington Palace. The grounds of 7 Buckingham Gate covered seven and a half acres and its 100 rooms had domed ceilings, panels of mother-of-pearl, oak and walnut everywhere, marble, gilding and panelling.

At roughly the same time Bonynge, who had now retired, came with his family to London. Well aware that as nouveaux riches they had no hope of becoming part of New York society, the Bonynges had decided to follow the now established custom of coming to England to achieve a brilliant match for Virginia. London, with its growing numbers of the American wealthy, and where a number of American heiresses had already married into

* *Daily Alta*, California, 18 March 1884, from a syndicated report.

the peerage, offered the best chance of this. They settled at 43 Princes Gate, Kensington.

But the couple they knew best, and who could have helped them most, the Mackays, could no longer be counted on, for by now relations between the two men had changed, turning sour when Bonynge publicly attacked Mackay for using, as he saw it, various schemes to milk the public. Soon this was to turn into naked social rivalry, with blood – literal and metaphorical – spilt across the floor.

Both families now set about conquering London society, competing with each other as they did so. On the same afternoon in March 1886 Louise Mackay, Virginia Bonynge and her stepfather Charles Bonynge were all presented to Queen Victoria at a Drawing Room, Mrs Mackay by Lady Mandeville and the Bonynges by the United States Minister, as the US Ambassador was then called, Edward J. Phelps. Mrs Bonynge too would have been presented, but shortly before the Drawing Room a London newspaper revealed that she had been divorced, which made her ineligible. To the Bonynges, who believed that either John or Louise Mackay had released that detrimental information, it was the opening of hostilities.

When it was further rumoured that the only way the Bonynges had been able to secure the vital presentation was because Bonynge had taken the financially imprudent son of Minister Phelps under his wing, advising him on profitable investments, and in his deep gratitude for this Phelps had made the Bonynges his social protégés, the Bonynges bristled even more.

Only two or three weeks later, Mrs Mackay secured the presence of the Prince of Wales at a dinner for twenty-two in her house in Buckingham Gate – something likely to have been organised for a huge fee by Consuelo Mandeville. There were two menus, one in French for the Prince and his retinue, and his favourite dessert was served – *tartelettes aux fraises*. Mrs Mackay wore a white satin gown made in Paris specially for the occasion and carried a bouquet of lilies of the valley, American banjo players provided the music at dinner and the whole house was filled with richly scented roses, with white orchids spilling out of white velvet sacks on each corner of the dining table. Princess Alexandra was there, and after dinner singers imported from Paris entertained the guests. With the Prince's imprimatur, Mrs Mackay became the fashion overnight. She, it appeared, was the victor.

But soon people began to ask, why was she living in Europe when her husband was in California? She had two young sons, she explained, and English schools were much better than Californian ones, where her husband's mining interests kept him.

'The triumph of Mrs Mackay is complete,' said the *New York Times*, kindly going on to remind its readers of her earlier embarrassments. 'She will soon forget all about her Meissonier misfortune and the Arc de Triomphe ... His Royal Highness has consecrated by his presence the new temple of hospitality in Buckingham Gate ... The crowd of ambassadors, ambassadresses, peers, peeresses, and American citizens soon became bewildering.'

This did not stop the derogatory rumours. One popular one was that she had financed a $100,000 expedition to New Guinea to trap 500 birds of paradise so that she could have an opera cape of their feathers – to refute this story she hung a parrot in a cage in her window; that having failed to buy the Arc de Triomphe she had offered for the Place de la Concorde; that her husband's study was carpeted in banknotes.

A few days after the dinner came something much more damaging. The *Manchester Examiner and Times*, and the *Echo* in London, declared: 'It is not generally known that Mrs Mackay, who entertained the Prince of Wales on Wednesday night ... was once what the Americans call a washwoman, what we call a washerwoman. She was a poor woman, with two children to support, and washed clothes for some of Mackay's miners out in Nevada.' Another article said that she had kept a boarding house in Virginia City; worse still, a third claimed that 'Mrs M ... with all those other seekers after bonanzas, sought relief in the sage bushes instead of a jaspar or alabaster lined, and rose of attar scented closet.'

Then came a further canard: that her husband had been one

of two little boys educated by a kindly uncle who was now a pauper in the Ulster County poorhouse, while 'one of the boys is none other than Mackay, the California millionaire'.

The day after this appeared Louise Mackay and Bonynge were at the same dinner party. Louise, clearly convinced that the Bonynges were behind the unpleasant stories, cut Bonynge dead. Next morning one of the papers had a paragraph saying that Bonynge, who had always said he was a colonel, had 'served in the Crimean war as a private where he was known widely as "Balaclava Charlie"'.

The response to this allegation appeared in a Californian paper, pointing out that, far from Bonynge being 'without antecedents', Charles II had granted John Bonynge, an ancestor, lands in County Longford, as shown in the Chancery courts. Louise countered with news of the expensive and amazing jewellery she had bought; Bonynge engaged the best-known portrait painter of the day, Bouguereau, to paint a portrait of his wife. London drawing rooms were enthralled by the promising feud that was brewing.

Then came gossip that fascinated everyone. Word spread that Mrs Mackay had given Lady Mandeville a diamond necklace in return for her presentation to Queen Victoria, a titbit that slipped out in the course of a row between Mrs Mackay and the hot-tempered Mrs Paran Stevens. Gleefully, *Town Topics* reported that 'it has long been an open secret that Lady Mandeville and one or two other ladies in London have made a regular livelihood this way. Mrs Mackay . . . paid a very high figure for her start in London . . . pressing bills have been paid, diamonds have exchanged hands, and receipts for house furnishings have been freely given. Everybody knows that Lady Mandeville has not a dime of her own.'

Both sides now engaged agents to publicise the other's lowly origins and bad behaviour and, in Louise Mackay's case, her movements and social triumphs. Bonynge was described in what *Collier's* magazine called 'obviously subsidised stories' as a former stable boy, Scrooge of working girls, and husband of a convict's widow. 'Mrs Mackay did not go unscathed,' said the magazine. 'She was derisively called . . . Mrs Bonanza, Silver Queen, boarding-house keeper and ex-washerwoman.'

Thanks to her husband's wealth, *Collier's* continued, she had been able to buy the Shah of Persia's $150,000 pearls, a maharajah's French palace, tapestries once owned by the Tsar of Russia – as well as a rumoured attempt to buy the Arc de Triomphe – but she had failed to penetrate French society.

In *Leslie's Weekly* of 21 September 1889 were several lengthy paragraphs setting out Mrs Mackay's background and stating that her husband had given her $5 million in US bonds and also her house in Paris, and that quite aside from the cost of her dresses and jewels, her current expenses were $100,000 a year. Louise instigated several lawsuits to try and quell the rumours. With most of these stories making their way to England, London was agog.

The person most affected by the steadily rising level of enmity was Virginia. When she had been launched into London society after her presentation at the age of eighteen her success had been instantaneous, and the Bonynges too achieved a royal connection when Virginia was taken up by the King's sister, Princess Christian. Rich and beautiful, Virginia was the target of many suitors until she finally agreed to marry the most persistent, the Hon. Ronald Greville, eldest son of Lord Greville. It seemed that the Bonynges' strategy for their beloved daughter had worked according to plan, with Virginia's engagement to Ronnie Greville announced late in 1889.

Ronnie Greville was a dandy, described by friends as a 'charming, unambitious man'. As the heir to a title, part of the social circle round the Prince of Wales, and with a genial, affable nature, he was considered quite a catch. For his part, as the family income had dropped drastically, he knew that he had to marry a rich woman – and Virginia came with a dowry of $4 million.

All seemed set fair, then rumours began to circulate about Virginia's innocent head: that she was not the daughter of the Bonynges, that Mrs Bonynge had a husband who had served a term of imprisonment in San Quentin prison for murder and then committed suicide on release.

London split into two camps: those who were glad to see off this threat to their own chances of marrying a daughter to this eligible sprig of the aristocracy and those who were indignant that the 'sins of the fathers' should be visited on a guiltless offspring – among these was Princess Christian. Being supported by royalty meant that the Bonynges could maintain their position in society and afford to overlook the slander.

But with the Mackays ranged against them, this state of affairs could not go on for long. 'The unforgiving spirit is very strongly developed in Mrs Mackay and forms one of the darkest sides of her character,' declared the *Chicago Tribune* in August 1890. 'Let an affront or injury be offered her and she seems utterly incapable of forgiving or forgetting. This trait has been evidenced in several cases, which have attracted more or less public attention, in which persons actuated by jealousy or ill will had sought to malign or injure her.'

It was true. That year, a small book entitled *Mrs Jonathan Abroad* had emerged in America. It gave more or less harmless descriptions of a number of American women who had succeeded in British society, each of a paragraph or two – but with thirty pages devoted to the Bonynges and their allegedly unsavoury and deceitful background. Mrs Bonynge, for instance, was described as an adulterous bigamist with a husband in San Quentin prison.

'The Mackay-Bonynge feud is bubbling at a lively rate once more,' said the *New York Times* of 18 May 1891, on learning that Bonynge had brought a case against Mackay to recover heavy damages, charging him with libel. *Town Topics* drew the attention of its readers to 'the systematic persecution of the Bonynges, who for years have made their home in England,' with The Saunterer describing the regular receipt of anonymous typewritten documents on the subject.

By now the feud, in full swing, had become known to the wider public. Quite apart from the rights and wrongs of the case, the Greville family became less and less happy about the future heir being caught up with a family involved in such an ugly business. Then, according to the *San Francisco Call*, which relished every detail of the battle between two of the town's former leading inhabitants: 'One fine morning the London mail carriers delivered to everybody in London society a marked copy of New York *Town Topics*. The article marked dealt with the history of the Bonynges, and alleged that Miss Bonynge was the child of a convict, during whose imprisonment Miss Bonynge's mother had married her present husband, etc.'

Ronnie, who had of course heard the rumours and now received a copy of *Town Topics*, confronted the Bonynges. Both Bonynges, and Virginia, agreed that they should disclose the true facts of her parentage. These were that when Daniel eventually emerged from prison he went straight to look for his wife and daughter, who had disappeared, although there were still men around who could tell him what had happened – that his wife had divorced him and married Bonynge. It was the first time he heard that he had conclusively lost them both and after his years in jail, living on what turned out to be false hope, he was shattered. He took to drink and crime and wandered off into the mountains, where his body was eventually found.

Hearing the story, or at least the basic facts of Virginia's parentage, Ronnie Greville broke off the engagement without an instant's hesitation and without even a word to his fiancée.* There had never, he said, been the slightest blemish on his lineage and his pride in his name meant that it was impossible to sully it with even such a remote slur. Virginia, devastated with both grief and humiliation, took to her bed and then developed brain fever. Thus stood matters just before the climax to the battle between these two warring tycoons.

In January 1891, Bonynge, who had returned to San Francisco on business matters, and driven perhaps by the misery and suffering of his daughter – for so he thought of Virginia – gave an interview to *Truth* magazine saying that when he and his wife had been up the Nile the previous winter, they had been followed by a dispatch from the *San Francisco Call*, stating that they had been driven from London.

---

* He successfully married another heiress, Margaret Anderson, who became the noted society hostess Mrs Ronnie Greville.

In the interview he discussed at length the attempts of a 'prominent American' to libel him. He said that various scurrilous rumours had been printed for several years, with around 500 copies of the newspapers in which they had appeared being sent to London and distributed at various clubs. 'So anxious was this party [to discredit me] that three papers of the same issue would be sent, one to the lady of the house, one to the gentleman and one to his club.

'Nothing gives so much mortification and annoyance to this individual as the contemplation that Mrs Bonynge is a lady by birth and education, the daughter of one of the slave-owning aristocracy of the South.' He then described how one of the lawyers of (presumably) Mackay had gone to her birthplace and had every one of her father's former slaves interviewed to try and rake up something against her.

Mackay was predictably outraged by the article. The day after it appeared, he happened to go to see the president of the Nevada Bank in San Francisco, of which he had been one of the founders in 1875. Walking into the president's office, he saw Bonynge there, talking to the president with his back turned to the door.

In strode Mackay and, without pause for thought, strode up to Bonynge and punched him in the face with a right and left, knocking him to the floor. Bonynge scrambled to his feet and both these sixty-year-old men, hardened by their early days in the mines, fought like tigers, knocking over chairs and desks and sending inkpots flying so that ink streaked the walls.

'Gentlemen! Gentlemen! This will never do!' cried the horrified president, but neither listened. Finally, they were separated by half a dozen of the bank staff.

'It was a regular possum and wildcat fight,' reported the *Lewiston Daily Sun* the next day. 'Their clothes were so torn and their faces so bloodied afterwards that they had to slip away unseen through a side door in a couple of cabs.'

Everyone attributed the cause of the fight to the social rivalry that had spread over the drawing rooms of two continents and several cities, though a contributory cause might have been that Bonynge had recently been talking of introducing an opposition cable line stretching across the Atlantic, which would have been a rival to Mackay's.

Many years later, it was said by Bonynge's granddaughter that there might have been a romance between Bonynge and Louise Mackay before she married Mackay in 1868, 'and nothing is as bitter as a lovers' quarrel'.

At this point both Mrs Mackay and Bonynge decided that enough was enough. The feud was called off. Mackay realised that his wife was securely established in London, and in 1892 leased an even grander house for her, No. 6 Carlton House Terrace. It had an art gallery, a marble staircase, a tapestry worth $250,000 on the wall, a ballroom that opened onto a terrace overlooking St James's Park and was decorated in sumptuous deep blues, silver, gold and red velvet.

For, finally, Louise Mackay had achieved the ambition that had caused all the problems in the first place: to become a social leader. Thanks to the feud, she now was famous, with everything she said, did or wore faithfully reported. 'Her fame as a social leader has been internationally established,' said the *New York Herald*.

Virginia, too, was on the verge of a happy ending. George William Coventry, the 13th Viscount Deerhurst, a fair-haired, blue-eyed young man of medium height, was the eldest son and heir to the 9th Earl of Coventry. He was imaginative and chivalrous and, so the story goes, hearing of Virginia's jilting and the reason behind it at his club, he was instantly struck by the pathos of the beautiful young woman lying ill with grief in the seclusion of her London home.

There could also have been another reason. Deerhurst was a gambler and had been in debt for a number of years (there is a thick file of letters between him, his bank, Coutts, and his solicitors discussing how to placate or pay off his creditors). 'What the creditors want is the payment of the remaining 10/- within a period of four years, and a charge on the unsettled real estate,' they tell him. Earlier, when his father had finally refused to pay his debts, he had been sent off to Australia for a while.

By February 1890 he had become desperate. 'Truly my state of affairs is awful,' he writes to his solicitor. 'I don't know what to do. I am miserable about the whole thing. It wants very little more money than there is in hand. If you offer my creditors 10/- in the £ and if such were done I expect that they would take it. If I could only get my father to do so it would save me and the family generally from this awful disgrace. I have lately been trying so hard not to run up fresh debts and have succeeded. If these proceedings are continued with I am sure sooner or later to do something which I ought not to and get into the most terrible mess.' Eight months later, he is writing desperately to his father asking him to insure his life 'or I will be made a bankrupt tomorrow'.

Although the story was put about that his chivalrous interest had been sparked towards the beauty who had been treated so badly by one of his own kind, it is also difficult to avoid the conclusion that now that a rival was out of the way he saw the chance of snapping up an heiress and sorting out his financial affairs. At the same time, his letters show him to be a man with many of the qualities likely to appeal to a woman – the ability to express his feelings and not be ashamed or embarrassed to do so, coupled with warmth, spontaneity and enjoyment of life.

He managed to achieve an introduction to the 'American Monte Cristo', as Bonynge was nicknamed; thereafter, the correct formalities having been observed by meeting Bonynge, he was able to call constantly at the Bonynges' house to enquire after the invalid, or to send presents of fruit or flowers. One day Mrs Bonynge, who happened to be there on one of his visits, invited him to tea, when she thanked him profusely for his presents. 'I promise you,' she told him, 'that when my girl is well enough to see a stranger, you shall be the very first to be introduced and she must thank you with her own lips for all your kindnesses.' They met, Virginia proved to be every bit the romantic heroine a young man could want, and it was not long before they were engaged.

Yet so broke was he that only a month before the wedding he was writing anxiously to his father about not being able to afford his side of the lawyers' fees for Bonynge's generous settlement on his daughter. 'I was amazed that they amount to nearly 350 [pounds]. Of course, as you know, I have not the ready money to pay this so I must make some sort of arrangement. Would you help me to borrow this money repaying it by stated instalments? It would be most good of you if you would, as to go to Mr Bonynge after his already great kindness to me would seem too much . . .'

For Deerhurst, the marriage took place in the nick of time. A fortnight later he was declared bankrupt, with liabilities of £25,000 and assets of only £500. He was able to offer his creditors ten shillings in the pound, 'with present security for the remainder of his liabilities'. It must have been a shock for Virginia, but both of them seem able to have brushed it aside. Later, Princess Christian stood sponsor to their elder daughter and the King was godfather to their son. Apart from the fact that Virginia disliked going into London society after her earlier experiences, the marriage was believed by all who saw them to be 'ideally happy'.* Perhaps the only person for whom events did not turn out too well was Mackay, wifeless and alone on the far side of the Atlantic.

* *San Francisco Chronicle*, 21 September 1919.

CHAPTER 12

Maud

Far from shrinking from society like Virginia Bonynge, Maud Burke could hardly get enough of it. No other American girl had such influence on the English cultural scene as the woman who became known as Emerald Cunard. Reinventing herself from unexceptional beginnings, this American heiress managed her love affairs discreetly, became one of England's most famous hostesses and brought English opera into the mainstream of life, financing many of the ventures of the great conductor Sir Thomas Beecham, her lover. Yet it all began because she was a girl for whom the acquisition of a titled English husband was not only a stepping stone but a way of showing how little she cared about a public jilting.

Born Maud Alice Burke in San Francisco on 3 August 1872, to parents who were well-off but not considered well-born, there is little known about the *soi-disant* Emerald's early life, as she never spoke of it and, conveniently, all documentation was destroyed in the San Francisco earthquake of 1906.

It was in any case questionable. She may not even have been the daughter of her mother's husband James Burke, as Mrs Burke, pretty, flirtatious and half-French, had many admirers. One of them, William O'Brien, a handsome, fair-haired, blue-eyed Irishman, one of the four partners who shared in the great Nevada Comstock Lode silver mine, was reputed to be Maud's father and she did indeed have the same colouring – she grew up to be a blue-eyed blonde and she certainly had the enterprise and vigour that had served O'Brien so well. From early on in her life, when she was brought up largely by Chinese servants, Maud regarded her mother as an adored friend rather than someone whose word was law and who would guide her into the future.

Her legal father, James Burke, died when she was in her early teens; after which her mother had a succession of influential admirers and protectors, some of whom were financiers and made profitable investments for her – something that would not have been lost on the adolescent Maud. One of these wealthy admirers was Horace Carpentier, a bibliophile and a cultured man who also had a habit of adopting very young women as honorary 'nieces' (as with his books, 'he liked them in mint condition', said a friend). The clever, pretty and lively Maud quickly became one.

Carpentier had had, to say the least, a chequered history, although he was also responsible for some philanthropic acts. He was highly intelligent, graduating from Columbia University in 1848 with a degree in law. Soon afterwards he left New York, drawn by the Californian Gold Rush, sailing with 200 other passengers in the ship *Panama*, a dreadful journey round the Horn, arriving in California in August 1849.

Once there, he decided against the goldfields, instead going into local politics and property. After a year or so in San Francisco, he settled on the other side of the Bay – the *contra costa* – and, with some cronies, proceeded to found the town of Oakland, becoming its first mayor and managing through various dubious manoeuvres to secure its lucrative waterfront for himself (he was ousted from the mayoralty by angry citizens when it was discovered he had finagled complete control of the waterfront for his own profit). Here he rose to become president of the California State Telegraph Company and the Overland Telegraph Company and was the man who sent the first transcontinental telegraph message – addressed to President Abraham Lincoln.

Maud soon became Carpentier's favourite 'niece'. He enjoyed directing her reading, and introduced her to the works of Balzac, the Greek and Latin poets and the plays of Shakespeare. Book-lover though she quickly became, she was even more enthralled by music. She heard her first opera, *The Ring*, at the Metropolitan Opera House in New York when she was only twelve years old. The impact was instantaneous, and lasting.

'It was as if a new world had opened out,' she wrote later,* 'revealing a race of men and women, very Titans of humanity endowed with superb gifts, and the musical setting within which they were enshrouded made an impression on me which was to last as long as life itself.' Carpentier loved to listen to his little 'niece' singing, playing the piano and, above all, watching her as she flitted in and out of his house.

As Maud grew older her mother, like so many other well-off Americans, began to take her daughter to Europe, where Maud fell under the spell of old-world civilisation, in particular French literature. When Maud was eighteen, her mother remarried. Mrs Burke's new husband was a stockbroker named Charles Tichenor, and at this point Maud began to make her home with Carpentier, to whom she now began to refer as 'my guardian'.

The remarriage also meant that, despite their love for each other, Maud's dependency on her mother – and her mother's influence over her – was far less than that of most girls of her age. She was, in a word, growing more independent and less likely to be guided by others. Finding a suitable husband, it soon became obvious, would be done by Maud rather than the new Mrs Tichenor.

Carpentier had returned to New York in 1883, buying a smart house on 37th Street. From the beginning of the nineteenth century, New York had expanded northwards, the former farms and estates on the island of Manhattan giving way to houses, stores and churches, laid out in a grid pattern by the 1811 Commissioners' Plan. One of these estates, belonging to Robert and Mary Murray, held out until 1847, when their descendants created the Murray Hill Restrictive Agreement, ensuring that future development consisted only of upmarket brick or stone houses, churches and private stables. Carpentier's house was in the midst of this exclusive area.

---

* In a publicity article for the League of Opera.

*

One day, when the twenty-two-year-old Maud and her mother were in London on a visit, Maud discovered that the writer George Moore was to be a fellow guest at a big luncheon party at the Savoy to which they had been invited. One of her favourite authors was Émile Zola, whom she regarded as trying to free the novel from the prudery and genteel obfuscations that then abounded, and she felt that Moore had the same crusading spirit. She also knew that he, like her, was an admirer of Zola.

Moore, the son of a former MP and horse breeder, was an Irishman whose family had lived in the same house, Moore Park, in County Mayo, for over a century. He was a popular writer and particularly renowned for novels that, tackling 'forbidden' issues like prostitution, extramarital sex and lesbianism, were frequently banned by circulating libraries.

Maud was so thrilled at discovering they would be at the same luncheon party, and so determined to meet him, that she slipped into the restaurant beforehand and changed the place cards so that she was now sitting next to him.

The luncheon was all she had hoped. George Moore held forth, talking passionately of his ambition to win freedom for the English novel, and praising what Zola had done for the French. Maud, wearing a becoming pink and grey shot silk dress, listened entranced and, during a pause, laid her pretty little hand on his arm, gazed at him enraptured and said: 'George Moore, you have a soul of fire!'

For any man, to hear these words uttered with adoring admiration by a beautiful young woman would be a near-erotic experience. For the forty-two-year-old Moore, newly emerged from a difficult liaison with a fellow writer, it was overwhelming. By the end of the luncheon he was in love.

They spent much of the next few weeks together, Maud managing to evade her mother's chaperonage – or, more likely, her mother tactfully ignoring their closeness. The enraptured Moore wrote of the afternoons he spent with the golden-haired Maud. 'While walking in the woods with one, she would say, "Let us sit here,"' Moore recorded, 'and after looking steadily at one for a few seconds, her pale marmoreal eyes glowing, she would say, "You can make love to me now, if you like."'

The idyll was not to last: at the beginning of summer Maud's mother took her back to America. 'Thinking of her my senses grow dizzy, a sort of madness creeps up behind the eyes – what an exquisite despair is this,' wrote the miserable George Moore; '. . . that one shall never possess that beautiful personality again, sweet-scented as the May-time, that I shall never hold that oval face in my hands again, shall look into those beautiful eyes no more, that all the beautiful intimacy of her person is now but a memory to be renewed by actual presence . . .'

In New York, it was back to the house on 37th Street. When Prince André Poniatowski, the grandson of the late King of Poland, arrived in New York in 1892, Maud met this attractive young man. She was taken with him, they got on well, and saw each other a number of times. The Prince's brother, Prince Charles, had married Maud Ely Goddard of New York a decade earlier and it appeared to the press, always chroniclers of the doings of a prince, that André was about to follow his brother's lead. Certainly, his friendship with Maud was close enough for a regular correspondence to start after he had returned to Europe and Maud and her mother had gone back to San Francisco. Therefore when Maud heard that the Prince was returning to the United States, and intended to come to San Francisco, she thought that it must be because of her – and that when he came he would propose to her. Unfortunately, she was so convinced of this that she told several of her friends of her belief.

The rumour got around and, inevitably, was picked up by *Town Topics*, which talked confidently of the 'approaching marriage' between the two. Other newspapers followed suit, referring to the Prince as Maud's 'fiancé'. When the Prince arrived he was horrified to find that everyone believed that he and Maud were either engaged or about to be – especially as he had his sights set on another, and considerably richer, San Francisco beauty. When a local newspaper actually announced the engagement between him and Maud it forced him to take action and he asked Maud to make a public denial of their betrothal.

She agreed, but not unnaturally did this in the way she thought would be least embarrassing for herself: she let it be known that the reason the engagement was broken was because her guardian Horace Carpentier objected so strongly to the match that he had threatened to cut her out of his will if she went ahead – another development that naturally fascinated the press.

When the Prince and the San Francisco beauty he had been courting in turn announced their engagement, it unleashed a further tide of gossip and press comment. 'It is authoritatively announced that Prince André Poniatowski, of Poland, the former fiancé of Maud Alice Burke, will marry Miss Sperry, daughter of the Stockton (Cal.) millionaire,' said the *New York Times*. 'Miss Sperry's father owns the Stockton Flour Mills and controls the California flour trade.'

For Maud, there was deep humiliation; although she had done her best to put a favourable gloss on the affair, it must have seemed like a public jilting. Unable to face the torrent of rumour and speculation, she and her mother left San Francisco for New York.

Here, a year after her fatal effect on George Moore, another man fell in love with Maud at first sight. This was Sir Bache Cunard, a dark, thick-set man with a melancholy expression, a drooping moustache and at forty-three old enough to be her father. As a grandson of the founder of the Cunard Line, he had inherited the baronetcy from his brother Edward, killed playing polo. He lived in a huge yellow stone house on the top of a hill in the heart of the Leicestershire hunting country; hunting was his passion in life and he kept his own pack of foxhounds. Other interests were carriage-driving, shooting, fishing and, surprisingly, working in gold and silver to produce decorative objects from his tower workshop. One of his presents to Maud was a cup carved from a coconut shell, with a scalloped silver border decorated with snowdrop heads made from seashells.

Maud was not in love with him, but like all young women then she had been brought up to believe that marriage was essential, the right and proper goal for all females. It was, too, as George Moore put it, the 'springboard to wider horizons'. Besides, Sir

Bache was rich, he had a title, he would raise her on the social ladder – and it would show how little she cared about what was seen by everyone as her jilting by Prince Poniatowski.

Essentially metropolitan herself, she disregarded the fact that with Sir Bache she would have to lead the quiet country life that he preferred – not even a plea by her future sister-in-law, who realised this, that she should break it off because of their essentially conflicting tastes and attitudes, caused her to change her mind. 'I like Sir Bache better than any man I know,' she declared – and that was that.

The twenty-three-year-old Maud married her baronet in New York in April 1895, far away from the scene of her earlier humiliation, and left a few days later for Nevill Holt, its gardens, its woods, its fishponds, its stables filled with well-bred hunters, carriage horses and hacks, its shrubberies where the box and bay were neatly topiaried by Sir Bache himself. Horace Carpentier remained alone in the house until his elderly niece (this time a genuine one), Maria Hall Williamson, moved in.

Maud, as her sister-in-law had predicted, did not enjoy country life. She did not care for hunting, or the conversations it engendered; her only pleasure was in rearranging the interior of the house. As she had brought plenty of money with her – some sources said she had a dowry of $2 million – she could indulge her tastes.

Her life began to open up only after she had met the Prince of Wales, with his penchant for young and pretty American women. Once the Prince's approval was known, weekends at Nevill Holt became fashionable, and Maud's long career as a hostess began. With her husband usually out hunting, shooting or visiting a friend for the fishing, Nevill Holt began to see the romantic intrigues that were so much a part of Edwardian house parties. Once, according to Maud, when Bache returned from a fishing trip he noticed 'an atmosphere of love' in the house. 'I don't understand what's going on in this house,' he said, 'but I don't like it.'*

* Quoted by Daphne Fielding in *Emerald and Nancy*.

Then, on one of her visits to London where, along with Paris, she bought her clothes, she spotted George Moore sitting, like her, in a hansom cab that was driving in the opposite direction. She waved, both cabs stopped and the delighted Moore, who had never stopped writing to her, asked her to go for a drive in his.

For him it was the most wonderful of reunions. A month after Maud's wedding he had lost his mother, and of that time he wrote: 'A man cannot lament two women at the same time, and only a month ago the most beautiful thing that had ever appeared in my life, an idea which I knew from the first I was destined to follow, had appeared to me, had stayed with me for a while, and had passed from me. All the partial loves of my youth seemed to find expression at last in a passion that would know no change . . . she had the indispensable quality of making me feel I was more intensely alive when she was by me than I was when she was away.'

A week later Maud wrote to Moore suggesting that he might come and stay at the house where she would be spending the weekend, without her husband. His hopes were raised, but to no avail. 'Every night she locked her door,' he wrote, 'and the sound is and ever will be in my ears.' All the same, after several months she wrote to him again, this time inviting him to Nevill Holt.

Again, his hopes were dashed – Maud was pregnant with her daughter Nancy, born a year after the Cunards were married. With the birth of her daughter, Maud obviously felt that her wifely duties were done. 'She had never really wished to have a child,' said Nancy later, adding that her mother maintained that no great woman had ever had one. ('[Queen] Elizabeth had none, and how about George Eliot and George Sand?')

After Nancy's birth, Maud moved into a bedroom far distant from that of her husband and handed Nancy over immediately to the care of nurses. Today we would call her treatment of her child inhumane: she scarcely saw her daughter, most of whose early life was made miserable by the regime imposed on her by a harsh, repressive governess (unlike the kindly Chinese servants who had cared for Maud as a child); then, there was nothing unusual about the separate lives led by well-off parents and children.

Maud did not keep her door locked for ever, and soon Moore was writing: 'Again I hear the soft sound of the door opening over the velvet pile of carpet . . .'

Of their affair, about which he wrote in his fiction, lightly disguising Maud as Elizabeth, he declared: 'It does not follow that because a woman sometimes reminds one of a dryad that she does not at other times remind one of Boucher or Fragonard, and that night Elizabeth seemed to me a very Fragonard, a plump Fragonard maiden as she sat up in bed reading, her gold hair in plaits and a large book in her hand. I asked her what she was reading and might have talked literature for a while, but throwing the vain linen aside she revealed herself and in that moment of august nakedness the mortal woman was forgotten . . .'

By now the Cunards were leading virtually separate lives. In Nancy's diary recording Maud's weekend house parties, her father is absent on all but two occasions during these 'constant arrivals and departures . . . Beautiful and exciting ladies moved about in smart tailor-mades; they arrived in sables or long fox stoles, a bunch of Parma violets pinned into the fur on the shoulder.'

Nancy also recorded that 'The men . . . became more intellectual as the autumn proceeded and the host was away shooting and fishing lengthily in Scotland.' One of them, the faithful George Moore, also took an interest in the child Nancy, talking to her not only of literature but also of sexual matters with a freedom unheard of in those days. Once, for example, he reported a female friend's attempt to become a better wife by going to Paris and taking some lessons from a superior cocotte – only to hear her husband say when she tried to put them into practice: 'Dora, *ladies never move*.'

Moore wrote to his 'dearest Primavera' constantly. 'There is no part of the house [Nevill Holt] I do not remember because you were there with me . . . I remember the chestnut trees at the back, Nancy and her governess, and the long roads, a little bare and dreary, that flow on over the hills – far away.

'But above all these things I remember your mien and motion, your brightly coloured cheeks, your fair hair, fair as the hair in an eighteenth-century pastel, and your marble eyes . . . How I live on memories of Maud.'

Maud's tireless social life continued: by now she knew not only the highest of society but politicians and their wives like the Asquiths and the Balfours, painters and writers such as Somerset Maugham and Max Beerbohm and, of course, George Moore. Some of those she met became her lovers; one was Lord Alexander Thynne, son of the 4th Marquess of Bath. Of this dashing man she remarked* that the witty and handsome Alexander 'was one of the world's great lovers'.

Although such liaisons were conducted with circumspection and discretion, they became known almost instantly in the circles in which both moved. 'Elizabeth was a constant but unfaithful mistress,' lamented Moore. 'In her own words "she liked not continuity", but was willing to pick up a thread again.' What he did not know was that she had met the great love of her life, the young musician Thomas Beecham, and by 1910 had begun an affair with him. Shortly afterwards he was cited as co-respondent in a much-publicised divorce case, but this did nothing to deter Maud.

Beecham was a powerful, imperious personality, a man of great determination and charm. He was as witty a lunchtime companion – once he described the sound of the harpsichord as 'two skeletons copulating on a roof' – as he was a superb musical interpreter and brilliant conductor. Maud found him irresistible.

Finally, the inevitable happened. In 1911, now thirty-nine, Maud left the husband from whom she had grown inalienably apart, rented their Cavendish Square house from her friends the Asquiths (H.H. was now Prime Minister and installed in No. 10 Downing Street) and proceeded to conquer London – and continue her affair with the married Beecham.

Her parties became famous for their mixture of guests, from

* Many years later, to a member of his family.

politicians and diplomats to writers, artists and musicians, drawn there by her signature purple invitations. The windows of her dining room had green lamé curtains, covering another wall was a hanging featuring leaf-eating giraffes among birch trees; in the centre of the huge round dining table of lapis lazuli stood a gilt-bronze epergne supported by naked nymphs and satyrs.

She treated her guests like a ringmaster, drawing out the shy and flicking the opinionated into life with a provocative remark or, as Osbert Sitwell later put it: 'she would goad the conversation, as if it were a bull, and she a matador, and compel it to show a fiery temper'. She herself wore dramatic clothes and many jewels, chiefly the emeralds by which she became known. She was rich, popular and famous; seemingly her only worry in life was her receding chin, which she fruitlessly tried to correct with massage and electrical treatment.

It made no difference to Moore. 'Dearest Maud,' he wrote in 1920, 'You brought into the world a hard heart as well as much beauty, grace and charm, and it is small wonder that I fell in love with you, remained in love with you, and shall always love you.'

Then came a step that caused him immense perturbation. He received a letter from his beloved Maud signed 'Maud Emerald'. He wrote at once, terrified that she had married a Mr Emerald. 'I beg you to send me a telegram. A yes or no will be enough. You cannot fail to understand that it is unfair to leave a man who has loved you dearly for more than thirty years in doubt.' He followed this up with a telegram: 'Who is Emerald are you married? GM'

Sir Joseph Duveen, to whom Moore showed the letter that caused him such anguish, described Moore as 'spending the morning pacing up and down the room like a caged animal'. Maud, explaining to Moore that she was nicknamed the Emerald Queen because she wore so many, confirmed that she had simply changed her name to Emerald. Henceforth that was how everyone addressed her, except for Moore, who continued to write to her as his 'Dearest Maud'.

She remained in love with Beecham all her life, just as she

remained George Moore's ideal and 'dearest Primavera'. With her devotion to music, fuelled by her passion for Beecham, she was largely responsible for introducing London's smart set to opera: she was a director of the Royal Opera House Company, she helped Beecham raise much-needed subscriptions from her wealthy friends, she took the Opera House's 'Omnibus' box, entertaining friends to dinner before the performance, and she did her best to win government support in establishing English opera. Nothing was allowed to prevent her from attending an opera or a concert when Beecham was conducting.

Nancy inherited her mother's love of the arts, becoming a writer and poet, and her flamboyance, wearing outré clothes and African bracelets of ivory and metal up to the elbows. But she rebelled against Maud-Emerald's way of life, choosing her friends among the more avant-garde writers, immersing herself in black culture, taking black lovers and supporting numerous causes. Soon the rift between them was irrevocable. 'I think of Her Ladyship, when I think of her at all, with great objectivity,' said Nancy. 'She was at all times very far from me.'

Sir Bache died in 1925. Neither he nor Horace Carpentier, who had died much earlier, mentioned Maud in their will. George Moore, though, left her his books, furniture and many pictures.

As the years passed, her wealth disappeared, much of it in funding Beecham's operatic projects. Estranged from her daughter, she now had to suffer another loss. She had accompanied Beecham to America, where he was giving a series of concerts, when she heard at a luncheon party there that he was going to marry a concert pianist. She managed to conceal her misery at the time but her heart was broken.

She died at the Dorchester Hotel, where she lived for the last part of her life. She had left instructions that after her death she wished to be cremated, but not as to where her ashes should be strewn. As all her friends knew, she hated country life, so that when someone said, half-jokingly, 'What about Grosvenor Square?', it seemed the perfect answer to most of them.

One of her regular guests performed this, and a wind blew them back into his face, so that he complained he was now full of his former hostess. It was just the sort of unexpected twist to the ceremony that the inimitable Emerald would have loved.

CHAPTER 13

Royal Connections

On Saturday, 14 August 1881, Belle (Leila) Wilson, whose sister May had married Ogden Goelet, wrote to her mother from Cowes, while she and Mr and Mrs Goelet were on board the yacht *Norseman*, 'I came away with the brightest and most pleasing reminiscence of English hospitality under the especial patronage of the Prince of Wales . . . I was very much amused, and at all the dances had delightful evenings and lots of partners . . . at one of the parties I was asked to go in to supper by *four* people . . .

'The fact is . . . the Prince's kindness to us *made* our visit to Cowes.'

The fact also was that the Prince looked favourably on anyone capable of entertaining him. It was this that allowed the borders of British society to become more porous than those of American. Unlike many of his contemporaries, he did not confine himself solely to those whom a royal prince might be expected to befriend, the landed aristocracy, but drew into his orbit those who amused or attracted him – and who could afford him.

His tastes were simple – that is to say, it did not require depth of intellect or strong intuitive powers to find them out. He liked good food, comfortable surroundings, staying in house parties in congenial company and pretty women, exquisitely gowned, who could amuse him, frequently with gossip about the love affairs of themselves or their friends, in which he took a keen interest. All of this required money and later, when he became king, a very great deal of money, so much so that many of his friends bankrupted themselves through trying to maintain their friendship with him.

He was the most longed-for guest in the country, admired so much that he was widely imitated: it was said that he could walk along Piccadilly without being recognised as so many gentlemen had modelled themselves on him, dressing and moving in exactly the same way. Once, when he had an attack of rheumatism in his shoulder, he was obliged to shake hands with his arm pressed tightly to his side, and this peculiar handshake was immediately adopted by fashionable London. Similarly, when Alexandra developed a slight limp after an illness, smart women also began to walk with the 'Alexandra limp'.

The Prince would often change his clothes half a dozen times a day. He had so many clothes that he never travelled with fewer than two valets, with two more at home cleaning, brushing and pressing his vast wardrobe. As everything he wore was instantly copied, he was what we would call a fashion icon, and was known as an authority on fashion – tailors from all over Europe would gather to watch him as he strolled through the streets of a favourite Continental spa.

The cost of entertaining him was prohibitive. When he stayed in a house party, for instance – and as Prince of Wales he stayed at most of the stately homes in England, quite often with the Princess – his retinue was large. As well as the two valets mentioned above, he would also bring his own footman, who wore the royal livery and stood behind his chair at mealtimes and served him with his food, two loaders if it was a shooting party, his horses and two grooms if there was hunting. He was usually accompanied by a gentleman-in-waiting and one or two equerries, all or both of whom brought their own servants.

The house in which he was going to stay had to be redecorated and refurbished, with one room converted into a private post office and sometimes a private train laid on: Daisy Brooke at Easton Lodge built Easton Lodge Station for his first visit in 1895 and a few months later had to sell some of her estates. There was also the cost of new clothes to meet his exacting tastes and food and drink of banquet standard. When he stayed five nights with his friend 'Sporting Joe' (the Earl of Aylesford), where the chief entertainment was shooting in the Capability Brown park, after every second drive each gun would shout 'Boy!' and a bottle of champagne would appear, to be drained immediately.

His appetite was enormous: he would eat a breakfast of haddock, poached eggs, bacon, chicken and woodcock before a day's shooting, lunch and dinner of ten to fourteen courses, elaborate teas, snacks of lobster salad or cold chicken, with a cold chicken left by his bed at night in case he became hungry. When he attended the opera he expected dinner to be as elaborate as at the Palace. 'Six footmen went down early in the day,' wrote one of the royal chefs, M. Tschumi, 'with hampers packed with cloths, silver, the finest gold plate and anything else that might add to the comfort of the thirty or so guests usually entertained.' A dozen hampers of food accompanied them, containing nine or ten courses, all served cold.

Then there were his special cigars, biscuits and bath salts, the choice of guests and where they would sleep – his own bedroom had to be discreetly near that of his current mistress – the composition of the bridge tables after dinner and the question of precedence. This, which had to be correct, meant that the senior peeress on his right was often elderly and rather dull – and Bertie bored was every hostess's nightmare.

He was fascinated by millionaires, usually the self-made ones, for whom money was no object. 'If the aristocracy wished to entertain the Prince, it had to accept the plutocracy on an equal footing,' wrote Virginia Cowles. He also forced society to accept acting as a respectable profession, and hostesses to invite opera stars to their houses. The only people he was terrified of were intellectuals. Believing as he did that there was an unbridgeable gulf between the ruler and the ruled, when he met his subjects he was able both to give rein to his natural friendliness and not worry about questions of status. Above all things he wished to be amused, and a hostess who saw him begin to drum with his fingers on the table knew that this was a signal she had better rescue him at once from boredom.

One way of getting to know the Prince was through a yacht. Cowes was close to his heart, if only because he did not wish his nephew the Kaiser to make off with the regatta trophies. Americans had the largest and some of the fastest yachts in the world, which they often kept in England, so for a rich American with a determined wife and pretty daughter, to meet the Prince at Cowes was not too difficult.

Most of the American heiresses who tangled with royalty were friends of the Prince: the court of the Queen, nominally the highest in the land, was so gloomy and depressing that attending it was a duty rather than a pleasure. Perpetually in mourning* for the death of her husband the Prince Consort many years earlier, Victoria did her best to enforce this state on everyone around her – made easier by the fact that she had so many relations that it was seldom a funeral had not recently taken place, when for weeks everything from dresses to shoes, fans, gloves and ornaments all had to be black, as had ink, pens and sealing wax. Writing paper and handkerchiefs were edged with black and underclothes frequently threaded with black ribbon.

'I am in despair about my clothes,' wrote Marie Adeane, a maid of honour, in October 1889. 'No sooner have I rigged myself out with good tweeds than we are plunged into the deepest mourning for the King of Portugal [Louis I], jet ornaments for six weeks! And he was only a first cousin once removed . . . it is a lesson *never*, *never* to buy anything but black!'

Mary Leiter was one of the few American girls closer to the Queen than the Prince; she regularly wrote long, descriptive eight-page letters to Victoria when her husband Lord Curzon was Viceroy of India. She wrote from Viceregal Lodge, she wrote from the Viceroy's Camp, she told the Queen how in one state caste was so strict that every Brahmin or high-caste Hindu must take a bath of purification after shaking hands with a Christian.

---

* Widows mourned two and a half years for a husband, in bombazine and black crêpe for the first year and dullish black silk for the next, twenty-one-month stage. During the last three months, embroidery and lace could make their appearance again. Many widows went into half-mourning – mauves and greys – for the rest of their lives.

'The dear little Princesses sat on my knee but were subjected to a good rubbing afterwards!'

To the Queen, she allowed her emotions to show, telling her as one mother to another of the sadness of planters' wives whose children had been sent back to England in early childhood. 'I think I have largely mentioned to your Majesty how very tragic and sad is this of every household in India. No father or mother ever seems to feel they have done their duty until they have packed their children off home. I cannot myself think the climate demands such complete renunciation of children.'

It was not an opinion likely to appeal to the unmaternal Queen, who would, one often feels, have liked nothing better than to get rid of her eldest son – and who certainly did not approve of his American lady friends. Of these, the three closest to him were Jennie Churchill, Minnie Paget and the Duchess of Manchester.

One of the earliest of the Prince's American friends – and later a part-time mistress – was Jennie Churchill. 'I don't know why,' wrote Clara Jerome, one of Jennie's two sisters, 'but people always seem to ask us whenever H.R.H. goes to them. I suppose it is because Jennie is so pretty and you have no idea how charming Randolph can be when *il fait des frais*! And I don't want to be conceited but I think I make myself agreeable too as they could easily ask them without me.'

In any case, the Prince loved women. 'A professional love-maker' was how Margot Tennant [later the wife of the Prime Minister H. H. Asquith] described him. 'Men did not interest him and like Disraeli, he delighted in the society of women. He was stimulated by their company, intrigued by their entanglements, flattered by their confidence, and valued their counsel.' To many women, he was an excellent friend.

After the Prince had made it up with the Churchills, he resumed his friendship with Jennie, inviting her to his Sandringham house parties – often without her husband – and attending her dinner parties. In any case, by then Randolph's health was deteriorating fast; it was thought he had syphilis (as a young man he had visited prostitutes), but later evidence suggests that it might have been a brain tumour.

At the time, Jennie was conducting a steamy affair with Prince Karl Kinsky, an attaché at the Austro-Hungarian embassy in London. It foundered when, travelling abroad with Randolph, she learnt of Kinsky's forthcoming marriage to the highly suitable Countess Elisabeth Wolff-Metternich zur Gracht. Unhappily Jennie wrote to her younger sister Leonie: 'From henceforth he is dead to me. I want to know nothing. He has deserted me at my hardest time in my hour of need & I want to forget him tho' I wish him every joy & luck & happiness in this life . . .'

But this dignified pose did not last. In November 1894 she wrote again. 'Oh, Leonie darling, do you think it is too late to stop it? . . . Leonie darling use all your cleverness and all your strength & urge him to put off his marriage anyhow until I have seen him.' With sadly misplaced assurance she added: 'The world wd forgive him and if he still cares for me the girl I am sure would be willing to give him up . . . besides, I could help him in his career. The future looks too black and lonely without him . . . don't let him marry until he has seen me.' Her letter was to no avail; the Kinsky marriage went ahead.

But Jennie being Jennie, it was only a few months before another man stepped in. This time, it was the Prince of Wales.

When, after a long and painful illness, Randolph died on 23 January 1895 the first letter of condolence she received was from the Prince, writing from Sandringham on the same day. 'My dear Lady Randolph, The sad news reached me this morning that all is over, & I felt that for his and your sake it was best so . . . there was a cloud in our friendship which lasted a few years but I am glad to think that it has long been forgotten by both of us . . . my thoughts are much with you, my dear Lady Randolph & I know what terribly trying times you have gone through . . .'

Soon he was seeing more of her, writing from the royal yacht *Britannia*. 'My dear Lady R. C., I am delighted you will sail with me on Monday' is typical of a whole sheaf of little notes in his black spiky writing that sloped to the right.

After a brief sojourn in Paris, Jennie established herself in a house in London's Great Cumberland Place and began an affair with the Prince – by January 1896 she was 'Ma chère amie'. A stream of letters followed. The ones indicating that sex was on the agenda would contain the sentence: 'Should you wish to see me, I could call at five tomorrow.' Some suggested he should visit her for a 'Japanese tea', when she was to wear a loose kimono, known as her 'geisha dress'.*

Although Jennie at that time had an occasionally overlapping succession of lovers (including a briefish affair with the widower William Waldorf Astor), in the Prince's circle this was looked on with latitude – always provided discretion was maintained. Otherwise, she did everything that could be expected of a royal mistress: she accompanied him to the Derby where his horse Persimmon won, her dinner parties for him were superb as she knew his friends and the food and the music he liked. The affair continued throughout 1896 and 1897, with Jennie blithely taking other lovers, many much younger.

But when, in 1899, the forty-five-year-old Jennie announced her engagement to George Cornwallis-West, a comparatively penniless young man the same age as her son Winston, the shock wave rippled round society. Even the Prince, now deeply involved with his last mistress, Mrs George Keppel, advised her against the marriage, telling her she was being foolish and compromising her position.

When the South African War broke out the same year, and off George went to fight in it, as did Winston, it seemed that more drastic events had supervened. Jennie was asked to organise an American hospital ship to care for the wounded in South Africa, which she did with great success.

And then she married George. His family, like hers, was horrified, her brother-in-law John 'Jack' Leslie writing to his wife,

* From letters shown to biographers Celia and John Lee by the widow of Jennie's grandson, Peregrine Churchill. 'Geisha' implies concubine and would in any case be an inappropriate word to use to any woman in the context of an ordinary, non-sexual friendship.

Jennie's younger sister Leonie: 'I hope G. West has survived the honeymoon.' (Jennie had once been described as 'more panther than woman'.)

Her friendship with the Prince, however, continued unabated. Entertaining him successfully often meant not so much knowing what to do as what not to do. He was extremely superstitious: mattresses could not be turned on a Friday, knives must not cross on a table, and above all thirteen must not sit down to dinner. Once, when he had learnt after a dinner in Germany that there had been thirteen at table, he had fretted for an hour until suddenly his face cleared and he turned to his secretary, Sir Frederick Ponsonby, to declare that it was all right after all because 'Princess Frederick Charles of Hesse is *enceinte*!'

Society was quick to notice the 'Jennie effect': the charm American women held for the Prince, and their looser, less hidebound attitude. As the Prince himself had said of them: 'they are not as squeamish as their English sisters and they are better able to take care of themselves' (both qualities useful to anyone in his circle).

Jennie was not the only Jerome girl to move in royal circles. Her younger sister Leonie, married to John Leslie, the heir to an Anglo-Irish landowning baronet, Sir John Leslie, met the Prince of Wales's younger brother the Duke of Connaught in 1895. Soon she, the Duke and Duchess became friends and Leonie would entertain them at the Castle Leslie estate at Glaslough, County Monaghan, Ulster.

By the time the Duke was appointed Commander-in-Chief in Ireland he was deeply in love with Leonie. Their close and intimate bond, which lasted forty years, became part of a curious tripartite relationship with the full knowledge and consent of the Duchess. She was a German princess who suffered from poor health and was no kind of helpmeet to a man who needed someone to support, soothe and advise him. She realised that Leonie was this person, so much so that when at one point Leonie, thinking her relationship with the Duke had become too intense, suggested that she withdrew, it was the Duchess who begged her to remain friends with them both. 'I know I still count for something & am not put aside,' she wrote to Leonie.

For the Leslies, their intimacy with the Connaughts meant a lively social life and, when they travelled together, luxury. 'Your letter is the event of the day,' she wrote to the Duke once, when she was alone with her children at Glaslough, adding, 'The Duchess has written me a most kind letter – and I hope I shall always be worthy of her friendship.' She signed herself, 'Votre Amie, L'.

'It was in the seventies that a new and powerful force began to make its influence felt in society,' wrote Lady Dorothy Nevill of the arrival of women like the Jerome sisters. Its impact was such that concern was expressed by a group of aristocratic ladies about declining moral standards owing to the influence of American women on the Prince of Wales. They went as far as approaching the Archbishop of Canterbury to request him to hold devotional meetings for women of their class to reverse this trend. Nothing came of this idea; the Archbishop must have realised immediately that he would find few takers, since most of society followed the Prince's lead slavishly.

One of the American women of whom they might have been thinking was Lady Mandeville, née Consuelo Yznaga (the model for Edith Wharton's character Conchita Closson in *The Buccaneers*).

When the Mandevilles returned to London after staying with Alva in New York, Kim went to live openly with Bessie Bellwood, for which he was ostracised by society. He borrowed from her, too: when he left her, she sued him for what she had lent him and spent on him.

Consuelo was now virtually on her own. Her position was ghastly. She was alone in a foreign land with a disreputable husband about whose unfaithfulness she could not complain ('any public recognition of it was unthinkable,' wrote E. F. Benson in *As We Were*), and divorce, then almost unheard of, would bring instant and total social ostracism. But she was young, extremely beautiful, determined and had the allure of difference: her friends listened enthralled when she played the banjo and sang the Southern songs of her childhood.

Many girls would have run home, back to the shelter and security of their families. Consuelo, however, was determined to make a life for herself in England. What she had seen of English society showed her that the life of a married woman in England could be far more interesting and stimulating than that at home. As one of her compatriots, Belle Wilson, later declared: 'There is only one place and one great society in the world and that is London and the English.' So she set her mind not just to surviving but to making an enjoyable life for herself. Soon she became a friend of the Prince of Wales and, because she could keep him amused, would be asked to evening parties at Marlborough House and to stay for his week-long house parties at Sandringham.

By the late 1880s they were close friends. 'My dear Lady Kim,' he wrote to her in a five-page letter from Hungary on 26 September 1888, 'many thanks for your long and amusing letter of 19th. Without the slightest flattery, I may say that nobody writes more amusing letters than you do.' So intimate were they that at her dinner table one of Queen Victoria's gentlemen-in-waiting, the Hon. Alexander Yorke, a brilliant mimic, was asked by the Prince: 'I hear you can take off my mother very well. Please do so.'

The poor man begged to be excused ('What will the Queen say if it gets to her ears? She'll never forgive me'), but HRH was adamant and he was forced to obey. Fortunately, his secret seems to have been kept, probably because, although the Queen knew he could mimic, as she had told one of her ladies-in-waiting, 'she would never believe that he could possibly be so vulgar [as to do so]'.

Consuelo's difficulty was to make her finances stretch to the sort of life she wanted to lead – like Wharton's Conchita, she was perpetually short of money. To make some, she began to give some of her countrywomen what they most desired, an introduction to English high society – for a price. If she thought a girl had the potential she would undertake, for a large fee* – or for settling outstanding bills or payment in kind, such as a box at the opera or a diamond necklace – to groom her, teach her how

* Thanks to the Married Woman's Property Act of 1870, Consuelo was now able to keep these earnings.

to comport herself, present her at court and, finally, to invite her to a select dinner party at which the Prince of Wales would be present.

If the Prince took to her, the young woman was 'made'; if she was looking for a husband among the aristocracy, Consuelo would introduce her to a suitable peer or, failing that, a younger son (marriage with the younger son of a peer held almost the same advantages: it brought the American bride into the closed circle of court and society, although without the burden of upkeep of a stately home).

Unless a girl had her imprimatur, though, she was so apt to get the thumbs-down from Consuelo that even the Prince noticed it. 'Whenever I ask Consuelo Duchess of Manchester about an American lady,' said HRH, 'I am invariably told, "Oh, sir, she has no position at home; out there she would be just dirt under our feet."'

(Consuelo must have been one of the women to whom the writer Marie Corelli was indignantly referring when she wrote that she could easily name 'at least a dozen well-known society women, assumed to be "loyal" who make a very good thing out of their "loyalty" by accepting huge payments in exchange for their recommendation or introduction to Royal personages . . . These are some of the very ladies who are most favoured by notice at Court.')

Kim's downward spiral had continued. By now his way of life had taken its toll and his appearance was thoroughly unappetising: as well as being small and insignificant-looking, his skin had become covered with pimples and he seemed far older than his years. In 1889 he was made bankrupt, and the following year his father died, leaving huge debts. Kim and Consuelo were now Duke and Duchess of Manchester. Then, two years later, in 1892, after being ill for some time, Kim too died, probably of cirrhosis of the liver or syphilis – with Consuelo at his bedside.

She was free – but not free of tragedy. In 1895 her daughter Mary died suddenly of double pneumonia. Shattering as it was for Consuelo, a devoted mother, she went on with the way of life she had chosen. In 1897 she brought her beautiful daughter Nell out, to great success, and after the season rented Egypt House in Cowes, as she would do every August bar one thereafter in order to entertain the Prince of Wales. As Commodore of the Squadron, he went to Cowes every year, strolling about among the other men in white flannels and navy blazers on the lawns overlooking the sea with its panorama of yachts.

But the sadnesses of her life were not over. In 1900 Nell died of consumption and her son – also called Kim – married without her knowledge an American girl called Helena Zimmerman whom Consuelo considered an unsuitable nobody.

At forty-seven, Consuelo was losing her fine-skinned blonde looks, and had put on weight. The following year, 1901, her brother Fernando also died. Here there was a silver lining, as he had left her everything – his $2 million fortune and $2 million's worth of property (on this she had to pay tax of a mere 1 per cent, amounting to about $25,000 dollars).

She was now rich, but she had lost much of what made life worth living. From then on she concentrated on what, now that she was a truly rich woman, she could do better than almost anyone else – entertaining the King, who had acceded in 1901.* She would organise dinner parties, some with the newly popular game of bridge, which the King enjoyed although he was not a particularly good player. ('My dear Consuelo, the party you propose for Monday will do admirably. I shall bring Captain Fordham with me as you know he is a "Professor" at bridge . . .')

She ordered the expensive delicacies such as pâté de foie gras, lobster and champagne that he adored, she sent him presents, she moved into a larger house, 5 Grosvenor Square, where she could give bigger parties for him and she rented houses wherever he might be, from Cowes to Monte Carlo. If she was not occupied with the monarch, she dined out every night, often going on to receptions and every year joined a party of fifty guests, along

* At his Coronation on 9 August 1902 his particular friends, who as commoners could not attend, were seated in a special box known as 'the Loose Box'. Among them were Jennie Cornwallis-West and Minnie Paget.

with 200 servants, at Chatsworth (when the widowed Duchess of Manchester* married the Duke of Devonshire as her second husband, house parties were often twice this size).

The third member of the American triumvirate on whom the King depended more and more was Minnie Paget, the daughter of Mrs Paran Stevens, who had married his friend Captain Arthur Paget.

The first impression Minnie made in London was poor: that of a tough, possibly unscrupulous social climber at a time when the female ideal was softness and submission. Worse still, she had attended various gatherings without her mother; and chaperoning was then essential for a well-brought-up young woman. The reason for this freedom, as the *New York Times* later pointed out,† was that there were 'houses from which Mrs Stevens was pointedly excluded, on account of her oddities of manner and status as wife of a hotel keeper'. This disapproval extended to Queen Alexandra, so that for a long time Minnie was never asked to Sandringham although her husband and children stayed there.

Fortunately for Minnie, she was not only rich but a friend of Consuelo Mandeville, who helped to smooth her path – her own looks, vitality and immense chic did the rest. She was presented at court by Lady Suffield, whose husband, like hers, was a great friend of the Prince of Wales. Like Consuelo, she supplemented her income by launching young American girls into society or, as the *New York Times* commented in veiled but unmistakable terms, introduced 'those of her countrymen and countrywomen who have secured her friendship and her backing into London society, or at least into a certain section thereof, since there are many houses where her sponsorship would not merely be valueless but might be detrimental'.

Minnie, beautiful and determined, was able to shrug off any such criticism, and was soon persona grata with the royal family, all of whom were impressed by her taste and elegance. 'You were

* She had been his mistress for many years and married him on the death of her first husband, hence she was known as the 'Double Duchess'.

† On 24 March 1912.

much admired yesterday,' wrote the Prince's younger brother Leopold, the young Duke of Albany. 'I thought you looked better than anyone else (*Don't* be offended at my saying so).'

Her friendship with Albert Edward grew warmer, at first through her husband and then in her own right. Thanks to her reputation for perfect taste, he entrusted her with buying small objets and bibelots at the Paris Exposition Universelle of 1889 for him to give as Christmas or birthday presents, and she would arrange exactly the sort of dinners for him that he liked, often at short notice. 'May I choose Tuesday next for dinner at 8.30,' runs one typical note from him. 'And please may it be a small party of friends not exceeding ten or twelve?' Often there would be bridge afterwards, when the dinners tended to be smaller. 'Let us be either four or eight at dinner, whichever you prefer,' runs one note from Sandringham. 'But they should all be bridge players. I am not sure that our last little party of four could be improved upon.'

Minnie made her intimacy with the King work for her. When she received a signed photograph or a present from him, she would quietly notify the American papers. This served both as an enhancement of her own prestige and a discreet signal to those interested that if anyone could get you the entrée it was Mrs Arthur Paget.

But his affection for her was genuine: when, in 1904, she had a terrible accident, falling down the lift shaft in her home and breaking both legs badly after returning from a dinner party, Edward VII sent a telegram at once and wrote the following day to her husband expressing his concern. 'Is there anything I can send her? Flowers or fruit, or both? Has she a table to put across the bed for reading?' (She had fifteen operations in two years but without much success, after which she went to a Berlin specialist, who improved her condition greatly.)

Her money also helped. Her mother so approved of her marriage to Arthur Paget that she had settled an annuity of $10,000 on him as a personal allowance, a help towards keeping up with the King. The cost of entertaining the King had in fact become something of a self-perpetuating cycle: those who could afford it became closer to him and, as more intimate friends, were then expected to entertain him more, with a growing extravagance.

It was not just dinners that had become more lavish. In the new reign, houses were redecorated more frequently and in a more 'feminine' style. Out went the heavy Victorian furniture, the solid fabrics in crimson and maroon, the thick fringing; in came French furniture, screens, little tables covered with silver-framed photographs and bibelots, lighter, more luscious colours and fabrics – Minnie Paget's boudoir had walls of a pale olive-green paper, and matching curtains of pale green silk, with French furniture; in her bedroom, with its toilet accessories of beaten gold, the furniture was carved and white-enamelled.

Ceilings were decorated with plasterwork and cornices, huge palms stood about in pots, china ornaments – rare ginger jars, Meissen figurines – abounded and almost always there was a profusion of flowers. Chandeliers hung from most of the high ceilings, chairs were often clustered in groups and decorative painted screens could be used to shield from a draught or enhance privacy.

The only rooms that remained determinedly masculine were studies, libraries and a new addition, the dedicated smoking room. With the King's blessing and as cigarettes became more popular, smoking rooms literally came in from the cold, furnished with comfortable sofas and chairs, often of leather. Women smoked too, though for the most part only in the house; the first woman of the King's circle to smoke in public was, unsurprisingly, an American, the Countess of Essex (née Adèle Beach Grant), when dining at the Carlton Hotel.

The King himself put many changes in motion; he dispensed with Osborne House and turned the private chapel at Balmoral into a billiard room. The royal yacht, the *Victoria and Albert*, gleamed with gold plate, there were footmen in scarlet livery and flowers everywhere. The Queen's cabin was large enough for a grand piano; there was a special room for the King's uniforms so that he could step ashore in whatever costume would most please the people of that country.

Above all, he refurbished the 'Mausoleum' (as he called

Buckingham Palace in his mother's day), installing electric light, new bathrooms and a telephone switchboard, so that it was no longer a neglected and gloomy building but the centre of fashionable life. Both Edward and Alexandra were determined to bring back proper royal entertaining: evening Courts rather than afternoon Drawing Rooms became the rule, with the King's throne on a new dais in the ballroom, there were glittering court balls and dinners, while Alexandra's beauty, style and clothes were emulated.

Again, it was an American who helped with some of the most important of these, including Alexandra's Coronation dress, for which Mary Curzon found the materials under oath of secrecy. 'The Queen wishes me to . . . ask you not to tell anyone in England about the dresses ordered in India,' wrote Charlotte Knollys, Alexandra's Private Secretary, 'or else they will be wanting to have some also.'

'H.M. is enchanted with them,' she wrote later. 'The one for the Coronation is being made up over cloth of real gold and will I am sure look magnificent. The black & silver is already made up and is to be worn at the next Court & the mauve & gold is in the dressmaker's hands & will also be worn for the Coronation festivities.' Alexandra herself sent a telegram apologising for her delay in writing to thank Mary, adding, 'am delighted with dresses and most grateful to you'.

What kept these American peeresses so firmly at the centre of the highest social circles in England was a factor that would have seemed nothing out of the ordinary in the more rigid society of New York: their extreme wealth and their willingness to spend it. The adoring Mary Curzon gladly underwrote her husband George's glittering career. Equally happily, other American women – especially in the King's circle – poured out their fortunes in an effort to outdo each other in entertaining the sovereign and his intimates.

The *New York American* estimated that Bradley Martin had spent $15 million on stalking, his daughter Lady Craven the same sum on shooting parties – both attended by the King – while her small dinner parties for him had cost Minnie Paget $6 million. The result was that, as so few could keep up with this spending level, as Jennie herself put it, 'the effect on society as a whole is towards exclusiveness'. Whether the English who perforce dropped out would have agreed is another matter.

CHAPTER 14

The Bradley-Martins

Cornelia Bradley Martin, daughter of parents determined to make their social mark once they had the means, was snapped up even before she was out of the schoolroom – the wonder is that her parents agreed to her marriage at just sixteen. But then, her husband-to-be *was* an earl. And her mother was very determined . . .

The Martins were people who, although well-born, had leapt from comparatively unobtrusive beginnings to an established position in both English and American society. Cornelia's father, Bradley Martin, born in Albany, New York, in 1841, was the son of a well-off merchant and her mother, also Cornelia, was the daughter of another, Isaac Sherman. The two had met at the wedding of a Vanderbilt daughter to whom Cornelia Sherman, a very pretty blonde, was a bridesmaid.

They began married life modestly, living with Cornelia Sherman's parents in West 20th Street in the winter and spending summers at Saratoga Springs, with occasional trips abroad. They seldom entertained and went out little.

Then came the surprise fortune that changed their lives. When Cornelia's father Isaac died in 1881 it was found that, far from being worth only the $200,000 everyone expected, he had instead left almost $6 million to his daughter Cornelia, his only child.

Almost at once, she and her husband began their upward trajectory. As well as acquiring a Long Island mansion near

Wheatley Hills they bought the house next to the parental one in West 20th Street, joined the two together and organised an extensive refurbishment, commissioning the high-end decorators Marcotte, of Union Square, at a total cost of $85,072.20. As the marble floors, gilded mouldings, mahogany and brass furniture, blue silk walls (for Cornelia's bedroom), Venetian mirrors and yellow silk music room complete with instruments were being installed, they took an extended trip abroad.

The setting prepared, they began to move into society. With Bradley Martin now a Patriarch, Mrs Martin cultivated the 'right' people by appearing with them as patroness of various fashionable entertainments such as the then new Assembly Balls. When Cornelia Martin formed one of the reception committee for these with Mrs Astor, her position was established, and duly acknowledged by Alva Vanderbilt with an invitation to her famous ball of 1883.

Once she was acknowledged by Mrs Astor and Alva Vanderbilt, Cornelia Martin could move on to the next step, knowing that it would not be resented as an attempt to insinuate herself into the inner circle. This was to give a series of grand, elegant dinners at the newly renovated and embellished house on West 20th Street. At about the same time, Bradley Martin leased a large house and estate in Scotland, Bal Macaan, fifteen miles from Inverness with its railway station, and thus convenient for guests.

It was a shrewd move. The castle of Bal Macaan was situated on a 46,000-acre estate that ran for nineteen miles along Loch Ness; it was known for the beauty of the scenery and its wonderful shooting, stalking and salmon-fishing – a great draw for the sort of people the Martins wanted to meet – and it was surrounded by other, nearby, estates. The fact that it was supposedly haunted, by the sounds of the spectral carriage of a former Lady Seafield (the Seafields were the original owners of the house) drawing up at the front door, gave no one pause.

In the winter of 1885 the Martins gave the first of the two great balls for which they became known. Cornelia Martin was anxious firstly to outdo the most famous one yet, that given by Alva Vanderbilt two years before, and secondly, as they now planned to spend most of their time in Scotland, to leave New York in a blaze of glory. Excitement rose as the date drew nearer. 'The Martins' ball has been the talk of the town for weeks,' said Anna Robinson.

The Martins asked around 400 people – whether or not in a conscious echo of Mrs Astor's Four Hundred is not known – to a ball that had one so far unique feature: an enormous temporary wooden supper room, sixty-eight feet long by twenty-five feet wide, built over the gardens of the two houses they owned at West 20th Street. It was entered from the billiard room that stretched along the whole of the rear of the double house, the three long windows of which, converted into doors for the occasion, overlooked it. The ceiling was painted as if it were a starry sky and the walls covered with red fabric and hung with antique armour. It was heated by steam and lighted by three great chandeliers and many side lights, and a long supper table was arranged in the centre.

Unfortunately, the night of the ball, 26 January 1886, was the coldest night of an exceptionally bitter winter. Not only did the Martins have to pay an enormous premium for insurance because of the possible fire risk to the adjoining buildings, but the steam heating of this sumptuous room proved inadequate when the thermometer plummeted to zero. After the guests had been received by Mrs Martin, wearing a gleaming white satin dress with a long train and holding several bouquets of flowers, they passed through the library and dining room to the billiard room and then on to the vision of the astonishing supper room before them. But most merely stood briefly on the broad flights of steps leading down into what must have seemed like a glamorous refrigerator, then turned back towards the warmth of the main hall – where two bands played continuously – to dance, possibly casting an admiring glance towards the stags' heads and other trophies of the chase from Bal Macaan glimpsed through a doorway. Alva's ball remained the *ne plus ultra*.

Gradually the Martins began to spend more and more time away from the US, visiting Europe in the early spring (a convenient time for those who wished to refurbish their wardrobes *chez* M. Worth). In June they would go to London for the English season, then set off for their Scottish home in the first week of August, where they stayed until December, and where they could be sure of meeting many of those they had encountered or danced with in London. Soon they began to regard Bal Macaan as their real home, although they would generally return to America for the first two or three months of the year. Here Mrs Bradley Martin would pay calls on friends, driving out in her black and red victoria, attended by footmen in the Bradley Martin livery of maroon breeches, with black and gold waistcoats.

During these years Cornelia Martin filled her jewel box. For Gilded Age wives, it was impossible to be over-jewelled: a wife festooned with gems was admired both as displaying her husband's wealth and being a credit to the society in which she moved, so that most loaded themselves with as many diamonds as they could lay their hands on. Mrs John Jacob Astor III wore so many that when she went out publicly it was always with a detective; when he accompanied her to her sister-in-law Caroline Astor's annual ball his practised eye estimated that there was, unsurprisingly, nearly $5 million in jewellery in the ballroom.

There were, in fact, so many jewels that it was sometimes difficult to find a new way of wearing them. Edith Gould, wife of robber-baron railroad developer Jay Gould's eldest son George, who owned gems valued at more than $1 million that she wore constantly, 'changing them from day to day,' recalled one acquaintance, never went motoring without her famous five-strand pearl necklace, bought for her from Tiffany's for half a million dollars. Some women wore diamond chains or ropes of pearls over one shoulder and under the opposite arm, like the sash of an order; one hung a huge uncut sapphire or ruby from a long chain of pearls hanging from her waist, kicking it gently ahead of her as she walked into her box at the opera.

When France's crown jewels were auctioned in 1887 there were further pickings. The Martins were among those who swooped down on the jeweller Tiffany's haul, around twenty-four 'lots'. This sale, unique in jewellery history, could have been designed to appeal to every instinct of those securing or wishing to secure a foothold in New York society, clothing the lucky winners in an invisible aura of prestige, conferring on them a touch of instant history and background and, of course, stating unequivocally that they were very rich indeed. Cornelia Bradley Martin achieved a pair of Marie Antoinette's ruby and diamond bracelets (that could be worn together to form a dog-collar necklace) and several other spectacular pieces. Alva Vanderbilt bought a magnificent pearl necklace once owned by the Empress Eugénie and valued at $200,000; the heiress wife of a wealthy lawyer and partner in the Morgan bank acquired part of Eugénie's emerald and diamond girdle, her ruby and diamond tiara, pendant and pair of bracelets.

The Bradley Martins' last notable entertainment in New York was a cotillion dinner for 300 given in February 1890 at Delmonico's, for which they retained the custom of Gilded Age New York for extravagant decoration of a party setting. Pictures, tapestries and bric-à-brac were brought from their house, palms and foliage banked the entrance to the restaurant, its dining-room walls were hung with blue silk brocade and small gilt mirrors, a Roman chandelier of orchids swung overhead instead of the usual circle of lights, small baskets of lilies of the valley scented the room and the dining tables were heaped with Gloire de Paris roses. Two bands played throughout dinner, after which the company – New York's finest – were entertained by the performance of two cotillions.

For the Martins, it was goodbye to New York for a while – they remained abroad for the winters of 1891 and 1892 – but their lavish entertaining went on. It was estimated that the average cost of a Bradley Martin dinner dance in London was $10,000. By now they had become a staple of the social columns, with constant comments on Mrs Bradley Martin's jewels and expenditure. 'Mrs Martin totters under . . . an extraordinary head ornament that is said to have cost a hundred thousand dollars and to weigh on an iceman's scales six pounds and a half. No chandeliers are necessary when this crown and Mrs Martin make their entrance either in the ballroom or in her box at the opera,' wrote The Saunterer in typical sardonic vein.

Significantly, sometime along this route, their name developed that tiny symbol of social cachet, a hyphen, so that in later years they were known as the Bradley-Martins, a change that did not go unnoticed by The Saunterer's column in *Town Topics*: 'In the elevation of the socially ambitious, the service it affords is frequently as effective as Mr Ward McAllister himself.'

When they went to Scotland for the autumn months it was an equally glittering affair. Forty-odd local people were employed permanently at Bal Macaan as indoor servants, gardeners and gamekeepers. The Bradley-Martins themselves would arrive in Inverness in a specially hired train, with servants, luggage, silver plate, horses, carriages and wagons. Guests would bring their own valets, lady's maids and loaders.

None of this was enough for the eldest Bradley-Martin son, Sherman. He had become bored with Bal Macaan and yearned for the bright lights of London and Paris. When his grandmother finally gave him the money to leave Scotland, he went straight to London, where all the things his parents must have feared, happened. He got in with a rich set, many of whom hung around stage doors, began to send expensive jewellery to a dancer named Ada Annie Nunn and finally became so entangled with this older woman that in 1889 she managed to persuade him to marry her. For the Bradley-Martins, this mésalliance came as a profound shock, almost worse when the marriage broke up a few months later, with Sherman departing for a tour of Spain.

So it was back to Bal Macaan, where their hospitality and the sport offered acted like a magnet. In 1892, when only fifteen, their daughter Cornelia met and became engaged to her future husband, the twenty-four-year-old Earl of Craven. Ten years earlier he had inherited from his father a total of 37,000 acres, which included the estates of Ashdown House and Coombe Abbey. A keen sporting man who loved shooting and stalking, William Craven had been the Martins' guest for the last shoot of the season (likely to have been in October or November) – Bal

Macaan was known as one of the best-stocked deer forests and grouse-shooting moors in all Scotland.*

It was then that he wooed and won Cornelia, a teenager still in the schoolroom and therefore known by sight to only a few of the Martins' most intimate friends. As one of her descendants related: 'One day she was playing with dolls and the next she was engaged and told she could no longer do that.' There were mutterings in England that Craven had stolen a march on potential rivals for the hand of this young heiress by snapping her up before she had even come out, when her debutante season would have given others a chance. The Bradley-Martins were obviously equally keen to acquire an earl for their daughter or they would have urged delay because of her extreme youth; as it was, the engagement was brief – an extraordinary break with the custom of their own society, where an engagement of less than a year was considered unduly short.

Town Topics, which never missed an opportunity to mock what it saw as the pretentious, greeted the announcement with its usual acerbic wit, this time scoring both a right and a left. 'I have no doubt that Mr Bradley-Martin (hyphenated) smoothes his chin with an affectionate hand these days,' wrote The Saunterer, 'and allows the opalescent light that falls through the stained-glass windows of his castle to gild and glorify his smooth and gleaming brow as he contemplates the grand coup that he has accomplished in bringing into the family a real live British earl.

'The Bradley-Martins (hyphenated) have been for several years the most conspicuous representatives of that class of Americans who revere English culture, habits and individuals.' He sweetened the pill by saying: 'It is nonsense for newspapers to say that Craven stole into the nursery to get the prize. He has been visiting the Bradley-Martins (hyphenated) since he was a minor.'

The wedding was planned for April 1893 and the Bradley-Martins, together with Lord Craven and his brother,

* A list of game slaughtered up to the beginning of 1889 included 3,000 rabbits, 2–3,000 grouse and pheasants, and numerous stags.

returned to New York two months earlier to prepare for it. The Saunterer was quick to point out that Mrs Bradley-Martin was putting on weight. '[Her] acquaintances have been obliged to welcome her home twice or thrice, as they believe she is two or three times the woman she was when she made her last visit home.'

When the Bradley-Martins arrived from England on the SS *Teutonic*, a ship of the utmost luxury that had won the Blue Riband the previous year, even by the standards of the *Teutonic*'s uber-rich passengers and even for a party of twenty-two (including servants), the luggage accompanying them seemed excessive – a staggering 128 trunks. Unsurprisingly, Customs officials became suspicious, imagining that there would be a treasure hoard on which to pay duty. Mr Bradley-Martin (by this time the hyphen was firmly in place) was interviewed by the Deputy Surveyor of the dock, but said he had brought nothing dutiable from Europe except a portrait of his son in oils, worth about $10,000, on which he then paid duty of $300. As for the trunks, Bradley-Martin stated that they contained only 'our old clothes. We brought nothing new over with us.'

'You could have knocked me down with a feather,' said the Deputy Surveyor of Customs later, but recovered sufficiently to ask, 'But how about your daughter's wedding trousseau?'

'That', said Mr Bradley-Martin, 'has been left at our place in Scotland, to which she will return immediately after the wedding. All that these trunks contain is our usual wearing apparel.'

'What about the wedding dress?' asked the Deputy Surveyor.

'Oh, it's here, of course – in that trunk there,' said Mr Bradley-Martin. 'But it's an old one that my daughter has worn to a ball in London and to several receptions, so that no duty can be charged on it.' Having repeated his question and received the same answer, the Deputy Surveyor had little option but, as he said, 'to take Mr Bradley-Martin's word for it'.

The excitement in New York at their arrival was intense. The Earl and his brother were entertained everywhere, Ward McAllister giving a dinner for the whole family. The *New York Times* instructed its readers on how the Earl was to be addressed, simply as 'Lord Craven', not 'My Lord' as 'one Anglomaniac with much money and little sense' did; other newspapers described in minute detail everything William Craven wore, from suits and shirts to underclothes, with illustrations of 'his most choice shirts and pants', which they had been shown by his helpful valet.

The wedding, in April 1893 at New York's Grace Church, filled with flowers and palms up to forty feet high, caused a frenzy. An excited crowd thronged the street outside waiting for a glimpse of the bride. Some of them managed to get into the church by means of forged invitation cards, which they held up to show the two struggling policemen at each door. Others, even the most well dressed, scrambled over the boundary picket fence when they could not force their way through the gates, leaving scraps of their clothing on the pickets. The entry of these uninvited guests meant that a church of which the capacity was 2,000 now held 3,000.

Inside the church it was even worse. The invited guests in the side aisles stood on the pews, and those farthest away piled hassocks on the pews and stood on those for a better view – most were women, as it was the custom among the clubmen of New York (and most of the smart set belonged to clubs) not to attend weddings. Bradley Martin's brother Frederick, one of the ushers, literally had to force his way in, arriving with his coat nearly torn off his back, while one guest, Mrs Van Rensselaer Cruger, who watched the scramble with horror and whose dress was almost ripped from her in the crush, told a newspaper: 'The people utterly ignored the fact that they were in the house of God. They talked in loud, vulgar voices. Ladies forgot the modesty of their sex in elbowing their way to the front, men forgot their manliness in pushing others aside, and even used the backs of the pews as a highway to reach the front.'

After the ceremony there was a near-riot when the public invaded the church, some stripping flowers off the altar until the police were called in. Afterwards, a number of the regulars at Grace Church stopped going to it and the price of the pews dropped from $200 to $50.

Inevitably, the youth of the bride, the speed of the engagement and the size of her dowry gave the gossips a field day. 'Poor little Miss Martin looked very nervous and even miserable as she walked down the aisle with her father,' wrote The Saunterer. 'Nor did her aspect become more cheerful when she drove back with the pale young earl, and I heard many expressions of pity uttered by the crowd, which was evidently of the opinion that she had been more or less forced into the match, the glowing satisfaction on the rubicund face of Mrs Bradley-Martin lending weight to the suspicion.'

Nothing had been spared that would express a sense of triumph. The floral decorations at the reception at the Martins' house outdid anything ever seen before on such an occasion. Even the champagne set a new standard: Bradley Martin had bought from London's Café Royal over 200 bottles of a vintage never served before in America, at a cost of $50 a bottle. Cornelia's dowry was $1 million, with a promise from her mother to make up the deficiency if her husband's income fell short of £15,000 a year. Her future mother-in-law gave her the family emeralds, Emily Countess of Craven (the Earl's grandmother) a magnificent diamond necklace, her mother gave her the diamond tiara once worn by the Empress Josephine, and her maternal grandmother a three-string necklace of pearls valued at over $50,000.

Not everyone viewed the couple's marriage kindly. One paper called it 'snobocratic', and as Elizabeth Cameron, wife of the senator from Pennsylvania, described it to Cecil Spring-Rice: 'The wedding of Miss Bradley-Martin, aged 16, to the Earl of Craven has been one of the most disgusting exhibitions of snobbery I have ever seen. Even New York was disgusted at such a palpable sale.'

Others condemned spending on such a scale when set against the beginnings of what became known as the Great Depression. Wheat prices had crashed – other countries were now producing wheat and cotton in quantity – and farmers in many states were encumbered with mortgages often between 40 and 50 per cent of the value of their farms, so that falling prices meant many foreclosures.

*

Two days after the wedding, the Bradley-Martins' house at 22 West 20th Street was burgled. Early in the morning the sharp metal spikes that topped the high wall protecting the whole length of the house up to 19th Street had been hammered downwards. Once the thieves had entered the garden, they smashed a pane of glass in the basement window, turned the latch and crept in while everyone was asleep. From the library they took a case holding thirteen antique watches, from the dining room forty-five pieces of silver, carrying everything away in a milk float, a vehicle that would have aroused no suspicion at that hour of the morning.

The burglary was discovered by a housemaid at 6.00 a.m. Fortunately for the newlyweds, none of the wedding presents was stolen. 'Thank goodness,' said Mrs Bradley-Martin when, swathed in a black velvet cloak, she emerged from the house that morning for her drive in Central Park, 'the wedding presents were in a place of safety.' Everything gold or silver was in fact locked in a safe.

The burglary did not stop the return of the young couple and the Bradley-Martins to England and Scotland respectively. Whether or not the Earl was in need of money, as believed by many, once in possession of Cornelia's dowry he immediately began the renovations and refurbishments to his main home, Coombe Abbey, in Warwickshire, that he could not afford before. Coombe, famous for its collection of paintings that had belonged to Elizabeth, Queen of Bohemia, who married a Lord Craven and left him her pictures, needed restoration of the fabric of the building, a partial re-roofing and improvements to the servants' quarters; later, electric light was installed. There is little doubt that without Cornelia's money Coombe would have passed out of the family far earlier than it did.*

In contrast to her husband, known as rather a dandy ('He wore turn-ups on his trousers!' breathed one New York paper in tones of awe; 'he is said to sport the longest cigarette holder in

* It was sold by the 5th Earl in 1923.

London!' noted an equally transfixed London journal), Cornelia was to begin with a rather staid dresser. She made her first public appearance in an iridescent black and violet shot-silk dress – to open a bazaar in Coventry – described even by the loyal local paper as 'rather matronly'. But she quickly adapted to the grand life, and the young couple were seen at all the smart social events and at fashionable watering holes abroad, Cornelia's success during her first London season even finding its way back to New York.

Much of their time was of course spent at Coombe, which Cornelia took to at once, though after her upbringing in a house made comfortable by her American parents, she complained bitterly of its lack of warmth. 'The house is so cold,' she told her mother, 'that the only time I take my furs off is when I go to bed.'

The year after the Cravens were married, the Bradley-Martins took a house in London, launching themselves with a cotillion ball, where favours were distributed by two small black boys carried in a floral sedan chair. They returned to New York that winter. 'It is confidently expected that Mrs Martin will devise . . . some novel form of entertainment that will keep her in the public eye this winter,' wrote The Saunterer.

'Since her last coup in the marriage of her youthful daughter to the Earl of Craven Mrs Martin has been, for her, very quiet . . . Now do the caterers smile, now do the florists laugh.' But it was not to be. In December 1894 Sherman died, and after his funeral the Bradley-Martins returned to Bal Macaan to grieve and to pass their months of mourning there.

By now many other Americans had discovered the joys of a Scottish sporting estate, so that by the early 1900s there was a strong American presence in the Highlands. Or as the *New York Times* put it: 'How refreshing it is while crossing English moorland or traversing Scottish glens to come suddenly upon some handsome shooting lodge or to see in the distance some splendid old castle flying the Stars and Stripes and to be told that these houses are peopled by Americans.' Mary Theresa Leiter, the American mother of both the Marchioness of Curzon and the Countess of Suffolk, had rented Tulloch Castle, while Henry

Phipps, the steel magnate from Pittsburgh, was ensconced in Glenoich, near Inveraray.

Such visits usually lasted several weeks, as they involved a long train journey to Scotland, then a much slower one on a Highland railway, followed by a drive often of many miles across the moors. The Bradley-Martins asked so many that they usually rented a nearby hotel for the overflow. Most people spent all day in the open, walking with the guns and enjoying the luxurious shooting lunches – game or meat dishes kept warm by hot water, sweets, ices, fruit, claret, champagne cup and liqueurs.

There was constant entertaining, with Highland reels, flings and jigs after dinner to the sound of the pipes. Not all the American girls staying there as guests had mastered these – the Duchess of Roxburghe (née May Goelet), although she had taken lessons from an old piper in Dunbar, had not yet dared to dance – but Cornelia Craven was noted as 'dancing the reels very gracefully'. Her mother, Cornelia Bradley-Martin, gave an annual ball, with Loch Ness lit up by carefully placed lights. If the evening was warm enough, a romantic alternative to sitting out was to be rowed on Loch Ness in the moonlight by kilted oarsmen who played the pipes.

In the winter of 1896 the Bradley-Martins returned to New York. There they began to prepare for the ball that would astonish New York. The *New York Times*, which reported that Mrs Bradley-Martin had promised to outdo the 1883 ball of the former Mrs Vanderbilt (now Alva Belmont), which had purportedly cost $100,000, confidently asserted that the forthcoming event would eclipse it. What they had no means of knowing was that in years to come the Bradley-Martin ball would become known as the kiss of death for the Gilded Age.

CHAPTER 15

Fitting In – or Not

'An English peer of very old title is desirous of marrying at once a very wealthy lady, her age and looks are immaterial, but her character must be irreproachable; she must be a widow or spinster – not a divorcée. If among your clients you know such a lady, who is willing to purchase the rank of a peeress for £25,000 sterling, paid in cash to her future husband, and who has sufficient wealth besides to keep up the rank of peeress, I shall be pleased if you will communicate with me in the first instance by letter when a meeting can be arranged in your office. I beg you to keep this confidential. The peer will pay handsomely for the introduction when it is arranged.'

By the time this advertisement appeared in England in 1901 in the widely read *Daily Telegraph*, the transatlantic traffic of dollar-laden young women on the one hand and impoverished members of the peerage on the other was so well established that it would have brought no more than a wry smile to the faces of those who read it.* Its message was even summed up by a song in a popular musical comedy of the time, *The American Girl*:

> 'The almighty dollar will buy, you bet,
> A superior class of coronet

---

* One estimate said that American girls had brought $50 million into the country.

That's why I've come from over the way
From New York City in USA.'

Yet across the Atlantic the attitude of Americans – or perhaps I should say that expressed in the American press – to titles or anything that smacked of an aristocracy of birth was ambivalent in the extreme.

There were now endless declarations of their innate republicanism, together with frequent quoting of that famous sentence in the Declaration of Independence: 'We hold these truths to be self-evident, that all men are created equal.'* There were ideological objections to hereditary aristocracies, with two main reasons why they should not be countenanced by the true-born American citizen. The first was that they concentrated land, wealth and power in the hands of just a few families, who would then try and hang on to these; only 'the threat and apprehension of revolution', commented *The North American Review*, 'wrung from the reluctant hands of the English aristocracy the reform legislation of 1832.'† The second was that while the original holder of the title might have deserved it, there was no logical reason why any of his descendants should. The effete Englishman and the dowdy Englishwoman were familiar figures of mockery.

Yet at the same time England, its culture, its mores and its fashions, was the model to which American smart society turned its enthralled eyes. The instant the Prince of Wales appeared with three studs on the front of his shirt instead of two the young dandies of the US rushed to their tailors, an English coachman and grooms were the *sine qua non* for the serious coaching aficionado, while hereditary titles seemed to hold an unholy allure for these sturdy sons of the Republic. 'I could not help thinking, as I looked on the unwonted throng, of how Thackeray's remark

---

* Except, of course, in those days, women and black Americans.

† The Great Reform Act, as it was known, was the first to effectively challenge the electoral status quo. It increased the size of the electorate (though not by very much) so that around one in five adult males could vote, and granted seats in the House of Commons to the large cities that had sprung up in the Industrial Revolution.

"Tommy loves a lord" applied even more closely to Americans than to his own countrymen,' wrote The Saunterer when the Duke of Marlborough arrived to stay with Alva in Newport.

Pages and pages, in even the smallest provincial newspaper, were given over to the doings of any aristocrats who visited; in the lengthy intervals between, the obligatory social columns focused relentlessly on the antics of their own upper crust, noting when Mrs Astor gave a dinner and how many for, who had been asked to lead a cotillion at the Bradley-Martins' dinner and dance, who sat in who's conveyance at the annual Coaching meeting – trivial social details that were lapped up as if they were Holy Writ.

Nowhere was this conflict between principle and worldly interest better exemplified than in the marriage of the various dollar princesses to the scions of aristocratic British families. There was a curious dichotomy between two opposing attitudes – triumph at an American girl having scooped up such a prize in the teeth of native opposition, interwoven with resentment at the thought that an American husband was not good enough – which were often found in uneasy reconciliation in the same article.

Such marriages were frequently treated as an implicit snub to Americans. Falling in love was not then given the weight it is now; and with a woman's absolute dependency on her husband, the head as much as the heart was concerned in marriage (if a girl did not see this, her mother certainly would). So that the reaction of her compatriots to an American woman falling in love with a foreigner was that she was demonstrating a conscious, unpatriotic preference for another country.

In England, where the best-selling romantic novelist Marie Corelli thundered, 'Heirs to a great name and title sell their birthrights for a mess of American dollar-pottage,' few of these heirs, envied by their contemporaries for this sudden shower of gold, took any notice. For one of the attractive qualities in an American bride was not only that her fortune passed to the possession of her husband, but that she actually approved of the spending of money. In her own country, the spending of money by the wife of a rich man was not simply a pleasure, an indulgence or a needless extravagance but a solemn, indeed a quasi-religious, duty.

If she did not spend, covering herself with jewels or bedecking her house with wonderful Louis XIV commodes, how would anyone know how immensely rich her husband was? His business rivals certainly would not broadcast any evidence of his success. Or how else could she entertain on a par with these rivals' wives? For without the stable caste system of England, constant jostling and struggling was needed simply to keep one's place in the competitive arena of high society. The wife who did not spend was failing in one important marital duty: that of proclaiming her husband's success to the world.

Yet although the transatlantic marriages continued, in the more puritan society of the US a zeal for moral reform was publicly taking hold from the mid-1890s. Journalists and preachers more and more frequently compared title-heiress marriages to prostitution, presumably hoping to shame their subjects by associating them with one of society's most disreputable activities. In 1901, the English journalist William Stead coined one of the more famous nicknames of the international marriage phenomenon: 'Gilded prostitution'.*

(There was an even stronger reaction if an American man left the country. When William Waldorf Astor, unable to stand the constant battles with his aunt, the social leader Caroline Astor, left the country in 1891, saying that 'America is no place for a gentleman,' American newspapers described his departure as flying to 'the land of lust and baccarat',† and there were even effigies of 'William the Traitor' burnt in the streets.)

There were also plenty of caveats from the other side of the Atlantic. There had been historic links with the South: many impoverished younger sons and English squires had gone out there to seek their fortune, and a Southern accent still charmed

* Quoted by Paul Jonathan Woolf in *Special Relationships: Anglo-American Love Affairs, Courtship and Marriages in Fiction, 1821–1914*. University of Birmingham, 2007.

† The year before had seen the Tranby Croft gambling scandal, in which the Prince of Wales was involved, which hinged on one of the guests in the country house Tranby Croft cheating at baccarat.

and reassured. But with the defeat of the Confederate States most English felt that all that was civilised and gentlemanly in the US had also been defeated, leaving only a tribe of voracious, unhealthily rich tycoons with little sense of how to behave.

As Jennie Jerome later wrote: 'In England, as on the Continent, the American woman was looked upon as a strange and abnormal creature, with habits and manners something between a Red Indian and a Gaiety Girl. Anything of an outlandish nature might be expected of her. If she talked, dressed and conducted herself as any well-bred woman would, much astonishment was invariably evinced, and she was usually saluted with the tactful remark: "I should never have thought you were an American" – which was intended as a compliment.'

The young American Belle Wilson bitterly resented the patronising attitude of the English upper classes towards herself and her countrymen and women. In 1886, when she was staying in Cowes for a week, she met a Mrs Cust, a woman with a tongue so sharp that her house, opposite the entrance to the Royal Yacht Squadron (familiarly known as the Club), was known as 'The Seat of the Scornful'. Mrs Cust lived up to her reputation by greeting Belle with the remark that she 'thought America must be a dreadful place, she had heard no one had any servants there'. Belle replied that one or two families had. Then Mrs Cust said that she thought no one there had a lady's maid and that she would hate to be without a lady's maid. Belle replied again that she knew those with lady's maids. 'I thought Americans did not like to be servants,' said Mrs Cust. Finally, driven beyond endurance, Belle allowed her good manners towards an older woman to slip slightly. 'They don't,' she replied, 'all our working class are English!'

It was true. Americans were used to a different kind of servant, who was very seldom a fellow countryman or woman: for an American, being a servant was looked down upon. Out of a sample of 562 American women, by far the largest number – 157 – gave as their reason for not wanting to be a domestic servant 'Pride, social condition, and unwillingness to be called a servant

– I don't like to be called a menial.'* Many would not wear uniform, a *sine qua non* in the houses of the rich, a habit that was catching. Delmonico himself, when asked to put his waiters in knee breeches with silk stockings and pumps for a special dinner, refused.† 'Servants who have been here even a very short time will not mark themselves out by assuming a distinctive livery of this kind,' he said.

Almost all those who did work in Fifth Avenue and its environs were foreign immigrants – many Irish – who had only gone into domestic service because, as one remarked, 'I was not educated enough for any other work' and because they could be certain of employment while picking up an ad hoc training as they went along, since servants in New York were in perennially short supply. 'Even now the number of servants employed in the town house of a Manhattan magnate is considerably less than would be thought indispensable in a Belgravia mansion of equal pretensions,'‡ said the *Nineteenth Century Magazine*.

One reason for this friction was the gulf in expectations and attitude. English servants, just as socially conscious as those they worked for – there was an equally strict hierarchy in the Servants' Hall – knew exactly what was expected of them and how they themselves should behave. They would have been well schooled in their duties by years in a great house under the supervision of the upper servants, and almost all would have gone into domestic service as a matter of choice.

To them, Americans, often including the new brides of their masters, were upstarts who had no idea of the traditions and responsibilities inherent to a great family. No English peeress, for instance, would have done as Alice Vanderbilt did, inspecting for dust and grime every morning by donning a clean pair of white gloves to run a finger along every surface and picture

---

* From *Domestic Service* by Lucy Maynard Salmon. Macmillan, New York, 1901.

† *Town Topics*, 5 January 1888.

‡ In 'A Study of New York Society' by Mayo William Hazeltine, *The Nineteenth Century Magazine*, 31 May 1882.

frame. If this had been done at all, it would have been done by the housekeeper.

Sometimes servants would discreetly sneer at their new mistresses; Consuelo Vanderbilt tells a story about sitting in her freezing drawing room in Blenheim and deciding that she needed a fire. She rang the bell and the butler appeared, but when she asked him to oblige her by lighting it, he looked at her with intense disapproval. 'I will ask the footman to see to it, Your Grace,' he told her, deeply shocked that she would ask him to perform so menial a task.

It was the same for Maud Burke, who often dismayed her husband Sir Bache Cunard by giving orders direct to the footmen instead of through the butler. Once, she committed a sin that would have been unforgivable in an English girl: when she saw Sir Bache standing at the window of his club, horror of horrors she waved to him from the street below. In the world of English society, women were not even supposed to walk down clubland streets.

Mary Curzon, too, found the servants incredibly difficult when she had to run 5 Carlton House Terrace. At one point she was served so little food that she had to send her plate back to the kitchen 'three or four times' to get sufficient. She found them tyrannical, goods were never delivered on time and when she said that the grocery bills were too high, the cook gave notice. It was not what a belle expected. 'English servants are *fiends*,' she wrote to her mother. 'They are malignant and stupid and make life barely worth living, and I should like to hang a few and burn the rest at the stake.'

Sometimes the new arrival was treated with sympathy. Sophia Wells Williams, who had been brought up in China, where her father had been the United States Minister in Peking, met the Hon. Thomas Grosvenor, second son of Lord Ebury, when he was a young attaché there. When they married, he took her to Moor Park, his father's wonderful Palladian mansion at Rickmansworth. As she stepped out of the train, the footman who met her at the station whispered to her: 'We are all very sorry for you.'

On her first morning at Moor Park she did not know what to wear. When she asked her husband Tommy, he simply begged her to put on 'something nice'. Not much wiser, she put on a dress she knew was expensive and smart, a black silk one that she had worn for a court mourning at The Hague and went down to family prayers, feeling worried and unhappy. After prayers, she stood beside a table in the hall, not quite knowing what to do next. Her new sister-in-law, Tommy's elder sister, came up to her and asked her not to stand about 'looking silk-gownified'. When she told the story later, Sophia always added: 'I could cheerfully have killed her.'

The ordeal of her arrival continued when her new husband took her to visit his father's old gamekeeper, who looked at her dubiously and said he hoped she would make Mr Thomas a respectable wife. But she was determined to love them and win them over and she did, writing later: 'It took a little time to learn all the ins and outs of life in that beloved household. None of them had ever really grown up; they had all [just] grown older doing the things they had always done, in the same way.'

Not everyone was greeted as warmly as Belle Wilson by her future sister-in-law, Lady de Grey. 'Mungo [Herbert] came down here yesterday looking much brighter and happier than I have ever seen him for years & he told me that there was perhaps some chance of yr marrying,' wrote Gladys de Grey in 1888. 'Knowing how much and how long he has cared for you, I am writing at the risk of yr thinking me intrusive to tell you how very much I hope it may be settled. I am so devoted to him that I cannot say how grateful I wld be to you for making him happy, and my one dream for him has always been that he should marry someone he loved very much as he does you.'

When the matter was finally settled, she was even warmer. 'I cannot tell you, my very dear future sister [in law], how joyful yr letter has made me. Now that Mungo has got the wish of his heart, I have nothing left to wish for and my gratitude towards the person who has brought us such happiness is beyond expression. I love him so much that even if you were to take him away to America for ever, I shld feel quite contented knowing he was happy with you. How glad I am to think that I shall see you next week.'

And when Mungo died aged only forty-seven (in 1903), Gladys wrote entirely from the heart: 'you are always in our thoughts, darling, & I wish that for a few minutes, sometimes, this could make you feel a little less lonely. More than this one cannot hope for, for when that overwhelming sense of desolation sweeps over you continually I know that nothing can be of any good. Good bye now, darling, I love you very much, & long for you to come back. Yr devoted Sister.'

Mary Curzon had a tougher time. After being fêted as a young and beautiful single woman, with the friendship and protection offered her by – among others – Margot Asquith, a close friend of George Curzon, the man with whom Mary had been hopelessly in love for several years, things changed when she eventually married her George. 'As yet I am not attached to my new country,' she wrote sadly, adding of her rather horrible father-in-law Lord Scarsdale, 'Lord S. is the most tyrannical old man I have ever seen, besides being the most eccentric.'

'Eccentric' was a kindly way of describing Lord Scarsdale's rude and irritating manner. When he asked his new daughter-in-law a series of questions implying that life in America was primitive beyond belief: 'Do you have sea fish in America?' 'I suppose you don't know how to make mince pies in America,' she was eventually goaded into replying: 'Why don't you ask if we are civilised or white in America?' Whereupon George leapt to her defence: 'Papa, what sort of notion have you of America anyway – I never heard such absurd questions in all my life.'

It took some time for acceptance to be reached, and at first she was bitterly lonely ('It is not all a bed of roses to live in a strange country and I am as strange to the people and their ways as they are to me'), although by marrying Curzon she had achieved the wish of her heart, hence the comment in her diary: 'My path is strewn with roses and the only thorns are the unforgiving women.'

Many of these, of course, were displeased that she had stolen Curzon, one of the most eligible of *partis*, from under their noses – one less eligible in the pool for their daughters to pick.

It was in any case far more difficult for the daughter of an aristocrat to marry than her brothers. She seldom had the advantage of a large dowry: after a few years of taking a house for the London season and subsidising the balls and dinners that went with it, the less well-off peers might jib at the expense and that meant fewer chances of meeting someone 'suitable'. There were, too, likely to be fewer of these than there were girls because of the aristocracy's own rigid, self-imposed caste system.

Just as a wife not only became a husband's property and took on his name, she took on his status as well, so that if a younger son, short of money as many were, married the daughter of a rich merchant, she immediately rose to his rank. But if his sister married the merchant's son, she moved down – and out of the close-knit circle of kinship. When Lady Charlotte Bertie married the wealthy Josiah John Guest, a successful ironmaster and Member of Parliament, the fact that he was much lower in status than his aristocratic wife caused her significant social strain for some years.

So unthinkable was such a fate considered that mothers often forbade their daughters to make such matches, or the daughters themselves rejected them. The arrival of American girls, irresistible to so many, cut down even further the chances of making a really good match – or even any match at all.

For the American girl who arrived in England unprepared, the clash of cultures was sometimes deafening. If she turned down an eldest son, the shock and surprise was considerable, not least to the peer himself who, having known from babyhood that he was *numero uno* in the family, had seldom been denied anything. Belle Wilson, who had been proposed to by several, wrote in a letter to her sister: 'the men get so *nasty* when they are refused over here'.

Others around her looked at the American girl as someone to be viewed with suspicion, if not avoided altogether. From the comparative freedom with which she had been brought up, her manner and expectations were quite different. 'I gathered that an English lady was hedged around with what seemed to me to be boring restrictions,' recorded Consuelo Vanderbilt, on becoming a duchess.

'It appeared that one should not walk alone in Piccadilly or in Bond Street, nor sit in Hyde Park unless accompanied; that one should not be seen in a hansom cab and that one should always travel in a reserved compartment; that it was better to occupy a box than a stall at the theatre and that a visit to a music hall was out of the question.'

The American girl might be pretty, well dressed and lively but – where did she come from? Few English could understand that Americans, too, had a class system which, though unadmitted, was every bit as meaningful as their own, that their opposite numbers in New York, Boston or Newport were hedged about with similar restrictions and conformed to shibboleths equally important in their world. (When the Metropolitan Museum of Art was founded in 1866, its backers had proposed co-operation with the New York Historical Society, in which lay many treasures that should have been in a museum. Their offer was rejected simply because the patricians who ran the Historical Society considered some of the backers of the museum unacceptable socially.) When Cornelius Vanderbilt IV, the son of the former Grace Wilson, as a small boy saw a woman hanging out clothes and asked his mother, 'What's that lady doing?', Grace smiled and said: 'That's not a lady, darling, that's a *woman*,' going on to explain that a lady never turned her hand to menial tasks, and always wore silk stockings and silk gloves. And while in Newport nothing was too grand or too formal, in the English equivalent, Cowes, everyone walked out to dinner as carriages would have been considered ostentatious.

To most English, all Americans were the same, so that it was a shock to realise that most of these girls were far better educated than the home-grown variety.

From the American girls' point of view, adjusting was just as difficult. They sparkled in an urban setting, but as much of the

British aristocracy's life was spent in the country the long months living either on their own in the great houses on their husbands' estates to which marriage brought them, or the weeks-long visits to other such houses, often tried them sorely. 'From my window I overlooked a pond in which a former butler had drowned himself,' wrote Consuelo of a winter at Blenheim. 'As one gloomy day succeeded another I began to feel a deep sympathy for him.' Even Englishwomen sometimes found life on the estate trying. 'Solitude at Studley, with de Grey out all day, breeds in me the germs of Melancholia,' wrote Lady de Grey. Then there was the question of physical comfort.

Despite these drawbacks, one of the great attractions of upper-class English life to American girls was that in England married women had a much better time than they did at home, something admitted even in America. 'Naturally, one of the chief reasons why American women have so great a liking for European society is to be found in the fact of the far more important position that married ladies occupy in that society than they do with us,' commented *Lippincott's Magazine*.

Thanks to their repressive upbringing, it was only after marriage that English girls blossomed, and thanks to the greater social mix – politicians, ambassadors, leading writers, the financiers befriended by the Prince of Wales – it was at their dining tables that the most fascinating conversations could be heard. In England, to be a beautiful young married woman with the talent and money to entertain was to be courted, admired and the centre of a circle.

In America, by contrast, most of the rich were too interested in and too busy at making money to involve themselves in politics. In New York, they spent most of their time in their offices or in the grand mahogany-walled bar of Hoffman House, with its famous cocktails and equally famous nude paintings; in Newport, husbands would depart on Sundays to return to their offices, leaving their rich, pampered womenfolk behind – politics, for most of them, happened in Washington. In England, most of the men in society did not do jobs but ran their estates, where they spent most of the year; when in London, many of them ran the country. In all this their wives, albeit only in a supporting role, were very much at their sides.

At home, the belle, so brilliant and popular while single, retired to the ranks of matrons once married, and although there was constant entertaining, but with writers and artists frowned on, husbands constantly involved in business, and few politicians – most were in Washington – conversation usually ran along narrow, predictable lines. The Four Hundred 'would have fled as a body from a painter, a musician, or a clever Frenchman,' said Mrs Winthrop Chanler, from a prominent New York family but with widened horizons from her upbringing in Rome.

'The English married ladies are like our American girls,' said Chauncey Depew, adding loyally that 'they never get the spring and dash, quickness of repartee and chaff that our girls have,' although he conceded that 'they are the brightest and most venomous politicians in English society. Their houses are frequently political centres from which emanate influences that govern the nation.'

So the girls from the US came – and they kept on coming. Between 1875 and 1905 over forty American girls married into the peerage, bringing with them the dollars that saved many a stately home from ruin. There were many attempts to calculate the total amount of American dollars spent in dowry payments; one estimate said that American brides had brought in $50 million to Britain, but the probability is that it was nearer a billion dollars – money that went straight into the pockets of the men they married.

Such was the concern about the economic drain on America of title-heiress marriages that when another Vanderbilt bride, Gertrude, married the son of an American railroad tycoon in 1896, the *New York Journal* reported jubilantly: 'it will be an American wedding. There will be no noblemen in this – no purchased titles. The millions all belong in America and they will all remain here.'

But not until the Singer sewing machine heiress, Marguerite Decazes de Glucksberg, married a young French duke in 1910 did the press spell out unambiguously what they saw as the sordid reality. For these nuptials, the *New York Tribune*'s headline was: 'She pays all the bills – he thinks himself cheap at the price.'

CHAPTER 16

Tennie Claflin: The Odd One Out

Tennessee Claflin's obituary in the *New York Times* said that she and her sister Victoria were 'the most widely known women in the country fifty years ago', adding that they then 'both went to England and married men with large fortunes'. It was quite true, but it is likely that she would have preferred *The Times*'s description of her as 'A pioneer of woman's suffrage'.

As the happily married Lady Cook, her life was full of pleasure and ease. She was perhaps happiest in the beautiful grounds of her baronet husband Sir Francis's estate of Monserrate, near Lisbon; one of the articles that had appeared about her, and pleased her greatly, had referred to the 'blonde, spirituelle Lady Cook', moving gracefully among the 'rare and gorgeous plants' of her garden. As well as this majestic hilltop castle in Portugal, she was châtelaine of Doughty House in Richmond, on the Thames, with its superb art collection.

For the former Tennie Claflin, this life of wealth and sophistication was a world away from the ramshackle, disreputable existence she had led as a child and young woman in America's Midwest. For of all the American husband-hunters who married into the British peerage during the late nineteenth century, Tennessee Claflin's was the most unlikely story. Although, like most of them, she was good-looking, unlike the others she was not rich, she did not have a mother to chaperone, support or dragoon her, she lacked formal education and had no superb clothes from

Worth. Instead, she had lived by her wits – managing en route to become one of the world's first female stockbrokers – and in her native US was trailed by an aura of scandal and sexual licence. Ironically, it was the latter which gave her her first real step up the ladder.

Tennie, as she was always known, was born on 26 October 1845, in Homer, Ohio. Originally, the family had been respectable and hard-working: on her father's side, her great-grandfather was a son of the Duke of Hamilton and their grandfather was the first senator from Massachusetts; another forebear was George Washington's great friend, the American legislator Colonel Alexander Hamilton; on her mother's side, she was descended from the old German families of the Hummels and the Moyers.

Her father, Reuben Buckman Claflin, always known as Buck, was however a confidence trickster, a one-eyed snake-oil salesman moving on from one small Ohio town to another when debts or false claims caught up with him; her mother Roxanna was illiterate, homely, small and fiery-tempered. Tennie was the youngest of the couple's eight surviving children (two died in childhood), all bar one exceptionally good-looking. Together the brood were noisy, self-assertive and given to disruptive behaviour – for which they were frequently beaten by their father with braided whips he kept supple for this purpose in a barrel of rainwater. They were lightly educated in a log-cabin school.

The Claflin tribe's wanderings continued until they reached a small town called Mount Gilead, by which time the remarkable handsomeness of two of the older girls had brought them respectable marriages. Victoria, the third daughter, had always believed herself to be psychic and in touch with angels and various notable figures of the past. And soon reports came that five-year-old Tennie, the youngest, sent some time before to stay with relatives in Pennsylvania, was showing signs of psychic gifts, this time of second sight, frightening playmates by 'reading their minds' and telling a farmer where he could find a lost calf. She even – accurately – predicted a fire in a seminary.

It was a time when fads, new philosophies and outré theories said to be science-based such as phrenology (reading character through the various bumps on the head) were taking hold in America. Most of these appealed mainly to the credulous, but one that interested and attracted the educated and serious-minded was spiritualism, believed in by many public figures both in England and the US.

This was tailor-made for Buck Claflin, who set Victoria up as a clairvoyant, with Tennie, already proven (in her own mind at least) to have occult powers, as a 'magnetic healer'. It was the start of the sisters' long closeness, largely with Victoria as pioneer and Tennie as able lieutenant.

One day Victoria, now a lovely girl with huge blue eyes, silky curling brown hair and a delicate profile, fell ill and the doctor who attended her, Dr Canning Woodhull, became smitten with her. He was a man from a good family but, unknown to the Claflins, such a wastrel that his family had cast him off. Victoria's parents, for whom life was a hand-to-mouth affair, thought the match too good to turn down and, two months after her fifteenth birthday, they were married.

As Woodhull's family could have foretold, he was constantly drunken and unfaithful – he ended up an alcoholic and a morphine addict. But at the beginning Victoria, prepared to give her marriage a chance, moved to San Francisco, then booming as a mining town, with her husband and their son, hoping to make a fresh start.

Soon Tennie, aged fourteen, was being billed not only as a healer but as a clairvoyant in her father's snake-oil 'show', where she sat in her booth for thirteen hours at a stretch. What aided her success at this was her utter conviction in her own powers, so that this became a life that continued in Canada, where her father advertised her as someone who could cure cancer. When this claim was, unsurprisingly, found to be fraudulent, the Claflin family left hurriedly, next settling in Cincinnati. Here Victoria and her two children had joined them there, leaving her feckless husband behind.

By twenty Tennie was a pretty girl who exuded friendly warmth, vitality and an earthy sensuousness, qualities that made her a magnet for men. By this time, the number of people interested in spiritualism had grown enormously, swelled by those who had lost loved ones in the Civil War. Buck was determined to cash in on this by means of his daughters. They moved to Chicago, again advertising themselves as mediums; here Tennie married a young man named John Bartels. But marriage did not put a stop to her free-and-easy way with men, and again the aura of illicit sex and the men that hung around the house caused complaints by the neighbours.

The family moved on, earning as they did so by fortune-telling and conducting séances. Tennie's youthful marriage broke up and her husband disappeared from her life for good. Then Victoria had a spirit vision telling her to go to New York, to 17 Great Jones Street. 'There you will find a house ready and waiting for you,' declared the spirit, after which a vision of the house and of its interior appeared. Victoria rushed to New York and there found the house exactly as she had seen it in every detail. It was on 3rd Street, between the Bowery and Broadway, a perfectly respectable district, and in 1868 the family moved there.

In New York, their fortunes changed dramatically, thanks to the impression they made on the richest man in America – Cornelius Vanderbilt. Vanderbilt, or the Commodore, as he was always called, was rough and unpolished in his ways, hard-bitten and ruthless – a real 'robber baron', as some of the more unscrupulous new millionaires were known. At seventy-six, he was tall, spare, hawk-nosed, looked and acted younger than his age and cared little what people thought of him: he had always gone his own way and was determined always to do so.

Despite his forbidding exterior, he was lonely: his wife of fifty-five years had died a few months earlier. This had lent an edge to his known interest in spiritualism, hitherto largely an effort to contact his dead mother. In short, for a man attempting to make money out of two pretty daughters said to have clairvoyant powers, he was a perfect target for Buck Claflin.

The Commodore lived not far from the Claflins, at 10 Washington Place, just off Washington Square. As he was a man happy to grant interviews – though dealing with those who came to him briskly – it would not have been difficult for Buck to bring Tennie to meet him, present her as a 'magnetic healer' and at some point also introduce Victoria.

From the start the Commodore found Tennie's gaiety, uninhibited freedom of expression and open, flirtatious manner more appealing than Victoria's more refined beauty. Tennie was used to down-to-earth language, she would pull his side-whiskers, tease him and perch on his knee. The healing sessions grew more intimate as the touch of her 'magnetic' hands inspired carnal thoughts. The good-natured Tennie took this in her stride, and soon the servants grew used to finding a flushed, tousled Tennie in the Commodore's bed in the morning, and the Commodore himself grew ever fonder of the girl he called his 'Little Sparrow'.

His personal physician and intimate friend, Jared Linsly, who had noted the Commodore's gradually declining mental powers, thought Tennie's presence 'invigorating' for the old man, adding in his diary: 'He is often childish and therefore lucky to have so attractive and willing a plaything as Miss Tennessee to divert him, while others, more capable, go about his material affairs.' His son Billy, although anxious that his father should not get too embroiled with the Claflins, realised that if he passed information to them, they would in turn feed it back to his father – who would then act on it.

While Billy was happy that his father was enjoying himself with Tennie, he certainly did not want him to marry her. Accordingly, he and his siblings tried to fix him up with a highly suitable widow, nearer his own age. But the Commodore was having none of it, and after the widow left, Tennie's visits continued.

Yet when the Commodore proposed to Tennie, to the mystification of those around him, she turned him down. From her point of view, she had her life ahead of her – thanks to the Commodore's stock-market tips the sisters were better off now than they had ever been – and he was old enough to be her grandfather. But the friendship remained, as did his help with investments, so that the girls continued to prosper.

By this time, investors had noticed that all the stocks the Claflins bought went up. Whether they thought that, as Victoria claimed, she was advised from beyond the grave or whether they simply assumed that she benefited from the Commodore's suggestions, investors began to follow her in large numbers.

At this point the Commodore was persuaded into marriage by his children, increasingly worried by Tennie's visits and presumed influence over their father. His bride was not the forty-nine-year-old widow Mrs Crawford but her thirty-one-year-old daughter Frank, and the marriage took place in Canada, safely away from Tennie. However, it was a marriage in name only, as Frank and the Commodore did not share a bed, and Tennie's visits continued.

At the end of 1869 two financiers, old enemies of the Commodore, tried to corner the New York Gold Exchange's gold market and the collapse of the economy seemed imminent, creating a panic that became known as Black Friday. The Commodore rushed back from his honeymoon and the takeover was foiled by the federal government. All through the crisis Victoria sat in her carriage, coolly playing the market, and at the end cried out: 'I came out a winner!', later declaring that they now had capital of $700,000.

Busy as the Commodore was, he kept the Claflin sisters under his wing. Recovery from Black Friday was slow, except for Vanderbilt and his protegées, whom he advised to buy as he bought: more holdings in his own railroads or in the ones that would soon be his at the current depressed prices. Soon the girls were rich.

Sometime in 1869 the sisters had spoken to the Commodore about opening a brokerage house. He must have been astonished at first – no woman had ever thought of such a thing before – but agreed to give them advice, aid and a certain amount of financial backing. They began by visiting Wall Street as speculators and, when their appearance was noted by the press, invited a reporter from the *New York Herald* to visit them. In a long article about them, he described this first office as 'a small comfortable room fronting on the avenue, profusely decorated with oil paintings and statuary, furnished with sofa, chairs, a piano and the various other articles, useful and ornamental, which go into the makeup of a ladies' drawing room'.

Ward McAllister, illustrated here with donkey ears, was often mocked for his social pretensions, founded mainly on English customs. In this cartoon, Uncle Sam is laughing uproariously at the English model he apes.

Grace Wilson, who as Mrs Cornelius Vanderbilt III succeeded Mrs Astor as the ruler of New York society.

Adèle Beach Grant, as Lady Essex, was one of the beauties of her time

Mrs Bradley-Martin as Mary Queen of Scots at her famous ball in February 1897

Cornelia (née Bradley-Martin), the Countess of Craven

Cornelia Bradley-Martin at the centre of a family group. Her father stands behind her with her mother on his left.

No. 4 Chesterfield Gardens, the London house of the Bradley-Martins – today it is the Egyptian Embassy. They bought its neighbour for their daughter.

Anna Gould and her husband Count 'Boni' de Castellane after their wedding in New York in March 1895. Boni was a noted dandy.

The Empress Eugénie was known for her taste and glamour and that of her court

The Angouleme rubies, bought by Mrs Bradley-Martin and eventually inherited by her daughter Cornelia.

Maud Burke, an heiress from San Francisco, who later rechristened herself Emerald.

Below Mrs Stuyvesant Fish (*right*) and a friend taking a stroll together

New York's financial centre: the corner of Broad Street and Wall Street, *c.*1900.

Right Tennie Claflin, who became the devoted wife of Sir Francis Cook

Above The beautiful Virginia Bonynge, whose marriage to the blond and handsome Lord Deerhurst, heir to the Earl of Coventry, was something of a Gilded Age fairy tale.

Right Minnie Paget (née Stevens) in her dazzling, bejewelled Cleopatra costume at the Duchess of Devonshire's Jubilee Ball in 1897.

The bustling streets of London's Knightsbridge in the late 1800s

Coaching in Central Park, where elegance of turnout was another form of social competition.

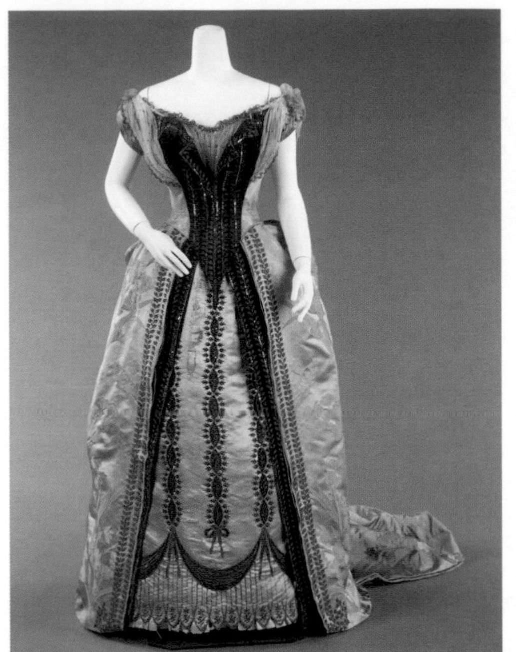

Top left A Worth dress of 1887, now in the Metropolitan Museum of Art, with sumptuous material enhanced by intricate detailing; *top right* another Worth creation worn by Mary Curzon *c.*1903; *above* a portrait of Empress Eugénie, wearing a dress possibly by Worth.

The Claflin sisters were now well known, and when in 1870 they opened an office on Wall Street, becoming the world's first women stockbrokers, 100 policemen were needed to keep the crowd in order. When the two good-looking sisters arrived to enter their new office, the crowd of male onlookers was not disappointed. Their skirts were short by the standards of the day – just down to the tops of their gleaming boots – and it was clear they had left off corsets and bustles. Their deep-blue jackets, out of which Tennie's magnificent bosom threatened to burst, were embellished with velvet. For the final, businesslike touch, each wore a gold pen behind her ear. All day men peered into the office, outside which hung a notice: 'Gentlemen will state their business and then retire at once.'

From the start they were feminists, believing that women could be equally as successful in business as men. 'Why cannot women be judged for their merits as men are?' asked Victoria. Tennie, whose ease of manner was invaluable with would-be investors, was always smartly dressed, usually in her favourite blue – sometimes a blue suit trimmed with black astrakhan, and an astrakhan muff, her hat black velvet trimmed with black feathers.

US newspapers such as the *Sun*, the *Evening Express* and the *New York Herald* hailed Woodhull and Claflin as 'the Bewitching Brokers' and 'the Queens of Finance' – in the first six weeks they had made $750,000. The *New York Evening Telegraph* of February 1870 depicted them in a chariot drawn by two bulls and two bears with the heads of the largest financiers of the time. Tennie is holding the reins and Victoria is whipping right and left, crushing other financiers under the wheels of the chariot. The *New York Sunday News* commented that in time they would 'have a standing equal to some of the oldest firms in the "street"'.

Not only were they a good-looking pair but it was clear that both exuded considerable sex appeal; all through their careers they had no trouble in attracting men to their sides to help them, often in the face of contemporary opinion. This was possibly also why many contemporary men's journals (e.g. *The Days' Doings*) published sexualised images of the pair running their firm, linking the notion of publicly minded, unchaperoned women with the concepts of sexual immorality and prostitution.

Once the sisters had proved that women could make money in a man's field, as firm believers in women's rights they cast about for the next step. They found it in the Fourteenth and Fifteenth Articles of Amendment, which declared that electoral rights belonged to every citizen without reference to sex.

'We will now prove that women can manage as well as men the interests of the country and, above all, that they have a right to do it,' declared Victoria in 1870. 'To do the good we wish to do, to be heard, we need a prominent position.' Accordingly, in a breathtaking opening gambit, she put herself forward as a candidate for election to the presidency of the United States in 1872, announcing this in a letter to the *New York Herald*. Tennie said that she would run for Congress. Both hoped that this move would boost the fight for female suffrage. As no woman had ever thought of such a thing before, at first most people thought this idea too preposterous even to notice.

Their first step was to start a paper to support their election. The first issue of the *Woodhull and Claflin's Weekly* appeared on 14 May 1870, and was soon selling around 50,000 copies every week. They campaigned vigorously, a crusade that included entertaining at the grand house they had bought with the money they had made. This stood at 15 East 38th Street and was lavishly decorated with large gilded mirrors, crystal chandeliers and painted ceilings.

Victoria's real object was of course not the presidency but the recognition of women as the equal of men, both in their enfranchisement and in their private lives. She hated the hypocrisy of the double standard – why should a woman who had 'fallen' once be condemned for ever, while a man was quickly forgiven – and she believed (though she had not yet said so publicly) that everyone should be free to love as they chose.

The first two national suffrage organisations had been established only the previous year, and a few women had tried to vote but had been turned away. Victoria, acting on her own, put their case before the House Judiciary Committee at the Senate in

Washington, on 12 January 1871. The hall was crowded, largely by members of the suffrage organisation who had originally fought shy of her because of her notoriety: news of her belief in free love had got about and the sisterhood were prepared for the appearance of a scarlet woman. Instead, they saw a dignified, ladylike figure in discreet dark clothing, visibly nervous. At first Victoria put her case forward barely audibly, in formal language, before launching into an impassioned, heartfelt plea.

'By what ethics does any free government impose taxes on woman without giving her a voice on how and by whom these taxes shall be used and applied?' she asked in her clear, sweet voice. 'Women constitute a majority of the people of this country and are entrusted with the most vital responsibilities of society. They bear, rear and educate men, train and mould their characters, inspire the noblest impulses in men, and often hold the accumulated fortunes of a man's life for the safety of the family – yet they are debarred from uttering any opinion by public vote.' Scandal was forgotten; applause swept the hall as she finished.

The decision to grant the vote or not hinged on the meaning of the word 'citizen', which had heretofore been taken not to apply to women (the suffrage associations were attempting to get the vote for black males on this basis). However, the second article of the Fourteenth Amendment stated: 'All *persons* [author's italics] born or naturalised in the United States, and subject to the jurisdiction thereof, are citizens of the United States . . . No state shall make or enforce any law which shall abridge the privileges or immunities of any citizens,' words which would appear to allow Victoria just as much right as any man to stand for President. But before the hearing she was firmly told by one of the Judiciary Committee: 'Madam, you are no citizen.' When she asked him what she was, he replied 'You are a woman!'

Victoria was a compelling and persuasive orator, gaining such influential personalities as General Grant to her point of view; eventually, although she lost, the Judiciary Committee issued a minority report in her favour. As for Tennie, her looks were widely admired. 'Oh, the irresistible Tennie!' wrote one enthralled reporter.

After the Judiciary Committee case there was a ferocious reaction from those who did not believe women should have the franchise, let alone stand for the highest office in the land. The sisters were turned out of the hotel where they were living and their baggage put on the street (they had to sleep on the floor of their office that night), they were insulted and the usual treatment of females as second-class citizens continued. One evening they went to Delmonico's, where they had often dined with their parents, arriving a few minutes after seven. They gave their order, and waited . . . and waited. Eventually, crossly, Tennie called the waiter. 'Miss Claflin,' he said apologetically, 'the rules are, not to serve ladies after seven in the evening unless accompanied by a gentleman.' 'Fetch Mr Delmonico,' said Tennie furiously. When Delmonico arrived he said that it was the rule, as 'we might be having women coming in from the street if I did'.

'You know very well that not half a dozen women outside in Fifth Avenue could pay your prices for a dinner,' retorted Tennie, adding that his rule 'would be obeyed'. Telling her sister to wait, she went outside, brought in her coachman, and loudly ordered: 'SOUP FOR THREE.' It came.

It was, however, the beginning of their decline. They were not behaving as women of the class they had risen to were expected to behave. There were battles when they presented their nominations at the polls and they were sued for illegally attempting to vote. But this was as nothing to the storm raised when, in the lectures they continued giving, they advocated giving a child sexual knowledge, albeit in the most decorous form imaginable ('Mamma carried you under her heart days, weeks and weary months . . . when people understand this mighty problem of proper generation, all the mock modesty will die').

Victoria went on to press for legalised prostitution ('a woman of the town can lift no hand or voice for defence'). Common prostitutes, she said, were at the mercy of policemen, and 'are compelled to pay them both in personal favours and money for the privilege of escaping arrest. In this way, large sums of money are drawn from them by men whose sworn duty it is to protect society.

'What we ask and demand,' she said, 'is equality everywhere.' She went on to a much more controversial theme: the double standard operating generally in society. 'If loss of virginity is a disgrace to unmarried women, then the same should be held of men. If the mother of a child out of legal wedlock is ostracised, then the father should share the same fate; if it is wrong to mother such a child, it is equally wrong to father it. If a life of female prostitution is wrong, a life of male prostitution is equally wrong. If Contagious Diseases Acts are passed, they should operate equally on both sexes.'

She went on to state particular cases, although without naming names, but made it clear that, as the campaign progressed, she would not hesitate to do so. 'We propose to tear off the hypocritical mask and expose their moral deformity to the gaze of all eyes. We know who they are and shall not hesitate to write and publish their history so definitely that all men shall know them.'

This was too much. The Claflin sisters must be stopped. Suits were brought against them and they were imprisoned a number of times on charges of 'offence against the United States', only being released on payment of large sums for bail. Their offices were closed and the *Weekly* had to cease publication. When their case eventually came to court, the judge – after saying that their business had been ruined and that they had been 'subjected to many indignities' – declared that no case had been proved against them. The jury was instructed to render a verdict of not guilty, which they did immediately, without even leaving their seats.

The judge went on to say: 'For the wrong which has been done to these women, they have no redress. The injury is irremediable.' He was right. The Senate refused all compensation.

Courageous as they had been at the time, they were so run-down and broken by their ordeal that they could not resume work until 1874. When they did, one of America's leading suffragettes said: 'Mrs Woodhull and Miss Tennessee Claflin have, with their prostrate bodies, bridged a chasm over which womanhood shall walk to freedom.'

Continuing with their work had become extraordinarily difficult as lecture halls and meeting places had been banned to them and police waited outside any venue where their appearance had been advertised in order to arrest them. On one occasion they got the better of the law, when a lady went onto the platform to announce that neither of them could come that night as there was an order of arrest for them. On hearing this, an old, shaky Quaker lady got up and walked to the platform with an unsteady step, to everyone's amusement, then disappeared behind a pillar.

The previous speaker then announced that, though Victoria could not be there in person, her lecture would be read to them. The next moment the 'old' Quaker lady, coalscuttle bonnet and simple grey dress shed, dashed out – and there stood Victoria. Her lecture set everyone alight; even the police forgot their duty until the thunderous applause rolled out. Only then was Victoria arrested and taken out to join Tennie, who was also under arrest and waiting in a carriage outside.

But the continued persecution, arrests and prison, coupled with an ostracism so severe that it was almost impossible for them to find anywhere to live – even Victoria's daughter had to be sent to school under an assumed name – made them realise their only hope was to leave America.

On 4 January 1877 their original benefactor, Cornelius Vanderbilt, died. As he had left almost his entire fortune to his eldest son William, his other nine younger children contested his will fiercely in a continuing battle, putting forward as one of their arguments the premise that Cornelius was senile when he signed this will, and bringing into court anyone who would testify to this. Among them were two men prepared to say that Cornelius had reneged on a promise to marry Tennie. In the event this testimony was irrelevant, but the rumour spread that William had paid the sisters, who had been out of his father's life for several years, $100,000 not to testify at the trial that November. Whether or not he had done so was never clear; in any event, they had already left for England three months earlier.

They continued their work in England, but on a much more moderate scale, so that lectures in St James's Hall on the *Human*

Body the Temple of God, for instance, aroused astonishment rather than hostility. In a new country it was important to arrive without trailing scandal, so to sanitise their image they denied that they had ever advocated free love, instead saying what they wished for was the 'teaching and elevation of their sex'.

It was a much safer subject – especially now they were meeting rich and influential Englishmen. Men who, in other words, would make suitable and substantial husbands.

Victoria was the first to meet such a man. John Biddulph Martin was a quiet, scholarly banker who was spellbound by her, to the horror of his family, so that rewriting her past became of paramount importance. She went back and forth to America to try and quell her detractors, she threatened libel suits, she wrote articles that denied some of the more outré of the statements she had made in the past.

Eventually, around 1880, Martin either ignored his family or they, perhaps, lost their hostility to Victoria, and the couple were married. Victoria now lived in a handsome town house or at Martin's country estate at Bredon's Norton in Worcestershire. Although shunned by most of his friends, she and Tennie remained close and Victoria, as the wife of a rich and devoted husband, seemed to have left her past behind her.

Sometime in 1884 Tennie, too, met the man she would marry. She was now thirty-five and, though prettier than ever, wanted to settle down. Francis Cook, recently widowed, considered one of the three richest men in Britain, was sixty-three, a tall, handsome, bearded man whose wealth came from the family textile business that traded finished wool, cotton, linen and silk. He was a philanthropic, cultured man with a passion for collecting art. He owned the magnificent Doughty House, on the Thames in Richmond, which was filled with statuary and many great paintings (on which he was advised by Sir John Charles Robinson, the former V&A curator); and the large estate of Monserrate, near Lisbon in Portugal, where he had built a Moorish-style palace and become Visconde de Monserrate.

More importantly, as a believer in the afterlife he had been trying to get in touch with his late wife, Emily Martha Lucas, who had died that August. When he heard that Tennessee was a clairvoyant he asked her to help him. It was a time when not only fervent religiosity but belief in supernatural forces and energies, ghosts, automatic writing, the new Ouija board and other spooky phenomena was swirling through the country, so that a country gentleman consulting a clairvoyant was not as odd as it sounds.

After a few sessions Tennie told Cook with conviction that she had a spirit message from his dead wife: marry Miss Claflin. The lonely widower, whose grown-up children were married and settled, found no difficulty in believing what this pretty, gay, good-natured young woman said. They were married in October 1885, reports of it reaching the New York papers. She was given away by her rascally father, dressed to the nines for the occasion, who died three weeks later of a stroke.

After Cook married Tennie, he allowed her mother Roxanna to come and live with them at Doughty House; she remained there until her death in 1890, aged eighty-five. He also added the Long Gallery to Doughty House to accommodate his growing collection, making this gallery open to scholars and, in a practical gesture towards the art he so loved, used some of his fortune to endow an artists' home in London, Alexandra House.

Its grand opening in 1887 was attended by the Prince and Princess of Wales and a host of grandees. Here Tennie, gay and animated as always and beautifully dressed in a blue suit trimmed with grey sable, made a great impression. 'The little American beauty', noted one visitor, 'was the nicest dressed and prettiest woman in the hall.'

Soon afterwards Cook was made a baronet and, now Sir Francis, took Tennie to visit Monserrate. As their carriage drove through the village below the hill on which the castle stood, the villagers sang and danced and pelted Tennie with flowers – Sir Francis had always been a very benevolent proprietor.

Tennie loved the pink and white castle, with its towers, cupolas, rose-marble pillars, its views of the surrounding countryside, the brilliant flowers in its gardens – Sir Francis had built the first irrigation system in Portugal. Here Lord Byron had been inspired to write *Childe Harold*; and Tennie's letters expressed her delight in this lovely place. 'I am out all day and happy as a bird,' she wrote to Victoria. 'Our cook is perfection and we have two big fires going all the time.' She added, as she often did: 'I have every thing that the heart could wish & perfectly happy & contented with my precious husband.'

At home, she liked to give garden parties, and because she often forgot just how many people she had asked, she sometimes had to entertain the overflow in a nearby field. But she was so cheerful and unworried by this that the guests did not mind either. She loved Monserrate best, though, and often went there, establishing a school in the village and sending several of the children to a convent in London.

The more colourful and scandalous incidents of the sisters' past continued to surface, sometimes affecting their new lives in England: once, when Victoria's husband invited them to a club dinner to which ladies were bidden, the wife of one of the other members managed to persuade all the other women that the two were not fit people to know – and next day's papers reported that Mrs Martin and Lady Cook had been the only ladies present.

There was a distraction from the constant efforts to clear their names when Tennie's husband was suddenly sued for breach of promise – an accusation that aroused all Tennie's fighting spirit. Twenty-five years earlier, Sir Francis had met a lovely young woman in the train from London to Richmond and, finding her alluring and, he thought, easy-going, had asked permission to call upon her. She readily agreed, and a sexual liaison began. At each visit he gave her £5 or £10, but fairly quickly tired of her and tried to drop her, although as she continually pestered him for money he went on paying her £1 a week. Seven years after their first meeting, she married. Through Tennie and her secretary, Sir Francis, now too tired and unwell at the age of seventy-seven to speak, said that he had never had any intention of marrying her (he was indeed married at the time). The case was soon settled in his favour.

Yet until the last there clung about Tennie the aura of the dark and forbidden. When Francis Cook died in February 1901, there were rumours that she had murdered him. To counter these she asked for an exhumation, but the courts turned this down.

Sir Francis left an estate of £1,600,000, of which Tennie inherited £25,000 and an income for life from an investment of £50,000. With his property left mainly to his eldest son and the rest to his second son, Tennie, now Tennessee Lady Cook, Viscountess of Montserrate, was a wealthy widow but without a settled home. At fifty-six she began a wandering life again, travelling the world in aid of various women's causes.

Tennie had managed more successfully than Victoria to leave her past life behind her: the days when she had averred that women who married for money were 'legalised prostitutes, no better and no worse than streetwalkers,' were conveniently forgotten.

She now began to make use of her title as an instrument to draw publicity and therefore audiences when she spoke out for the rights of women – at the age of sixty-four she attracted audiences of 7,000 to the Albert Hall – though not on such controversial themes. 'Home is heaven where the father and mother work together in trust and sympathy,' she would say; and audiences lapped it up.

She successfully used her celebrity and her title to inspire headlines in her fight for women's rights in England, France, Italy, Portugal and the US. She was frequently the star attraction at smart parties in London, and younger people, seeing this slim, elegant, dignified figure in sapphire velvet, found it difficult to believe that she had once been mocked, thrown out of hotels and spent nights in jail.

She even managed to sit down with President Roosevelt in 1907, when she told him, in her old forthright manner: 'By putting us on the same plane of suffrage with our servants and our former black slaves,* you could rise to the greatest height in the world.' But the President told her that he did not see much good had come of giving women the vote in the few places they had achieved it (Wyoming was one of the only states to allow it; in most others the idea had been voted down).

Tennie was now basking in the sun of approval for her outspokenness on the question of female suffrage. When she returned to America in 1909 a large contingent of American suffragettes came out in tugboats to greet this heroine of the movement as her ship arrived in New York harbour. 'Lady Cook in her old Cell' ran one headline as she took reporters to the jail where she and Victoria had been incarcerated.

She travelled, she lectured with enormous success both in the US, where she filled Carnegie Hall, and in London, where she repeated her earlier triumphs at the Albert Hall. She extolled the blessings of marriage (her fervour for free love might never have existed). She never gave up her fight for women's rights and in old age became a revered and inspirational figure to the younger generations of suffragettes now fighting for the same cause (British women achieved limited franchise in 1918, two years ahead of their American sisters). By any standards, hers is a remarkable story.

* Black franchise officially became part of the Constitution with the Fifteenth Amendment, adopted in 1870, that stipulated: 'The right of citizens of the United States to vote shall not be denied or abridged by the United States or by any State on account of race, color, or previous condition of servitude,' but in practice such things as white terrorism, literacy tests and local state laws meant that few blacks got the chance to vote.

CHAPTER 17

The River of Gold

By the late 1890s spending had become more than just a mark of status, a weapon for rising in society, a wish to be surrounded only by the best, a form of self-aggrandisement or even a way of giving pleasure to others, but simply an end in itself and even a validation of identity – I spend, therefore I am.

Gilded New York was pouring out its money in an endless cornucopia of extravagance, on houses, horses, clothes, paintings, marbles, yachts, cigars, wine, jewels and trivia. Bathtubs were cut from solid marble, waterfalls installed in dining rooms, vanloads of roses or orchids filled houses for the most 'informal' evenings. Hostesses used wonderful Sèvres, Dresden or Meissen china that museums would have leapt at. Around these tables sat women festooned with jewels, some of which had last been worn by a queen; later, the cigarettes passed round would be rolled, not in white paper, but in a 100-dollar bill with the initials of the host engraved in gold letters.

For the Vanderbilts, a family picnic meant two footmen, a maid and a couple of grooms going ahead in a carriage and setting up a table with a white linen cloth, silverware and china ready for when the family arrived on horseback. Fleets of lorries came up from the South to bring orchids to decorate a ballroom; cotillions offered diamond bracelet favours for the women, sapphire cravat pins for the men; at one ball an enormous papier-mâché watermelon was dragged in, out of which sprang a little Negro boy to distribute gold cigarette cases and enamel watches to the guests. Rivalry could now be measured in cash terms.

Frivolity ruled. 'The newspapers take much more interest in international matters than in Congress,' wrote the British diplomat Cecil Spring-Rice to his sisters in March 1895. 'When Miss Gould married a Frenchman there were whole sheets of vivid description for days . . . and one paper is prosecuting another for stealing pictures of the bride's underclothing.'

Social crazes became wilder and wilder – one woman drove down Bellevue Avenue in her victoria with a monkey on each shoulder and a pig beside her – and wealth was splashed in ludicrous, almost obscene, ways. The wife of one rich Westerner owned a pet monkey that had its own room, its own valet (to dress it in a selection from its wardrobe of clothes), its own dining table and solid-silver service, its own special carriage and trotting horse. The cotillion favours given at dances grew increasingly more expensive: engraved cigarette or card cases from Tiffany, ivory shirt studs, jewelled cufflinks, delicately painted fans, watches, brooches, golf balls inlaid with gold and vouchers to buy antique furniture.

Above all, there were parties, parties, parties, each more extravagant and outré than the last.

The most famous stag party of the day served dinner to white-tied guests on horseback in a hotel ballroom – they ended the evening playing polo. One party-giver hired Sherry's restaurant for the evening, turning its upper ballroom into a scene from the garden of Versailles at a cost of around $200,000, importing statues from France, framing them in orchids and covering the floor of the supper room in orchids. Mamie Stuyvesant Smith, one of the social queens of Newport, hosted parties with her court jester Harry Lehr at Crossways, her Newport 'cottage', that got sillier and sillier: a dinner where everyone had to speak baby talk and bring dolls and, at Harry Lehr's 'cottage', a three-course dinner party for 100 dogs, some dripping in diamonds (Mamie's wore a diamond collar worth $15,000), in honour of Mrs Lehr's Pomeranian, Mighty Atom. The gifts for Mighty Atom were said to be worth $25,000 and the night to have cost some $50,000.

To the rich of America everything, even a potential grand

family background, seemed buyable. The jewellers Tiffany had opened a 'blazoning, marshalling and designing of arms' department so that the wealthy could provide themselves with an ancient-seeming coat of arms. You went in, recorded Elizabeth Drexel, and said: 'I want armorial bearings in the name of Smith. Show me a large selection, please.' A massive book was produced, with illustrations of the arms of every known English family, and opened at the section headed 'Smith'. 'Which Smiths would you prefer – the Herefordshire Smiths or the Yorkshire Smiths?' the assistant would ask.

As the customer brooded over whether to adopt the Yorkshire or Herefordshire version of the armigerous Smiths, his eye might be caught by the arms of a duke or marquis and he would decide to include part of that in his own creation. The resulting shield, half-Herefordshire Smith and half-ducal, would be installed over his front door or perhaps in the stained-glass window of the ballroom. 'He had a coat of arms a very grand one, Bran-new besides, and not a second-hand one,' wrote William Allen Butler of a parvenu millionaire. Before he left for England, William Waldorf Astor had commissioned a family tree that traced his bloodline back to the crusader Count Pedro d'Astorga of Castile, a crusader killed at the siege of Jerusalem in 1100 by the Saracen King of Morocco.

Fifth Avenue and Newport's Bellevue Avenue were lined with huge, ornate mansions built by the new plutocrats that offended the old-school upper crust. When one of these nouveau hostesses announced, 'And this is my Louis Quinze salon!' Mamie Stuyvesant Fish, a woman noted for her rather acid frankness, responded, 'And what makes you think so?'

Yet little seemed to change the established social pecking order. Much of the serious in-fighting took place in Newport where, despite its rigid protocol, there was more scope for the unexpected coup.

Here Caroline Astor reigned at Beechwood, one of the oldest Newport mansions, in which she had had the architect Richard Morris Hunt build a ballroom large enough for her '400'. Here, for over two decades, she gave her famous Summer Ball. Next door was Beaulieu, on the sea cliffs, where lived Mrs William Waldorf Astor, Caroline's niece and only serious social rival. It was surrounded by acres of green lawn, tall copper beeches and gardens, and had sixteen bedrooms and thirteen bathrooms. Later it was bought by Grace and Neily Vanderbilt.

The smart set's joker was Harry Lehr, well connected and well educated, who from early on made a success first in Newport society, then in New York, solely by dint of keeping people amused. He was a protégé of Mrs Astor, who would reserve a seat for him in her box at the opera, and the particular pet of Mamie Stuyvesant Fish, who could be startlingly rude when she felt like it. 'Mrs Roosevelt dresses on $300 a year and looks like it,' she remarked of the President's wife. Mamie was one of those who battled constantly to keep her lofty place in society but who at the same time was often bored by its stuffiness and insistence on protocol. Only occasionally was she out-manoeuvred.

Her devoted husband Stuyvesant Fish, from a family at the heart of Knickerbocker society, was also president of the Illinois Central, a railroad in which Ned Harriman, a highly successful railroad-owner, held substantial interests. One day in 1906, the acid-tongued Mamie made some critical comments about Mrs Harriman at a ladies' tea at Crossways, the vast Fish 'cottage' on Bellevue Avenue – and Mrs Harriman overheard them.

She told her husband, and war to the knife was declared. 'I'll make those people suffer!' he told her. He laid his plans carefully; the most crucial step was the suborning of Fish's chief ally in his own company, a man whom he had raised up and befriended. At the board meeting a few days later, Stuyvesant Fish's protégé launched his attack. Fish, a big, powerful man who never wasted words, sat there stunned for a moment, then swung round and with one blow of his fist felled the man to the floor. But although the meeting was sympathetic he found himself no longer president of the Illinois Central.

Her defeat did not stop Mrs Fish exercising her sharp and often cruel wit even against those she counted as friends. She even stood up to the formidable Alva, a close confidante, when

Alva accused her of telling all their friends that she, Alva, looked like a frog. 'No, no!' cried Mamie, 'not a frog! A toad, my pet, a toad.'

No one was repelled more firmly than New York's Jews (though later, gradually, the ban was lifted). Although husbands did business with them, often lunched with them, regarded many as friends and frequently begged their wives to entertain a favoured Jewish friend or colleague, the answer was invariably No. And as New York society was run entirely by women, and no New Yorker dared stand up to his wife, No it was. 'These women are never crossed, never made to obey,' said the (American) author Price Collier, adding that though American men were not easily bullied by other men, they were entirely subordinate to their women. Because his wife Grace thought showers unsmart, Cornelius Vanderbilt III, who preferred them to baths, was not allowed one in any of the bathrooms in their home (which, naturally, he had paid for), so had to go to his club when he wanted one.

The extravagant party-giving rose to a final crescendo at the turn of the century; and ended by causing such public revulsion that several of the party-givers either left for Europe or spent more time abroad. This kind of needless ostentation was also a sign that the reign of Mrs Astor was drawing to a close and that she herself was losing her tight grip on the society that had for so long orbited her. In her heyday, she would never have countenanced this stepping over the line that separated limitless expenditure on whatever was considered the best from mere spending for frivolous spending's sake.

Already the would-be successors to her throne were jostling for position, with Caroline Astor and Mrs William Waldorf Astor as the two main contenders. When The Saunterer began denying that there was a rift in the Astor family but concluded 'that the words "In peace, prepare for war" just about covers the case', everyone knew that the battle would soon reach a climax.

Though William was desperate for Mamie to outdo Caroline

with dinners, parties and general entertainment, she was a gentler personality and did not have the stomach for such a fight. William on his own was unable to snatch the crown from Caroline, even when he had his own huge house in New York, next door to hers, pulled down and the Waldorf Hotel built on its site in his efforts to dislodge her. Caroline was indeed so infuriated and upset by this that she moved away from the neighbourhood; but nothing seemed to shake her grip on the social world and eventually, in 1891, William Waldorf gave up the struggle and moved with his family to England.

By now Newport had split into a series of cliques, presided over by the ruling queens, to offend whom was social disaster but who were united in their determination to reinforce the barriers. At the same time too many parties, too little exercise, too much rich food and little else to think about meant that quarrels often broke out between them. Underlying these squabbles was an intense rivalry as to who would become the next reigning monarch, all contenders prepared to battle for it down to their husbands' last dollar.

Eventually, it fell to Grace Vanderbilt, wife of Cornelius Vanderbilt III and a woman to whom the social life was all. She began her campaign with her great Fête des Roses, in August 1902. 'There was a harvest moon hanging low in the sky,' wrote her son Cornelius, 'fireworks cascaded down in gold and silver, airy lamps lit the velvety lawns and red roses were everywhere, their fragrance drifting through the house and filling the night air.' Grace had had a theatre constructed in the grounds and hired the entire cast and sets of *Red Rose Inn* from New York for two nights, perforce closing the theatre in New York for forty-eight hours.

It was fairyland, a glittering, glamorous confection of delights. All that was lacking was content. As Price Collier, accustomed to English drawing rooms where politicians, writers, leading ecclesiastics, diplomats and distinguished soldiers would be entertained by the great hostesses, asked: '[But] where were the statesmen, the soldiers, the men of letters, the men who are making America move, so to speak? . . . The best society of Europe is success enjoying an idle hour or so; the best society here is idleness enjoying its success.'

Grace was well equipped for the position she aimed to occupy. Her house at 640 Fifth Avenue was huge, run by thirty-three servants imported from abroad; her wardrobe was immense. She had 500 pairs of shoes, wore dresses by Worth and Paquin, some so heavy with gems that they could not be hung up but lay on twelve-foot shelves; there was a queen's ransom of jewels, said to be worth more than $1 million – one was a rose the size of a peony made entirely from platinum and diamonds. 'I hear that all the Italian papers speak of me and my jewels,' she wrote to her sister May Goelet. 'I wore my tiara, my emerald collar, my pearls with the emerald piece Belle gave me, my diamond fringe [this was three inches long and hung from shoulder to shoulder] across the front of my gown (they admire that extravagantly) and my other emerald piece, all this with my yellow and silver gown looked very pretty.'

She was thirty-two when she brought off the stunning coup that outflanked all her rivals and even Mrs Astor herself. New York, in the winter of 1902, was abuzz with the news that Prince Henry of Prussia, the forty-year-old popular younger brother of the German Kaiser, would be paying the city a visit – and who would have the honour of entertaining him? Everyone, herself included, believed that it would be Mrs Astor, who had even postponed going abroad in this confident expectation.

But no, it turned out to be Grace Vanderbilt, although the manoeuvre that brought this about remained unknown for years. She had quietly put herself forward in the most discreet and intelligent of ways, so that if she succeeded her success would appear to have come out of the blue and if she had failed there would been no trace of her gambit.

She had written a charming letter to the German Ambassador in Washington asking him for his advice. She had, she told him, been very kindly treated by the imperial family in Potsdam some years earlier when she had been the guest of her sister, and she would like to show her appreciation. What did the Ambassador think was the best way of doing this? When the Ambassador cabled the Emperor with the contents of the letter, Kaiser Wilhelm was delighted – he remembered Grace, and the name Vanderbilt was an impressive one – and sent her a cablegram requesting her to ask his brother Prince Henry to dinner.

The shock wave travelled round New York: the snub to Mrs Astor was unprecedented, signalling the end of a reign of more than thirty years. This seismic event was summed up by *Town Topics* with its usual gleeful malice: 'Young Mrs Cornelius . . . has succeeded beyond cavil in establishing herself as the representative of the most powerful family in America. Mrs Astor will sail before the dinner takes place.'

Finally came the event that brought the whole era to a close: the Bradley-Martin ball. With this, the river of gold burst its banks and flooded the plain – and after it had receded, life was never the same again. Conspicuous consumption, although not dead, became more discreet; instead of awestruck reportage of the breaking of each successive record of high spending, there was a new note of condemnation of excess, instead of admiration, obloquy.

At the time this huge expenditure on a night's frivolity was contemplated, life had seldom been worse for the city's poor. The Panic of 1893 still held its grip, unemployment was high and the economy low and stagnant. During these years banks closed, railroads failed, unemployment rose sharply (to 25 per cent in New York) and pitiful tales of poverty abounded. Soup kitchens opened, people chopped wood, broke rocks and sewed in exchange for food and sometimes women resorted to prostitution in order to feed their families. As miners were laid off, there were strikes: they would 'submit no longer to the cruel, heartless and inhuman conditions laid on them by unscrupulous employers,' said the president of the United Mine Workers of Illinois. The contrast with the life of the gilded few could not have been greater.

Although most people believed that the proposed ball was a further effort to outdo Alva Belmont, whose position since her remarriage had become unassailable, Cornelia Bradley-Martin always declared that her decision to give it was because she was so appalled by the sufferings of the poor that she had decided to do something about it (the Bradley-Martins were known for their generosity as landlords at Bal Macaan). The original idea, put forward by Bradley, was a concert. As his brother Frederick recorded, Cornelia Bradley-Martin disagreed. 'Pray, what good will that do?' she asked. 'No, I've a far better idea.'

Her inspiration was not a huge donation to some relief fund but a plan to give a costume ball; this would, she said, raise everyone's spirits as well as giving work to the florists, cooks, dressmakers, extra staff and food suppliers who would be involved. To keep this money within the US, the 1,200 invitations were despatched later than normal, so that no one had time to send to Europe – in particular, the House of Worth – for some spectacular creation.

From the moment the ball was rumoured, little else was spoken of. The Church weighed in heavily, some vicars – notably of the richer New York churches – supporting the Bradley-Martins ('Shots from the Pulpit' was how the press described this public argument), by saying that the ball and other social functions were a good thing in general because of the money distributed among poor people in consequence; others argued fiercely against it. 'With all the people who have to lie awake nights contriving to spend their time and money, and all the others who lie awake wondering how they may get food, there is danger in the air,' said the Rev. Dr Madison Peters bluntly. 'All history teaches us that the concentration of wealth is the forerunner of social upheaval . . . the situation is more serious than many suppose.'

The *New York Times* speculated on the costumes to be worn. 'Among the ladies, the preference will, no doubt, be given to those parts that can be dressed with diamonds. What is the use of owning, as New York is said to do, a thousand millions of dollars in precious stones if such an opportunity of showing them is not to be turned to the best account.' They were right.

The Bradley-Martins' legendary 'monument to vanity', as the *New York World* put it, took place on 10 February 1897, at the Waldorf Hotel on the corner of Fifth Avenue and 33rd Street.

Fifth Avenue and both sides of 33rd Street between Fifth Avenue and Broadway were cordoned off by the police before the arrival time of 10.00 p.m. and after. This did not prevent a massive traffic jam of horses and carriages in nearby blocks, complicated by the decision of many of the Bradley-Martins' guests to stop en route in order to have their photographs in costume taken at Gilbert's Studio at Fifth Avenue and 35th Street (Gilbert's wisely remained open all night to encourage business). Snow and ice added to the difficulties.

When the guests finally arrived at the Waldorf – the ball was held on its first floor – they found a scene reminiscent of Versailles. As they entered, a huge mirror directly ahead, framed with roses, reflected in an endless perspective the exquisite silks, satins and velvets of the sixteenth-, seventeenth- and eighteenth-century costumes and the profusion of jewels that were the order of the night. Even the waiters wore tights and powdered wigs.

Although some of the guests came as Egyptian princesses and Japanese noblemen, Pocahontas and George Washington, most paid tribute to the French court, from Madame de Pompadour to the Sun King. Far and away the most popular costume for women, though, was Marie Antoinette: fifty replicas of the doomed queen attended that night. J. P. Morgan was dressed as Molière; his niece, Miss Pierpont Morgan, came as Queen Louise of Prussia, John Jacob Astor was Henry of Navarre – his mother, Caroline, one of the Marie Antoinettes, wore a gown adorned with $250,000 worth of jewels. Dealers in antiques and fine jewellery had been cleaned out of old buckles, snuff boxes, lorgnettes, diamond- or pearl-studded girdles and rings.

There were eighty-six people, said the *New York World*, whose total wealth was 'more than men could grasp', with a dozen worth more than $10 million. Oliver Belmont wore a suit of inlaid gold armour valued at $10,000; Mrs Astor wore her famous diamond tiara worth $200,000, while the jewels of Cornelia Bradley-Martin herself, worth an estimated $50,000, were probably the most noticeable of all.

Cornelia, now a plump matron with a bow mouth, a generous bosom and incipient jowls, was an unlikely Mary Queen of Scots in a black velvet dress with white collar and a twenty-foot train of black velvet over a white satin underskirt. Against this chaste background she looked like a walking display cabinet. Her dress, embroidered with gold thread and hung with pearls, was adorned with clusters of diamond grapes ordered for Louis XIV; on her right shoulder was a quatrefoil pendant of rubies and diamonds in addition to a giant diamond brooch and the staggering ruby necklace that had belonged to Marie Antoinette.* Her toilette did not escape the eye of The Saunterer: 'Mrs Bradley-Martin was so ablaze with diamonds from head to foot that she looked like a dumpy lighthouse.'

The ball received immense press coverage, thanks to the expansion of society pages during the 1890s: as the rich grew ever richer and more ostentatious, so their doings were covered more fully by a growing breed of society columnists who became names in their own right, like the renowned Ivy Ross, who wrote the *New York Journal*'s famous Cholly Knickerbocker column.

Most of what was said was scathingly critical. Even for a country that had grown as used to, and admiring of, the making of money as America, this outpouring of almost $400,000 on a single night's entertainment for 800-odd people was too much. The country was still in a depression, with all its social consequences, and the Bradley-Martin ball, with its final total cost of $369,000 (over £7 million today), seemed to have taken the cult of limitless wealth to a new height – or rather, low.

Thus the remonstrances before the ball were as nothing to the flood of reproaches afterwards. One popular commentator, William Cowper Brann, described it as 'one more festering sore on the syphilitic body social'. All over the country newspapers wrote of it in blistering terms, ministers preached sermons on its scandalous extravagance – and the New York City authorities decided that if the Bradley-Martins could afford such luxurious entertainment they could and should pay increased property taxes. Promptly, they set about the necessary first step of proving

---

* She had bought both the grapes and the necklace from the sale of the French crown jewels in May 1887.

that the Bradley-Martins were residents of New York rather than Bal Macaan.

In vain did Bradley Martin testify that the lease of the 46,000-acre Bal Macaan estate, on which the castle was situated, still had three years to run. In vain did he swear that he always went to Scotland about the first week in August and stayed there until December, then he generally travelled on the Continent until the following June, or until it was time to go back to Bal Macaan. In vain did he swear that he was a subject of Great Britain, that his visits to the US never lasted more than three months and that he came to New York only about once in two years. None of this weighed a jot with the Supreme Court.

When asked if he was a member of many New York clubs and he replied that he was a member of the Metropolitan, Union, Downtown and Tuxedo Clubs and was a life member of the Knickerbocker ('I appear as a resident of several clubs because they have no non-resident list') and he still kept a pew in Grace Church, this must have appeared to the judiciary as a handsome piece of evidence. And when he replied: 'New York, of course, New York,' when asked where was the centre of his transactions, it was the clincher.

'It appears,' concluded the Supreme Court happily, 'that he still retains his citizenship and that there has been no change in his habits of life since 1882.' They doubled the assessed value of the Bradley-Martin mansion on West 20th Street, meaning that extra taxes* of $200,000 on each of the Martins' personal properties had to be paid.

On the Martins, the effect of the obloquy the ball had drawn on them and, no doubt, the determination of the Supreme Court to penalise their extravagance was such that they decided to sell their house in New York and settle in London for good.

In May 1899, the Martins said farewell to New York with a feast of huge splendour that was, crucially, not large enough to attract the same degree of disapproving attention. In any case,

* The War Revenue Act of 1898, to raise money for the Spanish–American War, introduced taxes on a wide range of goods and services.

they had taken care to arrange their passage to England for the following day. The *New York World* estimated that 90 per cent of the men present possessed personal fortunes of $5 million or more. The food was exquisite and, in a nice touch, the most popular piece in the accompanying music was 'If You Haint Got No Money You Needn't Come 'Round'. The price per person of this simple farewell was roughly $116,000.

It was time for the merry-go-round to stop.

CHAPTER 18

It Was All Too Much

Soon the procession of heiresses trooping across the Atlantic would also cease. So many of these marriages turned out unhappily – for the girls – that those at home began to think twice about the benefits offered by strawberry leaves. 'She never dreams that the coronet usually turns into brass and signifies nothing but a decadent race, profligate, immoral, poverty-stricken, and that instead of a crown of glory it will only be a weight of shame on her head to crush her to the earth in humiliation and despair,' wrote one New York vicar, summing up the American view of the tide of cash-for-coronet marriages, as they were popularly known. Although the majority of the marriages he cited involved European nobility, there were enough in Britain to serve as a warning.

After the first glamour had worn off, life in England, with its wretched climate, its lack of home comforts, the isolation of country life and a husband who spent the new wife's money while going his own way resulted in disillusionment, misery and – among the more spirited – a determination somehow to escape. Lady William Bagot, who had left her husband several times, finally separated; Sarah Stokes (of New York), who had married Baron Halkett, bringing $5 million, was divorced; as were Lord and Lady Rosslyn (Anna Robinson), while the divorced Lady Francis Hope (the actress May Yohé) 'ex-musical-comedy star and ex-duchess-presumptive, is, to earn her daily bread, reduced almost to the lowest depths. She is now giving nightly a song and dance turn in a cheap music hall in Sacramento,' reported the *Chicago Sunday Sun* with relish.

Better known still were three maritally unhappy American duchesses: Consuelo Marlborough, Consuelo Yznaga and her daughter-in-law Helena Zimmerman.

The archetype of these unions so fulminated against by the American press – indigent European nobleman cynically weds innocent American heiress to acquire her huge dowry – was probably that of the marriage of Alice Thaw and the Earl of Yarmouth, heir to the Marquess of Hertford. So innocent was Alice that she did not realise her future husband was homosexual; so determined was he to get hold of her money that the actual marriage ceremony was delayed by forty-five minutes as he negotiated for this while fielding a summons for debt.

Alice was one of the ten children of a Pittsburgh iron millionaire who had left each of them $1 million, with more to come from her even richer mother. She had met Lord Yarmouth through her half-brother, Harry Thaw. Yarmouth was known as 'one of the poorest peers in England',* but Alice was clearly determined to become a countess although many of her family disapproved of her marriage. They married in Pittsburgh and her mother, equally keen on the wedding, helped to organise a settlement of $1 million on the couple, plus an annual income that also amounted to $100,000.

The couple went to London, where Alice was presented, but her new life lasted a mere three years, when, unsurprisingly, the marriage was annulled on grounds of non-consummation. Fortunately for Alice, most of her money was securely in trust, although even when she was safely back in America she continued to pay Lord Yarmouth an annual income of $30,000 – it is thought as a quid pro quo for not contesting the divorce.

The story of Frances ('Fanny') Ellen Work, who would become the great-grandmother of Diana Princess of Wales, and the Hon.

* According to the *Portsmouth Herald* of 3 March 1903.

James Boothby Burke Roche is even more poignant, especially as her father had made his views clear.

'I am an American to my backbone,' he had declared. 'Therefore I have only contempt for these helpless, hopeless, lifeless men that cross the ocean to carry off the very flower of our womanhood. When they win our girls they use them, humble them and dishonour them, and then cast them aside for actresses or adventuresses of their own real class. If I had anything to say about the matter I'd make an international marriage a hanging offence.'

Franklin Work had built up his fortune in traditionally American fashion, starting from very little and working his way up, as he did so becoming an expert carriage-driver and owner of some of the finest trotting horses in the US. Through this sport, he met the legendary Commodore Vanderbilt, whose protégé he became – and increased his fortune even more. Fanny, his favourite daughter and set to inherit much of his money, was equally fond of horses. During her debutante seasons in New York she was much admired for her beauty, style and intelligence. She spent lavishly, enjoying parties and the excitement of being admired in beautiful clothes. At the same time, she was very well read, could speak French fluently and took a great interest in paintings and furniture.

She met James ('Jim') Roche for the first time when he spent a few days in New York. Jim was tall, good-looking, with good skin, dark eyes, a dark moustache, a sizeable dollop of Irish charm and, as his older brother then had no sons, heir presumptive to the barony of Fermoy.

Though Fanny could not know it, Jim was broke. His family's Irish estates had been gambled away, he was a younger son and he led a life far beyond what he could actually afford, scattering debts everywhere. He had gone to America with his great friend Moreton Frewen, already known as 'Mortal Ruin' for his ability to encourage his friends to invest in reckless financial schemes that failed, thus losing their money. Jim and Frewen, who was married to Clara, the eldest Jerome sister, had been friends since their days at Cambridge, where they had spent most of their time in hard riding to hounds and enjoying themselves.

When Moreton asked Jim to stay at his cattle ranch in

Wyoming, Jim accepted with alacrity, partly to try and make a fortune, partly for the opportunities of shooting, riding and general adventure in tough, open-air conditions. They took with them letters of introduction to many of the smartest families in New York, where they spent a few weeks after arrival. It was here that Jim first met the beautiful Fanny, but the friendship did not ripen until his second visit to the US.

In Fanny he saw a way out of his financial problems and she, for her part, was determined to marry the glamorous Jim although under no illusions as to her father's reactions. Their wedding took place in Christ Church, New York City, in September 1880, and although he disapproved, and indeed disinherited her, her father did, however, make her an allowance of $7,000 a year. The couple set sail for England almost at once, leaving Franklin – who had restrained himself after his daughter's wedding – to thunder after another similar one:

'It's time this international marrying came to a stop for our American girls are ruining our country by it. As fast as honourable hardworking men can earn their money their daughters take it and take it across the ocean. And for what? For the purpose of a title and the privilege of paying the debts of so-called noblemen.'

It was a true prophecy in Fanny's case. They set up house in London where Fanny, through the Jerome sisters and other American friends who had married into the peerage, was quickly adopted into 'society'; and gave birth first to two daughters,* then twin sons. After their arrival, her father increased her allowance to $12,000 a year – Fanny, as her father well knew, had been brought up to be a big spender.

Fanny quickly found that Jim was a philanderer and, what was almost worse, a compulsive gambler, meaning that even the social position to which she had aspired was compromised: she was cut by many in English society because Jim did not pay his gambling debts (where a tailor could be kept waiting for years, gambling debts were considered 'debts of honour' and had to be settled as quickly as possible). Appeals for more money, from

* The eldest died soon after birth.

Fanny, from her husband, and even from his mother, poured across the Atlantic. When Jim squandered $100,000 in one year, Franklin grew tired of subsidising these excesses and, in his own words, 'stopped pouring money down a rat hole'.

Finally, six years after her wedding and with their furniture in the hands of bailiffs, Fanny returned to New York in December 1886 with her tail between her legs. She took her daughter Cynthia with her – Jim refused to let her take the two boys, largely to keep a hold on her and as a bargaining counter for more money. In New York, Franklin agreed to reinstate her in his will, on condition that she divorced her husband and never returned to Europe. She agreed, taking up her American social life again, and initiating proceedings for an English divorce (American divorces were not then recognised in England). Spurred by this, Jim arrived in the spring of 1887 with the two boys, in an effort to extract more money from his father-in-law. With none forthcoming, he dumped the children on the doorstep of the Work mansion in fashionable East 26th Street and left.

The divorce, headlined in newspapers all over America, eventually took place in 1891 in Delaware. *Town Topics* was heartily on Fanny's side, The Saunterer expressing himself freely. 'Mrs Burke-Roche demands release from a husband she neither loves nor respects. The church and the law oppose her, and do all in their power to drive her into a state of desperation when sin would become easy and disgrace a natural consequence. If she is strong-minded, calm, and sensible, she will continue to fight the bitter battle to the end.'

She did, but during it, Jim's efforts to win money for himself infuriated Franklin. 'I have supported that man until I had to decline to pay his debts,' he told one newspaper. 'He wrote to me himself. He begged me to come to his assistance. He asked me to save him from bankruptcy. I helped him until I got tired. I deemed it wrong to assist him further after his wife and children had come to this country . . . I have letters from his mother where she begs me to save her son. Here I have telegrams and letters written by Roche both to me and my daughter.'

Eventually Fanny, who also seemed to have little idea of the value of money, left her father's house after quarrels with him over her extravagance, going to live at Two-Mile Corner Farm, given to her by her father and only a few miles from Newport, where he had a huge house, Elm Court, over which she presided. With public sympathy on her side, she led a lively social life.

This happy state was brought to an end by history repeating itself. Fanny was taught coach-driving (she became the first woman to drive a four-in-hand in Central Park) by a professional whip who went under the name of Count Aurel Batonyi (his real name, it later emerged, was Cohen). She fell in love with him and they married in 1903. Knowing what her father's reaction would be to another 'foreign' marriage, she kept her marriage completely secret from everyone, until a year later, only hours before they embarked for a trip to Europe, she told her father.

For the eighty-seven-year-old Franklin this was the last straw: he cut off her huge allowance – never less than $5,000 a month – and denied her the use of Elm Court, putting it on the market immediately. 'She is nothing more to me,' he said wearily. 'I don't know where they have gone; they will never come here.'

Where they went was to the farm near Newport. Here she saw some of her friends, although others cut her ('Passed Faxon in Bellevue Avenue. Did not bow'). Aurel was not accepted at all. Without her income – a bitter blow for one whose clothes and spending habits were part of her identity – and threatened by her father that her children would suffer in the future if she persisted in this marriage, Fanny finally caved in. Aurel was despatched and, after various ups and downs, her father reinstated her again and restored her generous allowance.

He continued to look after her children, giving them expensive educations, and when he died in 1911, aged ninety-two, left the twin boys, Maurice and Frank, huge fortunes – on condition they became American citizens and stayed in the US for the rest of their lives.

But the boys, with their romantic Irish heritage and their paternal roots overseas, did not see why they should allow a dead man to dictate to them as he had in life. After thinking things over, they decided to contest this clause of the will. As none of the other beneficiaries minded in the slightest if they travelled to Europe, or were unhappy about the elder twin inheriting his father's title, their case was successful. Maurice, who did not marry until he was forty-six, by which time he had become a close friend of the Duke of York, was granted a lease for Park House on the Sandringham estate. Here, no doubt, his small granddaughter Diana had her first sight of Prince Charles.

Some marriages were, of course, extremely happy, notably those where the bride was in her mid-twenties rather than her teens and where love, rather than ambition, had played a part. But adapting to a life so different in climate, attitudes, behaviour and general mores from the one they had known at home was a challenge that had faced all the American girls who married into the peerage.

Some surmounted it by simply winning over their in-laws by their general charm in the face of stiff opposition. One was Leonie Leslie, whose suitor, John Leslie, followed her to America and whose family violently disapproved of the match. 'Once married I am sure they will all like her,' wrote Mrs Jerome to her middle daughter, Jennie, in August 1884. 'She is such a nice clever kind-hearted girl. And will do all she can to make Jack happy & please his family.'

His father's uncompromising letter quickly followed these sentiments. 'Dear Sir, I believe my Son has sailed for America with the expressed intention of offering marriage to your daughter,' wrote Sir John Leslie to Leonard Jerome, in a warning shot across the bows that September. 'As he is acting entirely in opposition to my desire & without my approval in the course he has taken, I think you ought to know that I am in absolute possession of my estates. I remain faithfully yours.' On arrival, Jack Leslie quickly won over Mrs Jerome, who was soon reassuringly on his side.

A month later, Jack Leslie and Leonie Jerome were married – and went on to become favourites of both families, so that a year later Randolph was able to write to Jennie: 'I am truly delighted at Leonie having got over all her troubles,' adding, 'the son and heir is a great thing & must remove all remaining bad feelings in the Leslie bosom.'

Maud Burke, who quickly found that she had little in common with her fox-hunting husband, was one who managed to rebuild her life by discovering her talents as a hostess. At the start of her marriage she had tried to adapt to Leicestershire life, occasionally going out hunting with her husband to please him – though delighted when pregnancy gave her the excuse to stop – then on winter days standing listlessly looking out of the window at the mud, rain, snow and frost of the British winter, sometimes restlessly readjusting the furniture in the rooms she was gradually making prettier and more inviting. After approval by the Prince of Wales gave her social cachet she seized her chance and launched herself as a hostess, eventually moving to London and leading a life on her own.

Other girls tackled their transplanting with a kind of camouflage, adopting the customs, however eccentric they might have thought them, that they had seen in grand houses. One who did this, after a shaky start, was Katharine McVickar, the daughter of a commodore in the US Navy. She had eloped almost on sight with the 5th Baron Grantley in 1879, while being already married to his cousin. The startled and injured Charles Norton brought a divorce action and, as soon as it was absolute, Lord Grantley married Katharine, a mere week before their eldest child was born.

'Later,' wrote their son Richard (the 6th Baron), 'I continually urged my father to permit me to remove the evidence of this race with time from Burke's Peerage. He took the view, however, that nobody read that work except old-fashioned domestic servants, and said he did not care about their opinion anyway.'

Katharine quickly took to life as a peeress. 'I can remember being summoned to tea with my mother as a mite of four years,' wrote Richard Grantley. '[It was] a procedure of almost Germanic complexity. My nurse would lead me to the end of the picture gallery, a cosy little apartment 150 feet long. At the end of this interminable walk I was taken over by a footman-in-waiting and handed to the senior footman, two rooms on. Then, one room from my dear mother's boudoir, I was passed to the butler, and finally announced by the Steward, a sort of super-butler, in the way that still prevails at Embassies.

'He would throw open the door of the boudoir and trumpet: "Mr Norton."

'Tea with Mother was not very jolly. My sisters would be sitting bolt upright and nearly as terrified as I was, in spite of being older and wiser. I was always made to address them as "Miss Joan", "Miss Eleanor", "Miss Winifred" and "Miss Katharine". Our portion was one thin sandwich . . . I scored, because I was always given a bonus of a single lump of sugar, but only if I sucked it silently and did not crunch "vulgarly", as Mother used to say.'

Cornelia Craven, a bride at sixteen, managed her successful marriage through total immersion in her husband's way of life – aided by the fact that she had largely grown up in Scotland and that for much of the time her parents were nearby. As she grew older she became grander: once, when an elderly cousin whom she was entertaining to luncheon told her that he was over on business, she responded: 'How unfortunate you had to go into trade.' Living at Coombe Abbey in Warwickshire, where she was loved and respected, she took a close personal interest in the villagers' lives – to the extent that if a villager failed to appear in church on Sunday morning she would call round in her carriage and pair to find out why. If an employee was ill she provided medical attention, she distributed hampers at Christmas and (after she was widowed) financed a Christmas party and conjuror for the children in the village hall.

But it took Mary Curzon to sum up the more general view in a letter to her father. 'Just tell the dear girls once a month so they won't forget it never never never to marry away from home unless they find a George as it is always a sorrow to be an alien – and 50 years in a new country never alters your nationality and I shall never be an Englishwoman in feeling or character and oh! the unhappiness I see around me here in England amongst American women.'

EPILOGUE

By the end of 1902 the all-powerful Mrs Astor had fallen and there was a new queen of society, Grace Vanderbilt. Grace ruled, as ever, by insisting on the self-perpetuating mores of the society she had always known, relishing the routines of its seasons and days, the maintenance of the small but telling differentials between 'us' and 'them'.

But slowly, society itself was changing. Even in New York, the barriers were coming down – or rather, were being trampled underfoot by people who were hardly aware of them. No longer was it necessary to marry your daughter off to a title in order to ensure yourself a back-door entry into society, as had earlier been the case; the passage of years had cleansed many earlier fortunes of their 'nouveau' connotation and the younger generation found itself an outcast no more. Besides, there were plenty of ways other than balls, the ritual of calling and the effort of changing your clothes several times a day to make your mark or occupy your days.

Ideas of freedom, of education and above all of female franchise were sweeping through the consciousness of both nations. Alva Vanderbilt, whose whole life had once been dedicated to rising to the top of the social pile, was now drawn into the suffrage movement, founding the Political Equality League in 1909 to get votes for suffrage-supporting senators. She campaigned, she wrote articles for newspapers, she donated large sums to the cause, she focused all her formidable energies and independence of spirit on this new goal. Anything further from her life as a Newport and New York socialite cannot be imagined (although she carried on dyeing her hair a Titian red until the end. 'I don't want to die with grey hair', she told a friend.' 'It's so depressing.')

Organisations like the National Consumers' League were campaigning against sweatshops, there was general condemnation of excess, and those at the top were concerning themselves more and more with less frivolous matters.

It was the same in England where, as Consuelo Marlborough commented, 'A purely social life has no appeal.' It was not a remark that one would have heard twenty years earlier.

Lady Warwick, King Edward VII's former favourite, joined the Social Democratic Federation in 1904, giving it large sums of money and supporting its campaign for free meals for schoolchildren, while the suffrage movement steadily increased its supporters. Liberal politicians were promising welfare reforms (carried out a few years later); various *grandes dames* – Americans among them – were founding village schools or orphanages.

American newspapers, increasingly influential as their readership grew, were reflecting the changed attitude of the times, almost unanimously condemning what they saw as profligate spending. The tone of awed respect with which the huge dinners and wilder excesses of the Gilded Age were recorded had given way to acidulous comment on what the sociologist Thorstein Veblen called 'conspicuous consumption'.* A particular cause of resentment was that so many good American dollars had left the land of the free to prop up failing British estates.

As early as 1895 the *Los Angeles Herald* had pointed out that 'A laboriously compiled list of all the marriages of American women to titled men for the past thirty-five years shows that at least $200 million have gone away from these shores in the period. Eighty per cent of this is represented in the marriages of the past six years.'

Thoughtfully, the paper listed the names of those who had, as

* In his book *The Theory of the Leisure Class*, published in 1899. The term refers to the buying of expensive items to display wealth and status rather than to meet any real need.

they put it, exchanged cash for coronets, together with the size of the dowry that each had brought with her.

The flower of young American womanhood absorbed this expression of the zeitgeist. No longer did they, or their mammas, stalk the coverts of Mayfair for lurking eligibles. Perhaps, too, the girls were warned off by the fate that befell so many of them – again, zestfully chronicled by their own newspapers.

What is striking, though, is the effect, out of all proportion to their numbers, of the American invasion, not only – though mainly – on the upper classes, but on Britain in general.

The repair and restoration of many superb houses, now open to the public, is down to them. Most notable, perhaps, was the effect Consuelo's millions had on Blenheim Palace: the refurbishment began even on the new bride's honeymoon – tapestries, paintings and furniture were bought in Europe to fill the gaps left by the various sales, the Marlborough gems were replaced and immediately on the couple's return the Duke began a comprehensive restoration and redecoration programme, with gilt boiseries (in imitation of Versailles), the moving of various rooms to upper floors and the employment of a famous French landscape artist to create a water garden and fountains. Indeed, even after their divorce the allowance the Duke had secured from the Vanderbilts enabled him to continue not only with the improvements to Blenheim but its very maintenance.

In keeping with this grandeur more servants were engaged, with a staff of fifty outside, including electricians for the newly installed electric wiring, a cricket professional for the estate cricket team, lodge-keepers in black coats with silver buttons and cockaded top hats and twelve gamekeepers in green velvet coats and black billycock hats.

The money brought by Adèle Beach Grant when she married the 7th Earl of Essex supported the estate in the early years of the twentieth century and allowed the Earl to continue to host lavish parties. Their seat, Cassiobury House, enjoyed a high-society profile at this time; in 1902 the Earl and Countess received both King Edward VII and the young Winston Churchill there.

The series of renovations at Coombe Abbey, the ancestral home of the Earl of Craven, begun the year of his marriage to Cornelia, suggests that without this influx of American money Coombe Abbey would have been lost. Her parents, the Bradley-Martins, described as 'angels of generosity' by their English friends, greatly improved the castle at Bal Macaan and built a hall for the local people on the estate (they in turn were so appreciative of what Bradley Martin did for them that they subscribed to the erection of an obelisk memorial to him on his death).

Mary Leiter used her father's money to help her husband, George Curzon, become the Viceroy of India; it also secured Tattersall Castle in Lincolnshire, Bodiam Castle in Sussex and Montacute House in Somerset for the National Trust. Jennie Churchill's older sister Clara, married to Moreton Frewen, turned the surroundings of their house, Brede Place, into a magical garden. The beautiful May Goelet, happily married to the serious-minded 8th Duke of Roxburghe, brought wonderful tapestries as well as a superb collection of French furniture to Floors in addition to her enormous $20 million dowry; William Waldorf Astor adorned Cliveden with superb paintings and sculptures from Italy.

Culturally, the American effect was great, although more subtle. The Americans' style and smartness made Englishwomen make more of an effort; their vitality and openness to the new let fresh air into what had become formalised lives. They were responsible for a number of 'firsts': Maud Burke put English opera on the map and Nancy Astor became England's first female Member of Parliament. And their descendants, from the amazing 20th Earl of Suffolk (son of Daisy Leiter and the 19th Earl), hero of numerous incredible wartime exploits, to Winston Churchill, perhaps our greatest Prime Minister, made an indelible mark on our history.

ACKNOWLEDGEMENTS

My first and greatest debt of gratitude is to Simon, Earl of Kerry, for his huge help in researching this book and for his thoughtful ideas that led to new discoveries.

I would also like to thank Robert Bard for his generosity in making available to me so much of his material about the earls of Essex, as well as Lord Essex himself; Nicola Cornick for all she told me about Cornelia Craven; Sir Christopher Cook for confirmation of the story of his great-great-grandfather's marriage to Tennessee Claflin; Ian Curteis for his help on the Grantleys; Dr Elizabeth Kehoe for so generously making all her notes on the Jerome sisters available to me; David Donaldson and Sir William Molesworth for the Molesworth letters I was kindly allowed to see; Lord Grantley for letting me see the memoir of his great-grandfather the sixth Lord Grantley; Richard Jay Hutto for his wonderful photographs and great help over the Craven family; Sarah Lutyens for letting me see the privately printed *Warren House Tales* featuring her great-great-grandmother Minnie Stevens; Marge McNinch for her invaluable research into the letters of Anna Robinson in the Hagley Museum and Library, Delaware; Gill Neal (formerly of the Wiltshire and Swindon History Centre) for her speed and helpfulness over the Lady de Grey correspondence; Christine Sapieha for her decipherings of some appalling handwriting; the Earl of Suffolk and Berkshire for telling me about his grandmother Daisy Leiter; Sir Charles and Lady Wolseley for their kind permission in letting me use the letters of Anna Murphy; and of course the wonderful staff of The London Library, who seem able to find anything. I am also very grateful to the Royal Archives for letting me see the letters between Mary Leiter and Queen Alexandra. My thanks go to Paul Friedman of the New York Public Library who produced some wonderful stuff for me.

I would also like to say how much I owe to Bea Hemming, who was my editor for so much of this book, to thank Linden Lawson for her copy-editing skills; and to express my gratitude to Alan Samson for his help and kindnesses and to thank Holly Harley and everyone at Weidenfeld & Nicolson who worked on it, and of course, Isobel Dixon, my agent and friend.

BIBLIOGRAPHY

Adburgham, Alison, *A Punch History of Manners and Modes, 1841–1940,* Hutchinson, 1961)

Airlie, Mabell, Countess of, *Thatched with Gold* (Hutchinson, 1962)

Armstrong, B. J., *A Norfolk Diary* (George G. Harrap, 1949)

Ashenburg, Katherine, *The Dirt on Clean* (North Point Press, 2007)

Auchincloss, Louis, *Maverick in Mauve: The Diary of Florence Adèle Sloane* (Doubleday & Co., 1983)

Balsan, Consuelo Vanderbilt, *The Glitter and the Gold* (Harper & Brothers, 1953)

Banks, Elizabeth L., *Campaigns of Curiosity: Journalistic Adventures of an American Girl in London* (University of Wisconsin Press, 2003)

Bibby, E. K., *Making the American Aristocracy: Women, Cultural Capital, and High Society in New York City, 1870–1900* (Digital Library and Archives, Virginia Polytechnic Institute and State University)

Blumenfeld, R. D., *R. D. B.'s Diary, 1887–1914* (William Heinemann, 1930)

Blunt, Wilfrid Scawen, *My Diaries* (William Heinemann, 1953)

Brandon, Ruth, *The Dollar Princesses* (Alfred A. Knopf, 1980)

Buchan, Alice, *A Scrap Screen* (Hamish Hamilton, 1979)

Burke Roche, Mary, *Call Me Maurice: The Life and Times of Lord Fermoy (1885–1955)* (ELSP, 2008)

Burnett, John (ed.), *Useful Toil* (Allen Lane, 1974)

Cahill, Kevin, *Who Owns Britain* (Canongate, 2001)

Camplin, Jamie, *The Rise of the Plutocrats: Wealth and Power in Edwardian England* (Constable, 1978)

Cardigan and Lancastre, Countess of, *My Recollections* (Eveleigh Nash, 1909)

Carette, Madame, *My Mistress, the Empress Eugénie, or, Court Life at*

the Tuileries (Dean & Son, 1889)
Collier, Price, *America and the Americans from a French Point of View* (William Heinemann, 1897)
Cooper, Nicholas, *The Opulent Eye: Late Victorian and Edwardian Taste in Interior Design* (Architectural Press, 1976)
Cowles, Virginia, *Edward VII and his Circle* (Hamish Hamilton, 1956)
Crook, J. Mordaunt, *The Rise of the Nouveaux Riches* (John Murray, 1999)
Dakers, Caroline, *Clouds: The Biography of a Country House* (Yale University Press, 1993)
Darwin, M. F., *One Moral Standard for All* (Caulon Press, 191–?)
Davidoff, Leonore, *The Best Circles: Society, Etiquette and the Season* (Croom Helm, 1973)
De Castellane, Boni, *How I Discovered America: Confessions of the Marquis Boni de Castellane* (Alfred A. Knopf, 1924)
Decies, Lady, *King Lehr and the Gilded Age* (J. B. Lippincott, 1935)
De La Haye, Amy, and Mendes, Valerie D., *The House of Worth: Portrait of an Archive* (V & A Publishing, 2014)
De Marly, Diana, *Worth: Father of Haute Couture* (Elm Tree Books, 1980)
Eliot, Elizabeth, *They All Married Well* (Cassell, 1960)
Escott, T. H. S:, *Society in London* (Chatto & Windus, 1885)
Fane, Lady Augusta, *Chit-chat* (Thornton Butterworth, 1926)
Fielding, Daphne, *Emerald and Nancy* (Eyre & Spottiswoode, 1968)
Frewen, Moreton, *Melton Mowbray and Other Memories* (Herbert Jenkins, 1926)
Gabin, Jane S., *American Women in Gilded Age London* (University Press of Florida, 2006)
Gere, Charlotte, and Rudoe, Judy, *Jewellery in the Age of Queen Victoria* (The British Museum Press, 2010)
Glyn, Elinor, *Romantic Adventure* (Ivor Nicholson & Watson, 1936)
Good, V. K. L., *The Warren House Tales: A Social History since 1865* (Third Millennium Publishing, 2013)
Gordon, Lois, *Nancy Cunard: Heiress, Muse, Political Idealist* (Columbia University Press, 2007)
Hickman, Katie, *Courtesans* (HarperCollins, 2003)
Horn, Pamela, *Labouring Life in the Victorian Countryside* (Gill & Macmillan, 1976)

Horn, Pamela, *High Society: The English Social Élite, 1880–1914* (Alan Sutton, 1992)
Hoyt, Edwin P., *The Vanderbilts and their Fortunes* (Frederick Muller, 1963)
Hoyt, Edwin P., *The Goulds: A Social History* (Weybright & Talley, 1969)
Hutto, Richard Jay, *Crowning Glory* (Henchard Press, 2007)
Jackson, Lee, *Dirty Old London: The Victorian Fight Against Filth* (Yale University Press, 2014)
Kaplan, Justin, *When the Astors Owned New York* (Viking, 2006)
King, Greg, *The Court of Mrs Astor in Gilded Age New York* (Wiley, 2009)
Johnston, Johanna, *Mrs Satan: The Incredible Saga of Victoria C. Woodhull* (Macmillan, 1967)
Lambert, Angela, *Unquiet Souls* (Macmillan, 1984)
Ledoux, Kate Reid, *Ocean Notes and Foreign Travel for Ladies* (printed by J. W. Pratt, 1878)
Lee, Celia and John, *The Churchills: A Family Portrait* (Palgrave Macmillan, 2010)
Leslie, Anita, *Jennie: The Life of Lady Randolph Churchill* (Hutchinson, 1969)
Logan, Andy, *The Man Who Robbed the Robber Barons* (W. W. Norton, 1965)
Lucy, Mary Elizabeth, *Mistress of Charlecote* (Victor Gollancz, 1983)
Lutyens, Lady Emily, *A Blessed Girl: Memoirs of a Victorian Girlhood, 1887–96* (Rupert Hart-Davis, 1954)
McAllister, Ward, *Society As I Have Found It* (Cassell, 1890)
McLaren, Angus, *Birth Control in Nineteenth-Century England* (Croom Helm, 1978)
MacPherson, Myra, *The Scarlet Sisters* (Twelve, 2014)
Mackenzie Stuart, Amanda, *Consuelo and Alva* (HarperCollins, 2005)
Mallet, Victor (ed.), *Life with Queen Victoria: Marie Mallet's Letters from Court 1887–1901* (John Murray, 1968)
Moore, George (ed. Rupert Hart-Davis), *Letters to Lady Cunard, 1895–1933* (Rupert Hart-Davis, 1957)
Monkswell, Lady Mary (ed. Hon. E. C. F. Collier), *A Victorian Diarist* (John
Murray, 1944)

Murphy, Sophia, *The Duchess of Devonshire's Ball* (Sidgwick & Jackson, 1984)
Ponsonby, Sir Frederick, *Recollections of Three Reigns* (Eyre & Spottiswoode, 1951)
Renehan, Edward J., *Commodore: The Life of Cornelius Vanderbilt* (Basic Books, 2007)
Reynolds, K. D., *Aristocratic Women and Political Society in Victorian Britain* (Clarendon Press, Oxford 1998)
Ribblesdale, Lady Emma, *Letters and Diaries* (The Chiswick Press, privately printed, 1930)
Richards, J. M., *With John Bull and Jonathan* (T. Werner Laurie, 1905)
St George, Andrew, *The Descent of Manners* (Chatto & Windus, 1993)
Scarisbrick, Diana, *Ancestral Jewels* (André Deutsch, 1989)
Sewell, Lt-Col. J. P. C. (ed.), *Personal Letters of King Edward VII* (Hutchinson & Co., 1931)
Smalley, George W., *London Letters, Volume II* (Macmillan & Co., 1890)
Smith, Joseph Aubin, *Reminiscences of Saratoga; or, Twelve Seasons at the 'States'* (Library of the University of California, 1897)
Steinbach, Susie L., *Understanding the Victorians: Politics, Culture and Society in Nineteenth-Century Britain* (Routledge, 2012)
Strange, Michael, *Who Tells Me True* (Charles Scribner's Sons, 1940)
Taylor, Lou, *Mourning Dress* (George Allen & Unwin, 1983)
Titled Americans: The Real Heiresses' Guide to Marrying an Aristocrat (The Hand Book Library, 1890)
Tweedsmuir, Susan, *The Lilac and the Rose* (Gerald Duckworth, 1952)
Vanderbilt Jnr, Cornelius, *The Vanderbilt Feud* (Hutchinson, 1957)
Walkley, Christine and Foster, Vanda, *Crinolines and Crimping Irons: Victorian Clothes, How They Were Cleaned and Cared For* (Peter Owen, 1978)
Warren, Arthur, *London Days* (Little, Brown & Co., 1920)
Wharton, Edith, *The Age of Innocence* (D. Appleton & Co, 1920)
Wharton, Edith, *A Backward Glance* (D. Appleton-Century, 1934)
Wharton, Edith, *The Buccaneers* (Penguin Books, 1993)
Wilson, A. N., *Victoria: A Life* (Atlantic Books, 2014)
Wood, Mary and Alan, *Silver Spoon: The Memoirs of Lord Grantley,* (Hutchinson, 1954)

Manuscript Sources

'Alva E. Belmont, a Forgotten Feminist', PhD thesis of Peter Geidel, Columbia University, 1993.

New York Historical Society holds Log Book and Visitors' Book of the *Valiant*, saying who sailed on her, parties etc.

'New York Has a Ball: The Bradley Martin Extravaganza', by Robert Muccigrosso, *New York History*, Vol. 75, No. 3 (July 1994), pp. 297–320, published by New York State Historical Association.

Iris Capell's *Myself When Young and Other Writings* is a collection put together by her friends and printed by D. G. Seldon Printing, Ltd.

Certain of the Coventry papers are at Worcester Archives.

Lady de Grey letters are in the Wiltshire and Swindon History Centre, Chippenham, Wiltshire.

Letters from Edward VII to Lady Randolph Churchill (Jennie Jerome) are in the Churchill College Library, Cambridge.

The journals of Mary Theresa Leiter and Mary Leiter are at Chicago History Museum.

Shane Leslie papers, Georgetown University, Washington DC.

Lucy family archives, Warwickshire Record Office.

Anna Robinson letters are in the Manuscripts and Archives Department of the Hagley Museum and Library, Delaware.

The Isaac Sherman papers are at the Huntington Library, San Marino, California.

Edward Neufville Tailer's diaries are in the library of the New York Historical Society.

Alva Vanderbilt's unpublished autobiography and the Sara Bard Field correspondence is in the C. E. S. Wood Papers, Manuscript Department of the Huntington Library.

Gertrude Vanderbilt Whitney's letters and diary are in the Smithsonian, Washington.

Edith Wharton papers, Beinecke Library, Yale University.

Newspapers Consulted

Chicago Sunday Sun, article by Dr Madison C. Peters, a New York divine, 3 April 1910

Chicago Tribune, 16 August 1890
Collier's, 19 April 1947
Daily Alta, California, 17 March 1884
Lewiston Daily Sun, 20 January 1891
New York Times, numerous issues
Pittsburgh Daily Post, 15 July 1906
San Francisco Chronicle, 21 September 1919
Town Topics, weekly from 1885 to 1930, is available at the New York Public Library

INDEX